Training the Excluded for Work

Edited by Marjorie Griffin Cohen

Training the Excluded for Work:
Access and Equity for Women,
Immigrants, First Nations, Youth,
and People with Low Income

UBCPress · Vancouver · Toronto

09 08 07 06 05 04 03   5 4 3 2 1

Printed in Canada on acid-free paper

National Library of Canada Cataloguing in Publication Data

Main entry under title:

Training the excluded for work : access and equity for women, immigrants, first nations, youth, and people with low income / edited by Marjorie Griffin Cohen.

Includes bibliographical references and index.
ISBN 0-7748-1006-8

1. Occupational training for women – Canada. 2. Occupational training for minorities – Canada. 3. Occupational training – Government policy – Canada. 4. Affirmative action programs – Canada. 5. People with social disabilities – Employment – Canada. I. Cohen, Marjorie Griffin, 1944-

HD5715.5.C3T72 2003   374'.013'0971   C2002-911533-7

Canadä

UBC Press gratefully acknowledges the financial support for our publishing program of the Government of Canada through the Book Publishing Industry Development Program (BPIDP), and of the Canada Council for the Arts, and the British Columbia Arts Council.

The research for this book was undertaken with funds provided by the Social Sciences and Humanities Research Council of Canada for *Training Matters: The Labour Education and Training Research Network*. This network, which was located at York University, was one of five Strategic Research Networks in Education and Training.

Set in Stone By Brenda and Neil West, BN Typographics West
Printed and bound in Canada by Friesens
Copy editor: Joanne Richardson

UBC Press
The University of British Columbia
2029 West Mall
Vancouver, BC V6T 1Z2
604-822-5959 / Fax: 604-822-6083
www.ubcpress.ca

Contents

Figures and Tables

Acknowledgments

The Labour and Education and Training Research Network financially supported most of the research for the chapters in this book. The research benefited considerably from the ability of contributors to meet at Network conferences to discuss the ideas and issues under consideration. I am particularly grateful to the Social Sciences and Humanities Research Council for its funding of the Network and its meetings.

Several people deserve particular recognition for their support. These are Russell Janzen, Network coordinator; Carla Lipsey-Mummé, Network Leader; and Jean Wilson and others at UBC Press who assisted in the preparation of the manuscript.

I would also like to thank both Margaret Manery for her diligent editorial work and assistance in preparing the manuscript, and the anonymous reviewers at UBC Press for their insights and careful work.

Acronyms

ACTEW	Advocates for Training and Employment for Women
AFL/CIO	American Federation of Labor/Congress of Industrial Organizations
BCTFA	British Columbia Transportation Financing Authority
CAMO	Comité d'adaptation de la main-d'oeuvre
CAP	Canada Assistance Plan
CASP	Community Academic Services Program
CATEW	Committee for Alternative Training and Education for Women
CCLOW	Canadian Congress for Learning Opportunities for Women
CEIC	Canadian Employment and Immigration Commission
CHST	Canada Health and Social Transfer
CIFER	Centre intégré de formation et de recyclage
CJS	Canadian Jobs Strategy
CLFDB	Canadian Labour Force Development Board
CRF	Consolidated Revenue Fund
CSL	Canada Student Loans
CSN	Confédération des syndicats nationaux
DGP	Designated Group Policy
DPOT	direct-purchase-of-training
EBSM	Employment Benefits and Support Measures
EHEI	Enterprise in Higher Education Initiative
EI	Employment Insurance
EIC	Equity Integration Committee
ESP	Essential Skills Profile
FJIST	First Job in Science and Technology
FTE	full-time equivalent
FTQ	Fédération des travailleurs et travailleuses du Québec
HCL	Highway Constructors Ltd.
HRDC	Human Resources Development Canada
ISO	International Organization for Standardization

ITI	Information Technology Institute
KPI	Key Performance Indicators
LEAP	Local Employment Assistance Projects
LERN	Language Employment Related Needs
LFDS	Labour Force Development Strategy
LINC	Language Instruction for Newcomers to Canada
LIP	Local Initiatives Program
LMDAs	Labour Market Development Agreements
LMDS	Labour Market Development Strategy
LPNs	licensed practical nurses
MOTH	Ministry of Transportation and Highways
MOUS	Microsoft Office User Specialist
MS	MicroSkills
NATS	National Apprenticed Trades Survey
NGS	National Graduates Survey
NODECO	Newfoundland Offshore Development Constructors
NSSB	National Skills Standards Board
OAITH	Ontario Association of Interval and Transition Houses
OECD	Organisation for Economic Cooperation and Development
ODCCG	Oilfield Development Council Coordinating Group
ODC	Oil Development Council of Unions
PLAR	prior learning assessment and recognition
RAIS	Registered Apprentice Information System
RNs	registered nurses
SA	Social Assistance
SARS	social assistance recipients
SGEU	Saskatchewan Government Employees' Union
SIAST	Saskatchewan Institute of Applied Sciences and Technology
SIIT	Saskatchewan Indian Institute of Technology
SLG	Skills, Loans and Grants
SLID	Survey of Labour and Income Dynamics
SRDC	Social Research and Demonstration Corporation
SSP	Self-Sufficiency Project
UI	Unemployment Insurance
UIDU	Unemployment Insurance Developmental Uses
VIHP	Vancouver Island Highway Project
WITT	Women in Trades and Technology
WSC	Working Skills Centre
YMC	Yiasulth Management Corporation

Training the Excluded for Work

Introduction

The title of this book, *Training the Excluded for Work,* refers to people who are routinely marginalized from employment training and who are members of groups that are chronically disadvantaged in the workplace. The connection between the two – insufficient training and poor employment prospects – resonates with people who are unemployed or who are in low-paying and dead-end jobs. For all of the groups in this volume, receiving employment training that leads to decent jobs has been a struggle of sometimes epic proportions.

Employers in Canada are notoriously remiss in providing adequate job training even for people who are considered to be "core" workers.[1] And despite the general recognition of the significance of training in the new "knowledge-based" economy, the participation rates in employer-sponsored training dropped considerably during the 1990s.[2] The usual reasons employers cite for not developing more training programs is that extensive training is expensive and that it is a cost that cannot be re-couped if workers decide to switch jobs. As a consequence of this individuals are often left to seek out and pay for job training themselves, or governments are left to provide job training through funding specific training programs in both the public and private sectors and through community-based training.

The relationship between good, relevant training and employability is easy to understand, at least when specific individuals are concerned. But how this is achieved takes very different policy directions, depending on the general ideological and economic approaches of governments – approaches that bring about very different kinds of labour market policies. Getting a job at all depends a great deal on the willingness of governments to tolerate high levels of unemployment. While Canada has never pursued the full-employment objectives of many other industrialized countries in the post-Second World War era, its tolerance for high levels of unemployment has grown substantially: the last two decades of the twentieth century saw a consolidation of a dramatic shift towards a neoliberal economic model, where alleviating unemployment was low on the list of government priorities.[3]

The wisdom of the new economic policy directions in the neoliberal vein is that unemployment is the result of the wrong signals being sent to the labour market, which then leads to wages that are too high in some sectors. This thinking sees a variety of government programs, such as unemployment insurance, minimum wage, and social assistance as creating wage floors that price workers with low productivity out of a job. The solutions, according to this type of analysis, are to remove these so-called "barriers" to employment and to let wages fall to levels that reflect the productivity of workers in each sector. According to this theory, a sufficiently low real wage rate will generate employment for all workers. Fortunately, this theory has been too brutal to be fully put into practice, although governments throughout Canada have been progressively dismantling the income protections that were instituted during the Keynesian era. This has included a massive change in unemployment protection in Canada, the lowering of minimum wages for certain classes of workers, and arbitrary and wholesale reductions in the numbers on social assistance.[4]

Where does job training fit in this picture? If low wages are understood to be related to low productivity, as the neoliberal economists assert, then the best way for an individual to improve her or his employment circumstances would be to acquire more "human capital." The rush to prove that unemployment was something that was not the fault of government policy (a policy that was basically ignoring the issue) brought to the fore the oft-heard assertion that people were not trained adequately for the kinds of jobs that would be needed in a new economy – an economy that would focus on highly skilled and highly technical production.[5] As individuals each acquired better skills, they would become employable in jobs that were better paying and less precarious. The fault implicitly, then, lay less with the system for not creating enough jobs, less with the employers for paying workers too little, and more with the people themselves for failing to make themselves attractive as workers.

The focus on training as the solution to labour market problems greatly appealed to employer groups who stressed their need for people who were trained for specific jobs. This rhetoric about the significance of training supported very significant changes in social policy. Most notable was reducing the income protection the unemployed could receive through Unemployment Insurance, as funds that were normally paid out to the unemployed themselves were diverted into training programs. While the federal government was directly involved in training programs, those disadvantaged workers with a more tenuous attachment to the labour force had some opportunities to participate in creative training programs.

But in 1996 a major shift in the nature of government-sponsored training occurred – a shift that moved the responsibility for training from the federal government to the provinces. This was a radical change, and it has had significant implications for the people who are the subject of this book, particularly in those provinces that pursued a neoliberal economic agenda.[6]

Overview

In Chapter 1 Ursule Critoph documents the changes in the federal government's policy on training and its general implications for women. She shows that, under the new system, a bias has been created in favour of those who are easiest to serve in the new Employment Insurance rules and that the cost and responsibility of training has been downloaded to individuals. This has resulted in profound changes for women's training, mainly because it has effectively dismantled the apparatus that supported the training initiatives of women-only organizations. This chapter sets the background for understanding the context of training for workers with special training needs – those who face barriers to employment that are distinct and who cannot be adequately served without taking these into account.

Two other chapters focus directly on the implications of the removal of the federal government from training programs: Joan McFarland (Chapter 11) documents the effects of the changes in training programs for women in New Brunswick. While access to training for women has always been variable, some programs were successful, particularly those that involved the direct government sponsorship of places for women in women-only training programs. However, since the changes initiated in 1996, training has increasingly become the realm of the private sector, and the women-only programs have been eliminated. Karen Lior and Susan Wismer (Chapter 12) examine the bewildering context of training programs in the post-1996 period as individuals are required to "shop" for the training they need. The results are not encouraging and, as the authors show, seem to be particularly unhelpful for the most disadvantaged in the labour market.

Through examining programs that were designed specifically for workers with special needs – women, immigrants, First Nations, youth, and people with low incomes – this book intends to try to understand what works and what does not work in equity training programs. In analyzing these programs it attempts to distinguish between short-term, one-off training programs and those that provide training that is either both more sustained and long-term or that can be used as a model for other programs.

The programs cover provinces across the country and include very different types of work, ranging from clerical work to construction work. Some of the programs that are analyzed were spectacularly successful, such as the training associated with immigrant women in Toronto (Manery and Cohen), the training for women and First Nations on the Vancouver Island Highway Project (Cohen and Braid), the training for youth at risk in Quebec (Bourdon and Deschenaux), and the training for Aboriginal and low-income women in Saskatchewan (Little). The one feature that these programs have in common is that they were initiated either by or in close consultation with the communities they served. Other training projects were abject failures – most notably the training for women that occurred on the Hibernia Construction Project (Hart and Shrimpton) and the "low road" approach to youth training in British Columbia (Wong and McBride). Unfortunately, success has not guaranteed that innovative programs are replicated, and failure has not guaranteed that poorly designed and indifferently implemented programs are not replicated.

The chapters in this book focus on specific groups but examine them by taking into account a wide variety of issues. Kate Braid (Chapter 5), for example, looks at the culture of construction and what women need to learn as part of their training not only to cope and to survive in a virtually all-male workforce but also to change the culture itself. Her advice, which is offered after years of working as a carpenter, is funny and subversive, but it points to one of the most difficult issues in integrating the construction workplace – keeping women who receive training from leaving the industry. Margaret Little (Chapter 6) focuses on the barriers women with low incomes face when they try to break gender divides in construction work. In the training program she examined in Saskatchewan two-thirds of the participants were Aboriginal women. As she shows, with long-term training (this one lasted five years), and ancillary programs to deal with the specific conditions that they faced, these women were able to realize their dream of becoming carpenters. Shauna Butterwick (Chapter 9) examines the much-debated training initiatives known as "life skills" training. "Life skills" involve a set of skills that is supposed to aid workers who do not "fit" the prescribed workplace by showing them how they can change their behaviour in order to conform to expectations of employers and co-workers. Her examination shows both the negative aspects of these programs and their liberatory potential, which is revealed when they give people tools that enable them to function in a "risk society." Margaret Manery and Marjorie Griffin Cohen (Chapter 8) analyze the successes of two training programs in Toronto that were established and run by immigrant women for immigrant women. These programs were successful because they met the needs of these people by integrating language, job skills, and employment preparation, and they were supported by federal funding. However, the changes that have occurred in federal government support have considerably stressed these programs, forcing the women who run them to constantly shape them to fit funders' needs. This often means that the women who would most benefit from the programs no longer have access to them.

Two chapters look specifically at programs designed for youth. Linda Wong and Stephen McBride (Chapter 13) examine the implications for youth of two diverse training approaches – one that focuses on highly skilled occupations leading to good jobs and one that focuses on occupations requiring low levels of skills and that channels youth into jobs with harsh workplace conditions. They show how the youth of British Columbia are channelled into these polarized groups through the training process with virtually no vertical movement from one group to the other over time. This means that training programs are doing little to change the existing hierarchies in the labour force and that increasing numbers are channelled into low-waged employment. The other chapter dealing with youth training looks at an innovative training program designed for youth at risk in Montreal. Sylvain Bourdon and Frédéric Deschenaux (Chapter 14) analyze the unique features that make this program work; namely, its highly media-friendly character and its focus on recycling computers. However, they do not see the success of this program as easily replicated, mainly because it requires significant amounts of working capital, something few politicians are willing to commit on a large scale.

Two of the chapters deal specifically with training programs for women and/or First Nations associated with large construction projects. They look at what can make these projects succeed and what can make them fail. The construction trades are notorious for the closed nature of the workforces, and repeated efforts to change the colour and gender of the people in the workplace have been exceptionally unsuccessful. Susan Hart and Mark Shrimpton (Chapter 4), in their examination of equity initiatives on the Hibernia construction project, show that, while requirements for equity hires may give the appearance of access to jobs, without workable implementation plans that are closely monitored and given high priority women will not be integrated into the workforce. They recount the experiences of the women who undertook training on Hibernia and show that only with very specific and proactive work on the part of government will the barriers women face in the construction industry be overcome. This unsuccessful training program stands in stark contrast to the innovative and highly successful program that was carried out for women and First Nations on the Vancouver Island Highway Project. Marjorie Griffin Cohen and Kate Braid (Chapter 3) show that the equity initiatives worked well only because the government of British Columbia made equity hires a condition of employment on the project and ensured that they were implemented. In other words, successfully integrating equity hires in the workplace required some measure of coercion on the part of the government. But, most significantly, both First Nations and women's groups involved in the skills trades were actively involved in an ongoing way in the planning and oversight of the training program. This meant that women and First Nations were not only hired and trained but were also given the support necessary to stay on the job.

The changing nature of the workforce that has accompanied the restructuring of the economy has raised important questions about the nature of training in jobs and sectors of the economy that have experienced substantial changes. Alice de Wolff and Maureen Hynes (Chapter 2) are interested in the wide variety of approaches to training for clerical workers, and they assess the proposals for occupational and training standards for this type of work. While creating a universal set of standards is sometimes thought to put workers in a position to gain some bargaining power with employers, the authors suggest that these standards are more likely to be set by employers. They suggest that worker-focused organizing could better protect workers' rights.

The restructuring of the health care sector presents several alternatives for training health care aides. Larry Haiven and Liz Quinlan (Chapter 7) examine the tension that restructuring creates for the continued survival of health care training in public institutions in Saskatchewan. The peaceful coexistence that has historically existed between public and private trainers has changed as public institutions are increasingly deprived of their needed funding and the private sector is increasingly laying claims on the public purse. They show how the government is torn between a traditional devotion to public initiatives and the enormous pressure from the private sector to shift its support towards more private training.

Training Policy
The overriding theme of this book is that training for people who are either marginalized or at risk in the labour market can be highly successful if undertaken with their needs in focus. Too often the design in public training policy has a plethora of objectives and serving the specific needs of individual groups is an afterthought that is tacked on to programs whose main function serves some other aim. In Canada, active labour market measures (commonly referred to as ALMM) in the post-Keynesian era have focused on issues that are concerned with reshaping the labour market to become more competitive and reshaping social policy to reduce government expenditures. The attempt to redesign programs to make labour markets more "flexible" has been a high priority.[7] This pursuit of "flexibility" is in response to a sense that, as a result of a variety of public policy measures that have not allowed labour markets to work properly, labour productivity in Canada has fallen behind that of its main competitors. Related to this has been a growing emphasis on "moving people from welfare to work."[8]

The notion behind these two prongs of ALMM is that there is some problem either with the incentive systems or with the quality of the supply of labour that either makes Canadian workers less productive than their counterparts elsewhere or encourages too many workers to stay out of the labour force. The redesign of the federal government's training policy gives considerable lip service to meeting the needs of people who require training, but the latent objectives of the major changes that occurred were considerably less lofty. The shift from active federal government involvement in training programs to a series of labour market development agreements (LMDA) with individual provinces had very little to do with attempts to improve either training programs or labour market outcomes; rather, it was a direct result of interprovincial politics. As Harvey Lazar has convincingly argued, the desire to remove active labour market measures that were "an irritant in federal-Quebec relations drove the federal government's agenda."[9] In granting autonomy to Quebec, the way was paved for other provinces to argue for similar control over funds associated with training and other employment benefits previously controlled by the federal government.

While government officials tend to applaud the result of the changes because of the improvement in federal-provincial relations, the evidence indicates that the new system poses greater challenges for those marginalized in the labour force. As Gerry Boychuk pointed out in a presentation to a conference designed to review the experiences of the LMDAs, the combination of a shift in responsibility for training to the provinces, along with tighter eligibility requirements for both Employment Insurance (EI) and Social Assistance (SA), makes it harder to even identify the people who need training most.[10] This is because as, for a variety of reasons, people are eliminated from these programs, they cannot qualify for the training that is sponsored for those on EI and SA.

Understanding the nature of the barriers to training that specific categories of workers face is crucial to designing training programs to meet their needs. Too often the identification of barriers does not distinguish between different groups of workers in different circumstances. So, for example, in attempting to understand why an increasingly smaller proportion of the working population is involved in training, a large survey such as the Adult Education and Training Survey distinguishes the major reasons according to individuals' location, education, sex, age, and occupation.[11] However, it does not distinguish according to ethnicity, race, income, or whether one is an immigrant. The findings of this survey identified key barriers to training as being "too busy at work," "too expensive," "inconvenient time/location," "course or program not offered," "lack of employer support," and "family responsibilities." Having this kind of information could lead to significant policy changes, such as those that encouraged employers to lessen workloads, greater efforts to subsidize the cost of training, and shifts in the location and timing of training in order to make it more accessible. But it is unlikely to lead to changes in policies that get at the heart of some of the issues that exclude some classes of people from specific types of training. Discrimination in labour markets, for example, has an enormous impact on specific groups of people who are routinely excluded from access to training. This is a serious issue that needs to be identified in both designing training programs and in designing support programs for those who have been trained. As several chapters in this book have shown (Chapters 3 and 4), the culture of an industry or occupation frequently inhibits both the hiring and the retention of even those who receive adequate training. Similarly, the barriers that low-income people face require considerably more diverse programs to support the training initiatives (Chapter 6). Issues such as discrimination and poverty are the kinds of systemic issues that are hard to see through surveys but that are knowable through careful examination of the programs themselves and the populations they are designed to serve.

Too often the training programs that target designated groups considered to be more difficult to serve are minimal, tend to be remedial, and are not followed up with specific action to ensure that the trained receive long-term employment: it is the best educated workers who tend to get the most training.[12] One reason for this is that employee-sponsored programs focus on already employed workers with considerable background experience. But even in publicly sponsored programs, the better educated trainees result in "outcomes" that more neatly conform to the success criteria demanded of the programs. Measuring the success of training programs needs to be considerably expanded. The current discussion on measuring success tends to discount the value of government programs aimed at moving people from welfare to work and increasing employability and earnings. It is an issue that has captured the attention of policy makers in all countries that have substantial welfare roles and, perhaps a little too conveniently, seem to find that, overall, the programs are very ineffective.[13] This is not surprising, although not for the reasons usually given – that these people are hard cases that require too much in the way of public resources. When they are ineffective it is usually either because they were poorly designed or because their effectiveness could not be captured by the existing success criteria. Sometimes it is a combination of both. The primary indicators for evaluating the success of LMDA programs are (1) the number of claimants served, (2) the return to employment of claimants, and (3) savings to the EI account.[14] The limits of these indicators are considerable, and, for programs that need to show results in order to continue receiving funding, this greatly affects both the nature of the program and the selection of people who will be trained: the focus will be on short-term programs and people who are already relatively job ready. Measuring the success of programs is crucial because understanding what works and what does not work matters greatly to those who receive training. But the design of the measures and what constitutes success itself requires considerably more consultation with the communities and groups that are the subject of this book. The primary indicators currently being used inhibit the development of programs that best serve those who need them most.

The chapters in this book show that there is no magic formula for designing training that will best serve the needs of those who have been marginalized in labour market policies. Each group brings specific requirements that are best identified through their own communities: as the experiences of the successful programs examined in this book indicate, it is obvious that these communities have been remarkably adept in identifying both their training needs and how best to deliver the programs.

The significance of decent work to individuals' lives is a consistent theme in the international literature on training: "Decent work underpins individuals' independence, self-respect and well-being, and is therefore key to their overall quality of life."[15] Designing training programs that challenge existing hierarchies in the workplace is critical to meeting the objectives of decent work. As long as training programs merely replicate the existing hierarchies, youth will be segregated by class, immigrants will continue to underperform in relation to their potential, and women will continue to be segregated in areas requiring different skills from men.

A great deal is demanded of training programs, and the expectations for their success, in relation to the expectations about the future quality of the labour supply, are high. The potential exists for Canada's training schemes to truly serve the ambitions of those who place training high on the agenda for solutions to social and economic problems. But this potential will not be realized unless considerably more resources are put into these programs, governments actively ensure that issues of equality are an integral part of the programs, and affected communities are involved in their design from the outset.

Conclusions

The chapters in this book show that good training programs are highly effective with regard to providing workers who are disadvantaged in the labour market with the tools they need to acquire more secure and well-paying jobs. The multiple barriers that disadvantaged workers face require training programs that focus not only on providing skills but also on addressing other issues that inhibit their success in the labour market. The shift in recent years towards private and market-based training schemes has undermined the successes of training that focused on the "excluded."

While good training programs still exist, they struggle in the face of drastic funding changes and tend to shift their focus more to meet the directives of funding agencies than the needs of the communities they serve. Training matters a great deal, as does the nature of the training programs. Those that focus on the needs of the people being trained tend to be much more successful than do those that focus on the needs of their employers. But whatever the training regime, it is clear that training alone will not guarantee work: a great deal depends on the availability of jobs and the policies that governments pursue in order to ensure full employment. In a climate inspired by neoliberal ideology, training in Canada is moving in a direction that will see fewer and fewer of those who require training receiving it. If this continues, then those who have been excluded will remain excluded. This trajectory is not immutable. As this book shows, it is possible to understand, through the careful examination of specific cases, what mistakes have been made and can be avoided, and what policies deserve to be replicated. By recognizing what makes successful programs work well, future policy initiatives could be more focused on meeting the needs of those who are too easily excluded.

Notes

1 There is some debate in the literature regarding how far behind Canadian employers are in training. While, for example, Canadian employers train considerably fewer employees and offer fewer training hours than do American employers, their performance is not too different from that found in many other countries. See Constantine Kapsalis, *Employee Training: An International Perspective* (Ottawa: Statistics Canada, 1997).

2 André Léonard, *Why Did the Participation Rate in Job-Related Training Decline during the 1990s in Canada?* (Ottawa: Human Resources Development Canada, October 2001).

3 Stephen McBride, *Paradigm Shift: Globalization and the Canadian State* (Halifax: Fernwood, 2001).

4 The massive negative changes that occurred in unemployment insurance in the late 1980s and throughout the 1990s reduced the numbers and classes of people eligible to collect benefits when unemployed, reduced the amount of the benefits available, and shifted large amounts of insurance funds from direct payment to the unemployed to occupational training programs. See Human Resources Development Canada, *Employment Insurance: 2001 Monitoring and Assessment Report* (Ottawa: HRDC, 2002), Annex 1. Throughout Canada the minimum wage has not kept pace with the cost of living; however, in some provinces even its monetary rate has been reduced for some classes of workers. In British Columbia, for example, a "training wage" that is considerably less than the minimum wage was introduced in 2001 for new entrants into the workforce.

5 Gordon Betcherman, Kathryn McMullen, and Katie Davidman, *Training for the New Economy* (Ottawa: Canadian Policy Research Networks, 1998); Government of Canada, *Knowledge Matters: Skills and Learning for Canadians* (Ottawa: HRDC, 2002).

6 For a discussion of the effects of these changes, see Harvey Lazar, *Shifting Roles: Active Labour Market Policy in Canada under the Labour Market Development Agreements* (Ottawa: Canadian Policy Research Networks, 2002).

7 Ibid., pt. 3.

8 William P. Warburton and Rebecca N. Warburton, "Measuring the Performance of Government Training Programs," *C.D. Howe Institute Commentary*, No. 165, June 2002.

9 Lazar, *Shifting Roles*, 6.

10 Gerry Boychuk, presentation given in February 2002 in Edmonton, Alberta. Cited in Lazar, *Shifting Roles,* pt. 6.
11 Deborah Sussman, "Barriers to Job-Related Training," *Perspectives on Labour and Income* 14, 2 (Summer 2002): 25-32.
12 Ibid., 26.
13 Warburn and Warburn, "Measuring the Performance," 1.
14 Yvonne McFadzen and Jim Blain, presentation given in February 2002 in Edmonton, Alberta. Cited in Lazar, *Shifting Roles,* pt. 7.
15 ILO, *Learning and Training for Work in the Knowledge Society*, Report 4 (1) (Geneva: International Labour Office, 2002), 5.

1

Who Wins, Who Loses: The Real Story of the Transfer of Training to the Provinces and Its Impact on Women

Ursule Critoph

In early November 1995, Prime Minister Jean Chrétien made what appeared to be an off-the-cuff remark after the near loss of the Quebec referendum to the separatists. He offered to transfer responsibility for training to the provinces, something Quebec had been wanting for some time. By early 1998 all provinces except Ontario had signed Labour Market Development Agreements (LMDAs) covering three- to five-year periods.[1] It had been one of the smoothest and least acrimonious re-orderings of federal-provincial jurisdictions in the history of this country. However, the offer was not what it first seemed. Out of an overall system of about four billion dollars in spending on a multitude of training and related employment programs and services, the federal government was really only proposing to give the provinces limited administrative jurisdiction over programs covered by Part 2 of the new Employment Insurance Act. And, as we will see, this allowed the federal government to disguise and download the impacts of substantial cuts to spending, leaving many Canadians with the impression that it was the provinces who were responsible for a loss of access to training.

In this chapter the focus is on what really occurred over the 1995 to 1997 period and its consequences for women. After briefly outlining the system prior to this period of change, three substantial steps taken by the federal government for their impact on access to training for women are examined. The first step is the elimination of special Consolidated Revenue Fund (CRF) training and employment support programs for women; the second is the changes made to the rules for insurance benefits in the changeover from Unemployment Insurance to Employment Insurance (UI/EI); and the third, and in many respects the least significant except in political terms, is the actual transfer of responsibility to the provinces. During this same period, the federal government also abandoned the Designated Group Policy designed to mitigate the labour market disadvantage of the four equity groups: women, visible minorities, Aboriginal persons, and persons with disabilities. The focus in this discussion is on women, but much of what happened has also had a significant negative impact on all individuals seeking training, particularly those who are members of the other equity groups. Further, in the period just prior to and including 1995 to 1997, the provinces and territories[2] made substantial cuts to their own programs and changed the nature of social assistance.

Women's Labour Market Challenges

Women remain, even at the start of the new millennium, at a disadvantage in their effort to gain a strong attachment to the labour market.[3] Their participation rate at 58.1 percent in 1998 remains significantly below that of men, which stands at 72.4 percent. They represent only 39.4 percent of full-time, full-year workers, and almost half of employed women are part of the nonstandard labour market. Women's incomes are only 61 percent of men's and 50 percent of women had after-tax incomes ranging from zero to $13,786. As noted in Karen Hadley's recent report entitled *"And We Still Ain't Satisfied": Gender Inequality in Canada – A Status Report for 2001*, the situation for Aboriginal women, disabled women, and racialized women is much worse. The same is true for older women, with the largest income gap between women and men aged 45-64. The gap widens as educational levels decrease. Thirty-five percent of women have less than a high school education and, even with a university education, their incomes were only 70 percent of those of men. Women also represent the vast majority of persons in nonstandard (i.e., not full-year/full-time) employment.[4]

Women face multiple systemic barriers to labour market participation and achievement. These include attitudinal barriers and limited access to (and the high cost of) childcare. Women also bear the majority of the responsibility for family care of children and the elderly. Women in lone-parent families are the worst off.

Women also continue to experience labour market segregation. In spite of efforts to combat systemic gendered and racialized segregation, more than 70 percent of women "continue to be concentrated in a few female dominated sectors related to [women's] traditional social roles: clerical or other administrative positions, sales and service occupations, nursing and related health occupations and teaching."[5] Low-paying, part-time, and contingent forms of employment dominate these occupations. Increasingly, even the fields of nursing and education, two of the best paid and most highly unionized forms of employment for women, are being turned into contingent, part-time, and home-based or self-employed forms of employment.

Similarly, women face unique challenges in their efforts to pursue education and training in order to ameliorate these labour market disadvantages. Women get fewer opportunities than do men for job-related training; they get fewer hours of training; they face more barriers; and what they do get goes primarily to those already at the top. Furthermore, they and their families often have to pay for job-related training themselves.[6]

Women's needs with regard to labour market programming and services include:

- income support to carry them during periods of unemployment
- good quality, accessible training
- programs of longer duration
- more integrated programs (i.e., programs that combine the various support needs into one seamless approach)
- assistance to determine their needs and training (e.g., counselling, labour market information, case management)
- support to deal with life issues such as violence, low self-esteem, and discrimination
- extra supports to aid them in gaining access to nontraditional occupations along with the training that leads to them
- safe and confidential environments within which to receive services
- additional support for childcare and transportation costs.

Programs that ignore the interrelationship of these needs may bring about short-term results but do little to address the systemic disadvantages of women in the labour market.

Women's Programs Prior to 1996

Immediately prior to the shift in policy during the 1995-97 period, federal labour market programs and services for women operated at two levels and, to a degree, tried to address the above combination of needs. For women who had already formed a strong attachment to the paid labour force, income support during times of unemployment was available through the Unemployment Insurance Program. Additional services could be found through federal Human Resources Development Canada offices. These could include anything from counselling and assistance with job search and resume writing to enrolment in an extended adjustment or training program. Funds for these programs and services came from the Unemployment Insurance Developmental Uses (UIDU) fund.

During this same period, in recognition of their systemic disadvantage in the labour market, certain individuals not covered by UI were offered federal programs and services. These people included women, persons with disabilities, visible minorities, older workers, youth, social assistance recipients, and Aboriginal persons. In 1991 the commitment to assisting women, visible minorities, persons with disabilities, and Aboriginal persons was formalized in an internal directive known as the Designated Group Policy. The policy's "chief objective is to ... [eliminate] the barriers preventing the full productive contribution of the designated groups." Under this directive, the federal government was obliged to maintain its commitment to the equity groups in all its own arrangements and those with other stakeholders and labour market partners.

Programs for these disadvantaged individuals, if they were ineligible for UI, were funded from general government revenues under the Canadian Jobs Strategy (CJS). The two programs ran in parallel, and funding sources could be interchanged as long as the basic eligibility criteria could be met. In 1993-94 the amounts going to support training and related employment programs and services from general government revenues and the Unemployment Insurance Fund were roughly two billion dollars from each. In that same year, women, with over 124,000 participants, made up between one-quarter and one-half of the total number served and over three-quarters of the designated group participants.[7] Income support was allocated on the basis of the training allowances as outlined in the National Training Act and could be provided for a period of up to three years, although such an extended period was unusual. Additional funds were also available to cover childcare and other increased living expenses due to program participation. The programs themselves were often of an integrated long-term nature. Women-only programs and organizations were fairly common.

These four groups were "characterized by persistent characteristics reflecting disadvantage in the labour market [as evidenced by their lower labour force participation rate and] their tendency to be segregated in a limited range of occupations and levels within occupational groups."

(Human Resources Development Canada, "Designated Group Policy,"
Government of Canada, 1991)

Both the CJS and UIDU favoured an active programming approach. Individuals were provided with assistance and offered remedial support to encourage a successful return to work. These include training, job creation, and other labour force development strategies. The passive nature of UI income support, when used alone, was considered a deterrent to the smooth functioning of the labour market.[8]

The federal government contracted directly with providers on behalf of their UI and CJS clients. Under this system, known as direct-purchase-of-training (DPOT), the government paid the organization for the full cost of providing the training.[9] The allowable cost included not only the usual fees but also overhead. Many colleges and community-based organizations, including many women's organizations, developed their expertise and focus under the DPOT system. In the final years of the CJS, Human Resources Development Canada (HRDC) increasingly contracted for training with private and for-profit organizations, the expectation being that these would be more flexible than public sector programs and, consequently, a cheap source of tailor-made short-term programs.

Prior to the transfer of responsibility for Part 2 of the EI program, provincial and territorial governments played a relatively small role in targeted women's employment and training programs. In 1995-96, the provincial/ territorial governments provided only $13.75 million in dedicated funding for women's programs (of which $12.9 million was spent by British Columbia) and a further $176 million for other equity programs. Of this, $22 million consisted of federal monies transferred to the provinces.[10] In some cases, the provinces provided input and direction to the spending of federal dollars, although HRDC remained very much in control.

The Sea Change of 1995-97

As noted earlier, the period of 1995-97 was characterized by substantial changes on the part of the federal government in the manner in which it would deliver labour market programs in the future. The Designated Group Policy disappeared; there were massive cuts to CRF spending; the Employment Insurance Act, 1996, replaced the Unemployment Insurance Act; and LMDAs were negotiated with the provinces. Rather than compensating for, or rectifying, the imbalances in the labour market for women, the sum of the effect of the changes since 1995-97 has been to exacerbate the situation. In this section of the chapter, each of these changes is examined in turn for its impact on women's access to training.

Designated Group Policy Is Abandoned

Around 1995 it was determined that the practice of identifying a number of groups within the labour market as particularly disadvantaged and therefore in need of special programs should be abandoned.[11] As far as the federal government was concerned, the labour market situation of some of the equity groups was no longer a problem that required its attention.[12] The rejection of this policy had a profound effect on the choices the government made as it proceeded to "modernize" its policies in line with the active labour market programming approach dominating the thinking of Western industrial governments. Most important, when it developed new programs and services it was no longer necessary for the federal government to address the systemic disadvantage of the equity groups. Furthermore, the government could ignore this issue when negotiating the LMDAs with the provinces.

Loss of CRF Spending

The elimination of Consolidated Revenue Fund (CRF) spending on labour market programs for women has had the single most devastating impact on women. It has meant a drop in spending of about $700 million annually on women's training and employment programs. From its peak of two billion dollars in 1993-94, CRF spending for all groups fell to only seventy-nine million dollars in 1997-98, rebounding to between $200 and $250 million annually since. At the time of the negotiations between the federal and provincial governments, the effects of cuts had not yet been fully felt. It is not clear if the provinces fully understood that the federal government funded training from two separate pots and that they were being offered only one of them.[13] Most provinces had had little experience with labour market programming, having left it to the federal government for many years. Even those with experience running their own programs generally lacked expertise with the details of the federal government's financial arrangements.[14]

The loss of CRF funding for women's programs has been devastating for women, women's programs, and women's organizations. Without it, there is no longer a source of federal government funds targeted at women who have no pre-existing attachment to the labour market and are not current or recent EI beneficiaries.

Tightened Access to Insurance Benefits[15]
Unfortunately for women (and all other workers), the federal government's new legislation made becoming an EI beneficiary much more difficult than it had been before. In fact, for many, the new rules raised the threshold by more than double, particularly for those newly entering the workforce or returning to work after a period of absence.[16] This clearly discriminates against women, who make up the majority of workers in the nonstandard labour market.[17] The result was that by 1999 the percentage of unemployed women receiving UI had dropped to only 32 percent, down from 70 percent in 1989. Ten percent fewer women than men were receiving UI at this time. This gap is highest among young women and those in their childbearing and childrearing years. This represents almost 400,000 fewer women receiving UI than were receiving it under the pre-1996 eligibility rules.[18]

Women have been affected not only by the changes to the eligibility rules but also by a number of other changes to the EI rules. Contrary to the expected increase in access for women with the shift from weeks to hours, women are not only having more difficulty in qualifying but they are also seeing no improvement in their benefit rates (see Table 1.1). While the average benefit rate of women on regular benefits has remained constant, women receiving the family supplement have had the total amount paid to them decrease by 21.2 percent between 1995-96 and 1997-98. Men, on the other hand, have seen the total paid to them increase by 54.5 percent. The average amount was $211 for women and $283 for men.[19] To the detriment of women and their independence, the family supplement, previously based on an individual's income, is now based on the family's income. This loss of benefits can only have a negative impact on the ability of women to pursue training.

Introduction of Accountability Measures Causes Distortion

As part of the legislation, the federal government introduced accountability measures into the EI system for the first time. These measures focus on savings to the account and the number of persons who have returned to work. Targets have been set for each office and are part of the LMDAs. The impact of this is to distort the choices made about whom to serve. No longer are the criteria based on need and long-term impacts but, rather, on cost-savings and the rapid return to work. The faster an individual is off the system the more savings can be realized.

This shift has led to such undesirable practices as actively discouraging individuals from even applying. Some women have been asked if they really need EI or if they can manage without it and rely instead upon their husband's or father's incomes. Those who do apply find that the assistance previously available to them is no longer there. "Voluntary quits"[20] are not always helped to determine whether they have quit their job for allowable reasons, such as the need to relocate with a partner, to stop work to care for a family member, or to leave because of harassment or unfair working conditions.[21]

Those fortunate enough to receive benefits may be discouraged from taking the necessary time to secure comparable work if other, usually low-wage unskilled, work is readily available. To hold out is to risk disqualification. The goal is to get them on and off EI as quickly as possible regardless of the long-term consequences. Women with training and qualifications in a nontraditional area of female employment appear to be particularly vulnerable. A similar Catch-22 situation appears to occur for women with children. Some women have been told that they must have childcare in place or have their children in care while they are on EI in order to be considered "ready, willing, and available" for work. To disregard this is to risk being disqualified or penalized as "not available."

Transfer to the Provinces

On 30 May 1996 the provinces and territories were formally offered the opportunity to assume responsibility for certain elements of labour market policy and programs. Twelve LMDAs have been signed, leaving Ontario as the only jurisdiction without an agreement. The agreements provide a framework under which the provinces assume responsibility, alone or in partnership with the federal government, for the delivery of the Employment Benefits and Support Measures in Part 2 of the Employment Insurance Act,

1996. The agreements also spell out the amounts to be allocated for each year of the agreement. The LMDAs last three to five years, and the amounts correspond to the value of spending that would have occurred had the federal government maintained responsibility. The agreements do not transfer the funds previously spent by the federal government from general government revenues. Under the agreements, there is no requirement to adhere to any of the principles of the Designated Group Policy.

Contrary to what many believe, the LMDAs do not transfer control over training to the provinces.[22] Federal EI legislation remains the governing legal document and, as such, sets out the rules governing eligibility and the terms and conditions regarding the range of options available in delivering programs and services. By retaining control over the legislative framework, the federal government has maintained the de jure right to affect labour market policies and programs. Under the LMDAs, it also expressly retains a number of spheres under its direct control. These include a national labour market information system, interprovincial or sectoral development, and the responsibility for responding to national economic crises.

The Employment Benefits and Support Measures (EBSM) acquired by the provinces replace the former Developmental Uses portion of the Unemployment Insurance Act. A number of pre-existing policies continue. In particular, the rule that only individuals who qualify for Part 1 insurance benefits are eligible for Part 2 benefits continues to apply.[23] Two new rules are of particular concern. First, a new category of persons eligible for EBSM, known as "reach-back" clients, has been created. Second, there has been a shift from direct-purchase-of-training (DPOT) to individualized loans and grants.

Earlier it was noted that the number of women qualifying for unemployment insurance has fallen due to various changes to the eligibility and qualifying criteria. Without any compensating changes, the drop in the number of women with access to regular, maternity, sickness, and parental benefits would have resulted in rapidly decreasing numbers of women eligible to receive EBSM. As an offset, up to 35 percent of those receiving Employment Benefits can be reach-back clients, individuals with a regular claim in the previous three years or a maternity or parental claim in the previous five years. This also allowed the federal government to distance itself from the full impact of the loss of CRF spending and the tightening of access to Part 1 benefits. On the flip side, it also won support from the provinces by allowing them to transfer the cost of serving a specific group of social assistance recipients to the EI account.

As the only possible claimants of maternity benefits and the larger portion of parental and sickness benefits, women are potentially the largest beneficiaries of this change. However, the number being served in 1997-98

Table 1.1

Comparison of key characteristics of income and training support

Qualifying	Unemployment insurance	Employment insurance
Unit of measure	Weeks	Hours
New entrants	12-20 weeks (min. 15 hrs./week)	910 hours
Re-entrants	same as new entrants	420-700 hours
Part 1: Insurance benefits		
Maximum weeks	50 weeks	45 weeks
Rate	57%	55%
Benefit calculation	weekly pay multiplied by benefit rate	total hours employed divided by (# of weeks x 35) multiplied by weekly pay multiplied by benefit rate
Maximum benefit	$449/week	$413/week
No employment weeks	do not count	used in calculating benefit rate
Family supplement		
Eligibility	Individual income	Family income
Rate	60% to max. benefit	80% in 2000 to max. benefit

Training

Program name	UI Developmental Uses	Employment Benefits and Support Measures
Eligibility	Yes	Yes
Income support	based on Part 1 Insurance Benefits	individually negotiated
Tuition costs	by direct purchase from training provider	paid directly to client
Maximum duration	can be extended to maximum of 156 weeks	no extended benefits
Level of support	up to 100% of total cost to provider	usually 50% of client fees only

Source: Employment Insurance Act, 1 July 1996.

under this provision is far less than the numbers served under the old CRF spending. An estimated 34,000 former female claimants had access to EBSM programs in 1997-98 compared to 71,115 in 1995-96 and 124,567 in 1993-94 under the old CRF program. And this is without factoring in those women already served under the old UIDU program.[24]

Bias in Favour of the Easy-to-Serve

The provinces are bound by the accountability measures introduced with the new EI rules. The effect is to create an inducement for them to quickly shift current EI claimants onto Part 2 benefits and then into the workforce. Presented with two clients – one who would easily find employment with a minimum of assistance and one who would require considerable support – the incentive will be for the province to serve the first individual. By taking this individual into her/his workload and moving her/him quickly back into paid employment, preferably at very little cost, the province can claim the benefit of the savings to Part 1. In addition, the more of these easy-to-serve clients the province handles, the higher the savings (no matter how artificial) and the larger the number of clients placed in employment. Savings for the harder-to-serve client will be much lower; therefore she/he may be left to finish out her/his Part 1 claim (at federal expense and responsibility). Women, with their multiple barriers, may be more difficult to serve, particularly if they have a weak attachment to the labour market. Under a system that rewards serving the easy-to-serve, the most disadvantaged women may be considered simply too costly and too risky to serve.

Transferring the Cost and Responsibility to the Individual

The provinces must also adhere to the new rules governing training funded by EI. Each jurisdiction has developed its own answer to the requirement for some form of individualized funding to replace the old DPOT. They all share a number of common features. The amount of loan or grant for each client is based on an assessment of need and of the capacity of that individual and her/his family to contribute. All individuals are expected to contribute personally (or from family resources) to their own training. Although the amount of that contribution can vary from zero to 100 percent of the cost, it is usually in the 50 percent range. Guidelines are generally set at the provincial level, although local offices usually make the decisions on individual cases.[25] In a number of jurisdictions, loans are allocated first and grants are allocated only when the amount requirement exceeds the maximum loan level. For example, in New Brunswick applicants must assume a $3,500 loan before they will be considered for a grant. In addition, their suitability as an "investment" with a high enough rate of return (a well enough paid job) will determine their eligibility.

"The ideology imposed by the Employment Insurance legislation is that the individual is financially responsible for their own training."

(McFarland, 1999, p. 6)

For a number of reasons, women are potentially discriminated against under the new system. First, women are less likely to have financial resources of their own as they earn considerably less than men. Also, given the expectation that their earnings may never be as high as those of the men of the family, they may find it difficult to gain support for the expenditure of limited family resources on their training or education. Among single parent families led by women, the requirement to contribute even a small percentage of the cost of training in the form of living expenses and course and supplementary costs may be more than they can afford and may act as a deterrent to taking training. Furthermore, there are a significant number of women who, for a variety of reasons, have little or no access to the financial resources of their household or family. When attempting to seek funding for training, such women could find themselves dependent on the active support and assistance of their partners or other male members of their household.

"A participant who has been out of the labour force and living with a spouse would likely not incur incremental living expenses by taking training."

(Unidentified provincial government, 1997)

Women are also likely to be at a disadvantage when it comes to the negotiation process. Women who are already suffering from low self-esteem, have a weak attachment to the labour force, feel a sense of inadequacy, and are lacking in life skills are not likely to be strong candidates for carrying on tough negotiations to establish their level of need for financial support.

Faced with systemic discriminatory attitudes, women may also find themselves directed towards the same pink-collar ghettos from which they have been trying hard to break out. Training in traditional clerical and homecare work is of relatively short duration and is often less expensive than is training in nontraditional areas. When pursuing work in the high-tech sector, where shortages of qualified workers are supposed to abound, women are encouraged to consider the more traditional data and word processing while men are slotted into programming, networking, and software design training.

Search for Information

A key element of a woman's success in re-entering or remaining in the labour force is the ability to seek out and find the information she needs to make a good decision. Among the supports she needs are counselling and labour market information on employment opportunities, career choices, learning options, and financial and other resources available.

One of the most challenging elements of any form of labour market work involves finding good information that will enable one to predict what types of work will be available where. Governments, labour market specialists, education providers, and employers have all been daunted by this task. One need only look at the multitude of skill mismatches in the economy today to see just how unsuccessful their efforts have been. And yet, in the new world of training and employment programs, individuals are being sent out with little, if any, support to determine their best options for future employment. It is hard to see, given the sorts of information one is likely to be able to locate on one's own, how one woman can be expected to accomplish this task. And yet this is exactly what is now expected.

"[Clients] now have to piece it together themselves by finding job search seminars or workshops and technical classes to get needed computer skills. They have a very hard time getting a job without co-op placement that used to provide them with Canadian experience and a reference."

(National Women's Reference Group on Labour Market Issues, 1998, p. 14)

Information referral services, which are the starting point for many individuals, particularly for women, are offered in a sporadic, inconsistent, confusing, and often incomplete manner.[26] All too frequently services are offered on a group basis in the form of job-finding clubs and information sessions. Women are challenged to get enough from such a broadly focused session to meet their individual needs. It would be hard to imagine that these sessions could replace the one-on-one services of a trained counsellor in a dedicated women's organization. Alternatively, women can seek information services from the automated information systems available through kiosks. This option requires substantial computer and reading literacy levels.

The Dismantling of Women's Training Apparatus

The new funding and policy environment has profoundly affected women-only organizations, programs, and services, all of which have been important sources of support for meeting women's unique labour market needs. Traditionally, they have offered their clients low-cost and specifically developed and targeted women's programs. These services have often been delivered in an integrated manner and have covered the full range of women's needs.

"The women's training apparatus is being dismantled."
(National Women's Reference Group on Labour Market Issues, 1998, p. 11)

The introduction of the CJS in 1985 was the source of many such programs and services. In the end, it also became the source of their diminished role. The same rules that encouraged HRDC and its predecessors to seek out more effective alternatives to the traditional institutional providers of training for specific client groups – in this case, women – were used in the early 1990s to direct increasing amounts of funding to private for-profit providers. For-profit businesses began to be seen as the way to provide more flexible and cost-effective services to clients. For the first time, third-party agencies, for-profit and not-for-profit, are recognized as appropriate and legitimate potential service deliverers. Under the LMDAs the provinces are free to choose their own mix of preferred agencies. Long-term core funding has also been replaced by mainly short-term, project-based funding. With core funding virtually gone, women's organizations have been forced to spend their time applying for grants to cover services on a piece-meal basis and to justify their suitability as deliverers of these programs and services on a continuous basis. There is neither consistency nor predictability and, hence, no opportunity for long-term planning.[27]

Women's organizations that offer training or other services on a fee-for-service basis often set these rates very low to maximize accessibility for women. These rates do not normally reflect the full cost of providing the service. For-profit agencies or businesses usually set fees at 100 percent-plus of the actual cost of delivering the services or program. In the new environment of individualized funding, women are allocated only enough to pay the fees of the agency which they have agreed to use as part of their individual plan. If a woman goes to a for-profit provider, she loses because she must bear some of the cost of the higher fees. If she goes to a women's organization, the organization must either raise its fees to cover all costs or find other funds to make up the shortfall between the fees and the actual cost of delivering the service. Many women's organizations have had to dramatically alter their fee structure and their approach to conform to the new regime. The changes have seldom been to the gain of either the organization or their women clients.

"The new system is a market-driven one allowing the chips to fall where they may."
(McFarland, 1999, p. 6)

In an environment where all that is old is bad and all that is new is good, women's organizations have sometimes had difficulty holding their own. In some instances, the fact that much of their expertise and knowledge is hands-on and has been learned from peers counts against them in the world of paper credentials. In other instances, their very experience is a drawback as new creative (and often untested) approaches are preferred. Sometimes they simply lose because former HRDC personnel have set up the new agency with which they are competing.

Much of the strongest push for advancement in the career choices of women has come from women-only organizations. They are aware of the need for different career options for women, and they have built a singular body of expertise concerning the unique needs of women returning to employment. To lose these organizations is to move backwards. And the saddest thing of all is that, as women's organizations close and lose contracts, good jobs for women are often also lost. And, although women's organizations are not known for high rates of pay, they have often developed comprehensive compensation packages for their employees (in an effort not to do to their own staff what the labour market has done to women in general). Unfortunately, companies that hire their staff on a contract-by-contract basis and provide no such benefits and often remunerate their staff on a piecework basis are winning contracts for the right to deliver services. Hardly a step forward for women trying to break out of the nonstandard labour market.

Changes to Provincial Social Assistance

No discussion of the changes that took place during the 1995 to 1997 period would be complete without referring to the simultaneous cuts and shifts in focus that have also taken place within provincial social assistance programs. In times of extreme financial difficulty, provincial social assistance programs are key to the economic survival of some women and their families. They have also provided some women with income support while they have participated in training or other labour market programs and services.

In an effort to encourage all recipients considered employable to seek employment or to rely on other sources of support, such as their families, friends, or charities, the provinces have changed social assistance programs substantially. Provincial benefit rates have dropped and all provinces have tightened eligibility. In part these changes resulted from federal funding changes that involved moving from the Canada Assistance Plan (CAP) to the Canada Health and Social Transfer (CHST), which removed $26.7 billion over seven years from the provinces.[28] Some of these funds have recently been restored but have generally been used by the provinces to buttress health (and sometimes education) spending rather than social assistance.

The impact on women has been significant. Not only have rates been cut in many jurisdictions but most have also adopted mandatory work or training requirements for all women except those with very young children or severe disabilities. To refuse to participate is to risk being cut off. At the same time, many provinces have also cut spending on training. Between 1995-96 and 1997-98 provincial funding for all forms of training and employment programs decreased by $630 million. With access to federal assistance limited to current EI claimants and reach-back clients, women in need of training have few options. All forms of support, whether federally or provincially funded, are geared to a rapid return to employment regardless of the quality of work or its impact on women's rights to equity in the labour market.

Who Wins, Who Loses

In this chapter, a number of changes that took place in the labour market public policy arena and their impact on women have been examined. And as the title suggests, clear winners and losers have emerged from the shadows of these changes.

The first of the four changes was the abandonment of the federal government's Designated Group Policy. This abandonment meant that the federal government no longer imposed upon itself, or upon those with whom it dealt, the need to address the systemic disadvantage that women, visible minorities, Aboriginal persons, and persons with disabilities faced in the labour market.

The second change was the federal government's massive cuts to CRF spending on labour market programs. These programs had formed a large number of the steps taken by the federal government to give life to its Designated Group Policy. Although new programs for Aboriginal persons and persons with disabilities have been established, nothing has been done for women and members of the visible minority community. With the CRF cuts the federal government has saved close to five billion dollars over the past six years.

The third change was the introduction of new rules for governing (1) insurance benefits and (2) training and employment services for unemployed workers. In the shift from UI to EI and from UIDU to EBSM, the federal government tightened access, lowered benefit rates for many claimants, clawed back an increasing portion of benefits paid, and ensured that unemployed workers received substantive assistance with the costs of training only if they first qualified for insurance benefits. They also introduced a requirement for trainees to pay up to 50 percent or more of the costs of their training. And they used the EI system to spawn a burgeoning pool of for-profit, third-party service delivery agencies that do everything from running job-clubs to providing training. Many of the "changes" contained under Employment Benefits and Support Measures were nothing more than a confirmation of the trends HRDC offices had been implementing for some time. However, they were now written into legislation and could not be easily abandoned in the future.

The fourth and final change was the negotiation of a series of LMDAs with all provinces and territories except Ontario. This resulted in the balkanization of labour market programs and services, and the hamstringing of provinces, which were now caught within a legislative framework not of their own making. The provinces may have assumed responsibility for training, but they certainly did not gain control over it. Their options are limited, and they remain at the mercy of the federal government. Significantly, the federal government left itself lots of room to reassert itself in the field of labour market programming – something it never gave up except in a small way.

The incentives for the federal government were considerable. Billions of dollars in savings and the political kudos that came with giving the provinces something a number of them (especially Quebec) had been hankering after. Never mind that when all was said and done and the provinces woke up to the reality of what had in fact happened, they could say little without appearing like fools. It was a brilliant political move. Clearly, the federal government won much and lost little.

The provinces, initially thought by some to be the winners, have had mixed experiences. Ontario, which never signed an agreement, differs little from the other provinces in its basic approach to managing and delivering programs and services. This is testimony to the overriding effect of the federal EI legislation. On the one hand, the provinces have been left to carry the can for the cuts made to CRF spending; on the other hand, they have been able to transfer the cost of training some SARs to the federal government. It is not clear whether this is an improvement over the numbers previously paid for with CRF dollars.

Provinces such as Alberta and Quebec, which for practical and/or ideological reasons were the most keen to assume responsibility, are unlikely to give it up. Provinces such as Nova Scotia, Newfoundland, and Prince Edward Island are harder to evaluate, in part because they have continued to have considerable federal government involvement. British Columbia and Manitoba will be particularly interesting to watch as they have both experienced a change in government since they first signed their agreements. Although no provinces have been public about their dissatisfaction with the arrangement, persons at both levels of government have suggested that it cannot be assumed that all agreements will be renewed. With the impacts of the worst of the cuts behind them and lots of room left within which to manoeuvre, the federal government has little to lose either way.

Unfortunately the same cannot be said for members of the equity groups, particularly women. They have already been the losers. They bore much of the brunt of the abandonment of the Designated Group Policy and the cuts to CRF spending. With the disappearance of close to $700 million annually and the introduction of a whole series of detrimental policy changes, women and women's organizations have been severely negatively affected by the policy choices made since 1995. Those who can ill afford to contribute to training must now do so. In many cases they are on their own when it comes to childcare and other necessary supports to their efforts. And they risk facing discriminatory attitudes and practices that go against everything the women's movement has tried to do by improving labour market conditions for women. They are more likely than ever to find themselves relegated to the pink-collar ghettos from which they have only slowly begun to emerge. And the organizations they created and nurtured as sources of support and expertise have been under siege in the new world of for-profit providers and short-term contracts.

"Fewer women appear to be availing themselves of training opportunities; federal and provincial policies are undercutting services targeted to women; there are no requirements that women have equal access to training; and providers specializing in working with women are disappearing from the field, reducing the range of future options."

(National Women's Reference Group on Labour Market Issues, 1998, p. 1)

The federal government and some provinces may be applauding what occurred during the dark days of 1995 to 1997, but there are not likely to be many women or women's organizations among those celebrating.

Notes

1 By the time Ontario was prepared to negotiate an agreement, the federal government had lost its appetite for the initiative. This was particularly true in Ontario, where 101 federal Liberal MPs were not happy at the prospect of handing over one of their sources of largesse to the Harris government. On the provincial side, there was a desire to acquire, at minimum, what the government considered to be a "fair share" of the total funds at stake, based on the percentage of UI premiums paid by Ontario workers rather than on the percentage received back in benefits (which is considerably lower). Unable to find common ground, both sides have abandoned negotiations for now.
2 The provinces and territories are hereafter simply referred to as "the provinces."
3 Good examples of more detailed reviews of these issues can be found in any one of many publications. Possible sources include: Federal/Provincial/Territorial Ministers Responsible for the Status of Women, *Economic Gender Equality Indicators* (Ottawa: Status of Women Canada, 1997); Winnie Ng, *Women's Work: A Report by the Canadian Labour Congress* (Canadian Labour Congress, Ottawa, March 1997); Shauna Butterwick, *What Works and What Doesn't Work in Training: Lessons Learned from a Review of Selected Studies of Labour Market Training Programs* (British Columbia Labour Force Development Board, Vancouver, December 1996); and Heather Menzies, *Women and the Knowledge-Based Economy and Society* (Ottawa: Status of Women Canada, 1998).

4 Statistics Canada, various years, as quoted in Ursule Critoph, "Recent Labour Market Policy and Program Changes: A Synthesis of the Impacts and Implications for Women"
   (unpublished, prepared for the Status of Women, Canada, October 1999); and Karen
   Hadley, *"And We Ain't Satisfied": Gender Inequality In Canada – A Status Report for 2001*
   (Toronto: National Action Committee on the Status of Women and the CSJ Foundation
   for Research and Education, 2001).
5 Hadley, *Ain't Satisfied*, 31.
6 Human Resources Development Canada and Statistics Canada, *Adult Education and Training in Canada: Report of the 1994 Adult Education and Training Survey* (Ottawa: Human
   Resources Development Canada and Statistics Canada, February 1997).
7 Human Resources Development Canada, unpublished financial data, 1997.
8 This philosophy, which continues to dominate policy approaches today, was promoted
   and popularized among Western industrialized countries in the mid-1980s by the work of
   the Organization of Economic and Development Cooperation.
9 Some clients, called fee-payers, were required to contribute some of their own funds.
   Although the use of this cost-sharing arrangement between individuals and the government expanded in the years prior to 1996, it remained limited in its application until the
   introduction of the Employment Act, 1996.
10 Canadian Labour Force Development Board, *Inventory of Programs and Services, 1995/96*
   (Ottawa: Canadian Labour Force Development Board, 1997).
11 This decision was made without consulting the broader public and groups such as the
   Canadian Labour Force Development Board. As a body established and funded by the federal government to provide it with advice on labour market issues, and with a network of
   reference groups from among the designated groups, this would have been a logical place
   to go to discuss this possibility.
12 Although no longer bound by the Designated Group Policy, HRDC has continued to provide specially targeted programs for persons with disabilities and for Aboriginal persons.
13 It has been rumoured that, when the federal offer was first made, in at least one province
   cabinet ministers fought over who would have control over this new pot of federal money.
   They quickly learned their mistake.
14 Making sense of the federal government's data on training has always been a challenge.
   What data and information are available are often outdated and confusing as accounting
   systems and programs change frequently, sometimes more than once in a year.
15 This section focuses only on those changes made to Part 1 (i.e., the Insurance Benefits portion) of the EI Act. Changes made under Part 2 of the act are covered in the section on the
   transfer to the provinces.
16 In the changeover from a weeks-based to an hours-based system, the government raised
   the threshold from a range of 180-300 hours (12-20 weeks) to 420-700 hours for most and
   to 910 hours for new or re-entrants to the labour market.
17 In the recent case of *Kelly Lesiuk* v. *the EI Commission,* the umpire ruled that the EI eligibility requirements for new and re-entrants in ss. 6(1) and 7(2) violate Section 15 of
   the Charter of Rights and Freedoms. In his decision the umpire noted the substantive disadvantage of women due to their prevalence in the nonstandard, and the unpaid, labour
   force.
18 Based on Statistics Canada and Human Resources Development Canada data presented in
   Canadian Labour Congress, "An Analysis: The Lesiuk Case" (Ottawa: Canadian Labour
   Congress, 2001).
19 Critoph, "Recent Labour Market Policy."
20 Now a voluntary quit not only prevents an individual from collecting benefits but also
   negates all qualifying time earned to that point, unless it has been accepted under the
   exemption provisions of the EI Act.
21 Much of the material in this section was obtained as part of thirty-nine focus groups
   undertaken in 1998 under the auspices of the Canadian Labour Force Development Board.
   Although some improvements may have occurred since that time, contrary to what
   was suggested by HRDC officials (who claimed the problems were simply transitional)
   such practices have not disappeared. Part of the source for this change in attitude may be

traced to inspection officers trained in fraud detection replacing front-line staff trained in counselling and providing assistance. It should be noted that the union representing employees in HRDC offices have condemned the changes that have brought about this situation.

22 Although legislative responsibility has not been transferred, the federal government could face significant political opposition should it try to unilaterally terminate the agreements. However, the federal government has simply found new ways to remain actively involved in this very visible area of public policy, regardless of the views of their provincial counterparts.

23 Employment Insurance is a self-funded insurance program and, as such, it is open only to those who meet certain minimum requirements, the most important being an attachment to the labour market and the payment of premiums. It has been suggested that this should change or that the program itself be eliminated and replaced by a universal income support system, a negative tax system, or a guaranteed annual income system. For now, however, the insurance principle remains.

24 Critoph, "Recent Labour Market Policy," 41.

25 For administrative purposes, some provinces have combined it with their student assistance programs. In Ontario, where no LMDA exists and where HRDC continues to make the decisions, over thirty different schemes were being used to calculate client contributions.

26 All unemployed individuals, regardless of their status in relation to the EI account, are intended to have access to these services. The increasing use of third-party agencies is resulting in a highly fragmented system that is becoming increasingly difficult for the unemployed to navigate. In some instances, all services are being contracted to the same agency in a particular region. However, several agencies are often selected to provide different services, sometimes to different client populations. The result is confusion among clients, and even among agency and government staff, regarding who should go where for what.

27 In both the National Women's Reference Group on Labour Market Issues report, *Voices from the Field,* and in Shauna Butterwick's report to the British Columbia Labour Force Development Board, *Training for What,* the importance of stable funding and the negative impact of having to continuously seek out and secure funding are highlighted.

28 Ursule Critoph, *Training: Is There Still a Public Commitment?* (Ottawa: National Union of Public and General Employees, 1996), 16.

2
Snakes and Ladders: Coherence in Training for Office Workers
Alice de Wolff and Maureen Hynes

> It's so confusing. I might be wasting a lot of my time and going
> into debt if I take this course. They will give me a diploma, but
> will it be worth anything?
> – Office worker, Office Workers Career Centre, June 1999

The current training industry in Ontario displays a profusion of programs, diplomas, and certificates for office workers,[1] from short-term on-line software certification offered by software manufacturers to multiple-year college programs. Trainers, counsellors, researchers, adult educators, and office workers themselves are constantly grappling with a key problem: the privatization, proliferation, and lack of coherence in training mirrors chaotic changes in office work itself, and makes it very difficult for workers to figure out whether, or how best, to invest in their own future. In this discussion we are not attempting either to find some previously hidden coherence in the current training market or to impose our own order; rather, we explore the issues that contribute to the fragmentation of training as well as a range of existing institution-based approaches that attempt to address it. In particular, we examine the limitations to the proposal that the development of training and occupational standards would establish coherence and transparency in the current system.

This discussion is based in the experience of a group of workers, trainers, community-based advocates, and union representatives who have been involved in a series of initiatives to support office workers in Toronto. Our efforts have been motivated by several observations. The first, made in the early 1990s, was that this large group of workers was not well served by federal and provincial adjustment and training programs and that, without changes in policy and approach, a quarter of the women in the labour force would continue to be systematically excluded from these resources.[2] The second was that most office workers in the private sector do not have strong unions or associations and that, even in the unionized public sector, many struggle for recognition within their broad bargaining units.[3] Consequently, most office workers have not had the means either to influence the changes taking place in their work or to advocate for the training or labour adjustment programs that will assist them. The third observation, made in the mid-1990s, was that office work itself was in the midst of not simply technological change but, rather, something more like an industrial revolution.[4] Even experienced workers had a hard time staying on top of the changes, and this was happening as workplace and public training resources were decreasing. The fourth was that, in Toronto at least, office workers formed the occupational group that has experienced the largest and the most permanent job loss through the last decade and that the resulting labour market has become highly competitive.[5]

And, finally, the Metropolitan Toronto Clerical Workers Labour Adjustment Committee found that a central training problem for workers was not in program content but in lack of transferability from one program to another: "accreditation for clerical training is not transferable: it is not developmental, does not accumulate, and does not assist individuals in progressing either though clerical occupations or into other occupational areas."[6]

The experience of attempting to support the development of a more coherent training system has prompted our title: "Snakes and Ladders." Much like the classic board game, we have discovered opportunities for office workers to move in one training direction only to then find them either blocked or fruitless; and many of the "ladders" touted as solutions turn out, in fact, to be "snakes." We hope to provide some cautions about the snakes we have encountered and to identify some ladders that could be included or strengthened in strategies adopted by organizations of office workers and their advocates.

Changing Office Work: Why Nontransferable, Fragmented Training Is a Current Problem for Office Workers

In the last decade and a half, office workers have experienced the equivalent of an industrial revolution in their work. This process has been largely equated with technological change in workplace, union, or training discussions and has remained remarkably invisible, much like the work itself. Office work has intensified, and the work processes, the tools office workers use, who they work with, where and when they work – all have changed and continue to change at an extraordinary rate.

The more recent moments in "the information revolution" have had the most dramatic effects on the work. In the 1970s the introduction of mainframe computers, which ran word processing and accounting programs, changed the technical skills required by a small number of workers. Throughout the 1980s, as personal computers were introduced to most offices, most office workers learned about more complex text production; but the occupation continued to grow and tasks and divisions of labour did not significantly shift. The loss of jobs, along with significant changes in the work process and in divisions of labour, did not begin until the recession and downsizing of the early 1990s, which coincided with the introduction of reliable, relatively inexpensive in-house networking of personal computers.[7]

E-business, or the use of the Internet for most business transactions, is the current phase of the networking transformation, and it is taking place on a scale that can be described as the reconstruction of business administration infrastructure. It makes externally networked administrative work processes available to all sizes of workplaces in all industrial sectors. The work is increasingly complex, involves a higher volume of communications, and uses a wider range of software. Office workers will increasingly analyze data for trends and anomalies, gain access to a wider range of databases, use the Internet to source information and supplies, and coordinate in-house systems with a wider variety of outsourced databases and services.

It is likely that these changes will precipitate further job loss over the coming decade. Further, because the Internet makes it possible to deliver a wide range of administrative support systems and services from a distance, a growing number of workers are displaced from traditional workplaces and employment relationships and are employed on individual contracts as distance workers or by administrative and financial services contractors.[8]

An ongoing effect of restructuring is the increasing permeability of more traditional divisions of labour between office workers and other professionals and managers. Managers and professionals are doing more text production and communication than they were in the 1970s, while support workers are increasingly doing components of what used to be other people's work. In the course of our research over the past five years, we have come across receptionists who vet manuscripts for publishers and payroll clerks who maintain the local area network. Accounting clerks regularly handle smaller workplace accounts up to the point of audit; administrative support workers handle preliminary design tasks using computer-assisted design applications; office support workers solve basic technical support problems; and receptionists are maintaining Web sites.

Figure 2.1 captures the kinds of knowledge that office workers need in these new jobs. We use the term "knowledge" here very deliberately. Office work is often described as "low-skilled" and is regularly reduced to a set of measurable, practical tasks. Skill-based descriptions rarely capture how office workers provide the glue that holds most offices together, and they are not designed to reflect the complexity or breadth of the knowledge that is required. Our studies suggest that the traditional core knowledge of office procedures and information management continues to be the foundation of most current jobs. The tools needed to carry out most tasks are changing constantly, however, and this requires the continual learning of software applications and some knowledge of how to maintain or service the hardware. The range of knowledge about clients, types of transactions, and organizational information that most jobs now require has expanded, sometimes to include tasks formerly in the domain of other occupations or professions. Computer-assisted design, for instance, makes it possible for support workers to do routine technical tasks. And the last decade's downsizing has resulted in the merging of many jobs: receptionists now handle entry-level counselling in health, education, and social service settings; payroll clerks are responsible for maintaining the local area network; and general office clerks maintain libraries.

The "invisibility" of the occupation means that most employers, and many trainers, do not easily recognize the changes in the knowledge and skills required of a contemporary office worker, particularly in the knowledge illustrated by the outer ring of Figure 2.1. Consequently, the implications of the intensification of the work and its permeability into other occupations are double-edged. On the one hand, most office workers find that they are handling more complex responsibilities and are not recognized for it either in their pay or in the respect that they receive. On the other hand, new responsibilities can open up new interests and, for some, a route out of a shrinking occupation.

Some office workers are forging new career paths, and this should act as signposts to trainers. Traditionally, office support work had an internal mobility: payroll clerks became human resource assistants; typists became secretaries, administrative assistants, and office managers; accounting clerks became accountants; and purchasing clerks became buyers. Restructuring has restricted these opportunities in many workplaces. Instances of the newer paths include workers who have been good at providing others with

Figure 2.1

Kinds of knowledge required in office work

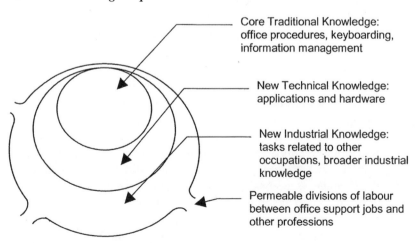

Core Traditional Knowledge: office procedures, keyboarding, information management

New Technical Knowledge: applications and hardware

New Industrial Knowledge: tasks related to other occupations, broader industrial knowledge

Permeable divisions of labour between office support jobs and other professions software support and trouble shooting moving to a help desk, to computer instruction, and to becoming application solutions providers. Administrative assistants responsible for in-house publications have moved to specialized desktop publishing, to multimedia design, to Web mastery, and to e-business consulting.

These observations raise several challenges for trainers. The first is to make it possible for workers to assess whether or not they need training: many displaced workers are highly trained, although they may not have the credentials to prove it to a new employer. In an increasingly competitive labour market, credentials rather than experience may be what distinguishes one worker from another. Trainers need to be more prepared to use extensive prior learning assessment and recognition in order to assist workers as they navigate the current labour market. The second challenge is to design coherent training for entry to, and upgrading in, occupations in which the tools are changing dramatically and in which the responsibilities are expanding into areas traditionally related to other jobs. The third is to design training that reflects the mobility of work tasks and that creates bridges out of this shrinking occupation into an expanding group of related occupations.

Fragmentation and Privatization

There is a growing disjuncture between the new work, the training needs of office workers, and the kind of training available. The occupation is becoming more complex, and its links with other occupations need to be made more specific. The available training, on the other hand, is being delivered in shorter, more fragmented pieces that focus on technical training – the middle circle in Figure 2.1 – or on the so-called "soft" employability skills such as communication and dressing for success. Entry-level training is getting shorter, while the entry-level requirements for many office support jobs are becoming more complex.

Office workers learn about their work in many different ways: in public and secondary school, from each other on the job and on their own at home, through on-the-job training, and through public or private courses or programs, usually taken at their own expense.[9] But the informal learning and the certificates rarely accumulate or contribute in any predictable way to further training or employment. This issue – "lack of transferability" – is actually a bundle of issues and is the result of a particular history.

For much of the century the training office workers needed and received was predictable and relatively stable, as were their work and its related career paths. Many students received keyboard training in secondary school. Public colleges, technical institutes, and a small number of private business schools provided up to two years of postsecondary diploma programs in typing, shorthand, bookkeeping, office procedures, and business English.

The public colleges provided the most consistently recognized diploma, which set a commonly recognized standard. Some colleges offered refresher diplomas for people returning to the workforce, which included more complex courses like report writing. In the bigger institutions courses could be taken separately and credits could be applied over time to a diploma. Even though they were similar, the programs were treated as proprietary to each institution, making it difficult for students to transfer credits between programs.

The broad transformation of office work processes that began in the 1970s not only revolutionized the work but it also contributed to the fragmentation of training provision. In the early 1980s employers spent significant resources training their office support staff to use new office technologies.[10] This short burst of employer demand established the model for much of the development of the short, modularized, technical skills-based courses that dominate the current market. As a result, on-the-job training has become synonymous with software applications training. Subsequently, many software producers recognized that product training was a revenue generator and have developed and marketed their own programs and certificates, and franchised instructors and training institutions to deliver them. Established public and private programs have struggled to keep up with what employers and the software industry claim to be state of the art training: they have been encouraged to develop distance learning capacities, shorten and modularize their courses, and become certified deliverers of manufacturers' certificates. Training for office workers has fractured into a mosaic of mostly technical, skills-based courses and programs.

The last decade's drastic cuts in public funding to college and community-based programs have resulted in a decrease in the number of seats in public programs and, at the same time, a proliferation of shorter courses. In 1996 the federal government transferred the responsibility for administering Employment Insurance (EI) training funds to the provinces. The legislation signalled a significant policy change: at the same time as it was getting out of the business of training, the federal government set up mechanisms that support the development of a private training market. In 1997, in the form of vouchers and loans, the EI program began to transfer training funds from block purchases of program seats to individuals. As of 2001 the Ontario provincial government had not picked up the transferred responsibility – a position that complemented its other actions regarding training, including a 20 percent cut to colleges, the reduction of access to student loans, and the elimination of support for workplace literacy programs.

While these federal and provincial actions have not been articulated in one coherent training policy, their effect can be seen in the programs that are currently available in Toronto. In 1995 there were twenty-seven community-based programs that delivered clerical-related vocational train-ing.[11] In 2001 many of the same agencies existed; however, because of the elimination of federal support for training, most were focused on pro-viding employment and career guidance rather than vocational training. These short "career readiness" courses included components similar to former programs, but they cannot be called "training." Only four or five programs found funding that made it possible for them to continue to offer "training."

Colleges have restructured programs in response to a 20 percent cut to their provincial funding in 1996 and the federal EI shift from purchas-ing block seats to individual vouchers in 1997. The Toronto colleges went through a consolidation process to avoid duplication, which resulted in the elimination of one of four office administration programs. The remain-ing programs have significantly cut back on their enrolment, shortened their diplomas, added multiple entry points, and established single courses offered through their continuing education departments. In part, these changes have developed in response to the demands of students. But every-one involved acknowledges that the concerns of many students are related to the EI vouchers that offer support for only twenty-six weeks of training, which means that students must get into a short program as quickly as pos-sible after their claim is approved.

In the private sector, there has been a proliferation of training institu-tions offering diploma and shorter certificate programs related to office work. A federal government Web site that hosts an admittedly incomplete list of training programs reports 240 office administration and related computer courses offered by fifty-one private institutions in Toronto.[12] Fee structures, course length, and start dates of private courses are tightly matched to EI provisions and have changed accordingly over the decade. Private programs have also been affected by the 1995 provincial decision to stop providing student loan assistance to welfare recipients: enrolment dropped immediately in many office-related programs. And because the province has begun to hold both public and private training institutions responsible for student loan defaults, a small number of private institu-tions have closed, and most have become more cautious about the risks involved in offering more comprehensive, longer programs that have higher fees.

Both private and public trainers are struggling with remaining both rele-vant to the occupation and economically viable. In interviews, instructors in four diploma courses (public and private) illustrated the challenges: their entry diploma program used to provide students with enough time to progress from no experience with a keyboard to typing sixty words per minute. Now most diplomas require only fifty words per minute, and even this is very difficult to accomplish within the shorter time period. Students whose English is not strong have even less of a chance of getting through such a compact program. Interviewees reported having very little time to teach the kind of broader knowledge of business and the world that office workers increasingly need – basic geography, general current events, and English grammar.

As the student quoted at the beginning of this chapter says, the resulting array of training is confusing. This confusion cannot be fixed solely by encouraging students to be more informed consumers of training. This confusion is in the lack of coherence in courses offered, in the speed with which the occupation itself is changing, in its relative lack of importance in the view of employers, and in the reduction of time and space, even in the multi-year diploma programs, within which students and instructors are expected to develop an overview of these changes along with adequate responses to them.

So Why Don't We Develop Training Standards?

In the course of our attempts to support office workers, we have encountered a striking interest in developing training content standards, even within the context of increased competition among programs. Trainers, workers, union representatives, employers, Human Resources Development Canada (HRDC) representatives, and employment counsellors have all said that training standards are an obvious solution to the problem as we stated it.

On the face of it, the development of training standards appears to have the potential to solve a number of problems. It would presumably map out the occupation and its possible future directions and require an analysis of different levels of expertise. Workers and union representatives have indicated that, if it were done thoroughly, the extent of both technical and nontechnical knowledge needed in the occupation would become more visible. Students and workers have said that, with standards, it would be easier to assess and describe their own level of expertise to new or current employers. "Shopping" for courses might be easier; the differences among programs and how they apply to a possible career path would be more obvious. Employers echoed this, saying that they are not familiar with the full range of diplomas and certificates available, nor do they know what to expect from programs outside their personal experience. Counsellors have observed that standards recognized by both trainers and employers would make it far simpler to counsel people about their career plans. And trainers anticipate advantages: more students might be in the right courses, keeping up with changes in the occupation might be less time-consuming, and curriculum would more likely align with employers' needs.

Because of the consistent interest in standards, we have reviewed existing standards related to the occupation and have conducted interviews with trainers. The resulting observations problematize the apparently obvious way forward. The interests of all parties involved – workers, trainers, employers, government, and office equipment and software manufacturers – are different and at times conflicting. The creation and maintenance of standards are often sites of intense negotiation and struggle, and the results tend to reflect the interests of the party(ies) who bring the most effective resources to that struggle.

What Standards Exist?

> The value of every diploma is different. It depends on the reputation of the school and how well it is accepted by employers, not on whether it is from a college, private vocational program or a university.[13]

We discovered that, rather than an absence of standards, there are many standards. Private training programs, government-funded programs, large employers with training programs, and some professional associations all have established training standards. It is, however, just about as difficult to make sense of the profusion of standards as it is to find coherence among the profusion of training programs. In fact, in the new environment of competition among trainers, standards are being used as a promotional tool, a way of setting programs apart from each other, rather than as a tool that easily establishes commonalities and coherence.

First, we should briefly describe two different kinds of training standards: performance standards and content standards. Performance standards describe how well learners should know or be able to do something (e.g., the accepted number of error-free keyboard words per minute or the grades needed to pass portions of the curriculum). Content standards in vocational programs generally detail a course and/or program according to their academic, technical, and employability content. Academic standards usually refer to school and university subjects; technical standards relate to job-specific knowledge and skills; and employability standards relate to thinking, problem solving, communication, interpersonal skills, responsibility, and integrity.[14]

The Standards Industry
A small industry has emerged that assists workplaces, training providers, and associations to produce their own standards. Its product is a range of organizational standards designed for specific training programs or workplaces. The Work Keys system is a prominent example because it is promoted by the Association of Community Colleges of Canada as a tool that tightly integrates the needs of business with those of trainees and trainers.

It provides tools to measure skill levels; to develop detailed job profiles; and to assess individual trainee/employee performance, the potential of job applicants, and trainee/employee development. The system connects the descriptions and measures needed to establish a set of skill standards and those required to create workplace job descriptions and performance appraisals, and it facilitates a practical interchangeability between each.

Employer Standards
Some large employers have developed in-house training programs for their office workers using the standards industry's tools. The International Organization for Standardization (ISO) has created an influential and widely recognized template for workplace management practices that assure quality service and products. The ISO itself does not set standards but, rather, establishes management practices that detail expectations of work processes and introduce measurable performance standards. In many companies these programs are a component of a competitive strategy, and management takes steps to establish their difference from those of other companies.

Experience in one of the major Canadian banks illustrates concerns many workers have about employers' use of training standards. This bank has invested significant resources in electronic training modules that are available at every branch and bank office.[15] Employees are expected to log on during their (increasingly pressured) workday and to work through the units at their own pace. Employees are assured that their supervisors do not see the results of the on-line "self-testing." However, the system does not allow individuals to progress from one module to the next unless they can meet a set of performance standards at the end of each module. Supervisors electronically monitor how often they log on as well as their progress through each course, and they use this information in performance appraisals. Performance standards are the central mechanism in this system, and they make it possible for the employer to turn training standards into criteria against which individual job performance is measured.

Software Manufacturers' Standards
Manufacturers of software provide a plethora of certificates and standards related to office software. One that is familiar to many office workers is the Microsoft Office User Specialist (MOUS) certificate. In this case the manufacturer uses a set of standards as the basis for examinations of different levels of expertise; publishes study and self-examination tools; and selects testing centres, authorized instructors, and course outlines.[16] Other manufacturers, including Novell (Local Area Network Administrator and Certified Internet Professional), IBM, Oracle, Lotus, and many others, certify users and trainers in a similar manner.

Existing Government Standards

The Ontario government establishes standards for both publicly funded and private office work training programs. For the twenty-six Ontario colleges, the content standards-setting process is actually the "soft cop" to the harsher ministry requirement that a high proportion of graduates be placed in jobs. This requirement was formalized by the introduction of the government's Key Performance Indicators (KPI) Project for colleges in the fall of 1998. The KPI's are a "performance-based funding initiative" in which survey data in five areas (graduate employment, graduate satisfaction, employer satisfaction, student satisfaction, and graduation rate) are compiled and ranked.

When fully implemented, up to 10 percent of the ministry's grants to each college will be tied to KPI performance. The implementation of this system has been enormously controversial, focusing on the exclusion of faculty in consultations and the need for broader evaluation terms, including, for example, measures of the colleges' accessibility, equity, and responsiveness to community needs. It is likely that the funding incentives will preserve the disadvantage of the colleges scoring at the lower end of the indicators. And, while providing students with an opportunity to give feedback on the quality of the learning experience, the KPI project is another example of a project that privileges employers' needs to "ensure an even more job-ready graduate from the Ontario college system."[17]

The discussions that occurred during the 2000 revisions to the content standards for the colleges' office administration diploma programs provide a glimpse of several concerns. First, students were only marginally involved in the process, and it was assumed that their interests in employability were essentially the same as those of employers. Second, the prioritizing process emphasized that the only "givens" were employer requirements and government spending limits. A focus group found it easy to establish consensus about increases in the kinds of knowledge and skills required by entry-level office workers. But when pushed to prioritize the content of their year-long, multiple-entry-point, first-level programs, the educators expressed strong concern about being able to teach all of what was needed. The ministry was not prepared to take a position that suggested that colleges could not deliver what employers wanted, nor was it prepared to intervene in the funding tensions that have forced colleges to shorten programs. Consequently, many faculty feel that they have to appear to do the impossible:

> Office workers have to know something about how business and government work. Our students don't know how to read newspapers, don't know the geography of this country let alone that of the globe, don't know the

names or positions of politicians. We need more than a year to prepare them to be anything like "information workers in the global economy."[18]

Most of our students are recent immigrants. They must have a certain level of fluency in English to enter the program, but for many of them this is the first learning other than ESL that they have done in English, and they are still struggling with the language. They are fine learning office software, but keyboard skills involve language skills, and most take the full program to work up their speed and accuracy.[19]

We are developing a short component on the Internet, but we can't go into it in much depth. They just barely get through the current curriculum.[20]

These observations by faculty suggest that office work should no longer be treated as an entry-level occupation, and they point out how a standards-setting process can contribute to the increasingly stretched and fragmented nature of public programs.

The Ontario government also licenses private vocational programs but sets no common content standards. The standards for licensed private trainers are business standards: an institution must show that it is a responsible business, that it is properly governed, that it provides an adequate facility, and that it has taken care of safety and liability issues. Each institution must also show that it has a course of studies with its own content standards that will prepare students for a vocation; a government adult training design specialist then reviews this program. Most important, programs must find employers who will state that the program will produce the kind of workers that they will hire.

The federal government has devolved its jurisdiction over training and education to most provinces, although it has retained some responsibility for labour market development. Human Resources Development Canada has, however, established a little known guide for curriculum development and employment performance standards that specifies entry-level skills for office workers (among a wide range of other occupations). The Essential Skills Profile (ESP) is intended to define entry-level requirements for literacy, numeracy, computer literacy, oral communication, thinking skills, working with others, and the necessity for ongoing learning.[21]

Unions

Few unions representing office workers have developed strategies to use training standards and certification to strengthen their members' ability to capture jobs or to improve their bargaining position. The British Columbia Government Employees' Union has developed a proposal that would make clerical/administrative support work an apprenticeable trade. This strategy recognizes the extent to which office workers learn on the job, and it would ensure that the members involved would receive consistent training over a number of years.

Professional Associations

Professional associations establish credentials for their own membership by establishing standards for the training that they should receive and by certifying specific training providers to issue a certificate. This is a "guild" strategy, the goal of which is to establish a legitimate claim that only certified association members have the required background to adequately do the job. This strategy is successful when the association has (1) control over all the relevant training or (2) all workers in the occupation are members. In the field of office work, the International Association of Administration Professionals and the Payroll Association both detail several levels of achievement, outline courses that need to be taken in order to achieve each level, and identify approved course providers. Neither association, however, has a large membership in Canada, and their credentials are not widely recognized by employers, workers, or trainers.

Concerns about Organizational Standards

Significant concerns arise from this review of existing organizational standards. First, it appears that standards-setting processes commonly equate the interests of students/employees with those of employers. Other researchers have described this effect: "skills development is being transformed from the chance for individuals to gain bargaining power in the labour market, into an opportunity for employers to gain workers whose knowledge and skill is already tightly harnessed to the interests of business."[22]

The current interests of office workers diverge from those of employers in two central ways. Because significant numbers of office workers are being displaced from the occupation, both displaced workers and those in less secure positions need to move out of the occupation and beyond the requirements of their current employers. Further, it is generally not in employers' interest to identify the increased responsibilities and knowledge required to do the redesigned work.

The second concern is related: tools like Work Keys are most easily used to measure the technical tasks noted in Figure 2.1, and they are less likely to be used to describe the increased knowledge required to handle the new work. Third, the difficulty of preparing workers for the current workplace suggests that trainers, employers, and workers all need to reconsider the assumption that office work is an entry-level occupation that can be supported by short-term and fragmented training. Fourth, the content of skills or competency standards is not significantly different from that of detailed job descriptions and workplace performance criteria, and it can be easily translated for these other purposes. Without vigilance on the part of employee advocates, standards to which students/workers can be expected to perform in the workplace can easily be used in employee performance assessments. And finally, those employee associations that do use training and certification standards to demonstrate the employability of their members are not currently strong enough to significantly influence the training or the employment market.

Problem of the Dominant Standard

The previous section's examination of the proliferation of existing standards and their limitations makes it clear that the impulse to establish standards that would enable workers to sort their way through the maze of available training is really an impulse to create a dominant standard – a meta-standard that can articulate existing standards and programs to each other. However, a review of experience elsewhere suggests that, in a political climate that is encouraging the formation of a private training industry, the development of meta-standards is most likely to create a mechanism that articulates privately provided training to a publicly sanctioned credential. It might address the broad concerns about the lack of coherence in the system, but it is likely to compound the concerns that emerged in our discussion of organizational standards.

The Existing Dominant Standard

The current system actually does have a dominant performance standard that operates in both the public and private training systems: programs must demonstrate that their graduates are employable and employed. Publicly funded programs are required to demonstrate that a certain proportion of graduates find employment in a related job after graduation. Private programs use graduate employment statistics as part of their promotion, and there is an assumption that previous successes influence enrolment. Because private programs are not, however, required to publicize whether students' jobs are program-related, this measure is unreliable in helping students understand a program's specific place in the training mosaic, its links to a particular kind of job, and/or its ability to open up other occupational or education opportunities.

Industry-Wide Standards

While the employability standard is a defining mechanism of the market-driven training system, efforts do exist to develop more effective and directed training. Many governments recognize that a meta-standard is not likely to arise from a strictly market-driven system and that they are not achievable without complex negotiations. In Canada the federal government has supported the formation of over thirty industry-specific sector councils whose mandate is to anticipate and develop the human resources for each industry. Each council has a structure that involves representatives of employers and employees. Many of these councils have established industry-wide standards and certification programs. Several function like employee associations in that they outline a course of study and levels of achievement, identify and approve training providers, and certify individuals.

The most immediate difficulty that office workers encounter with this system is that it is industry-specific and not easily adaptable to an occupation that crosses all sectors but is not definitional to any one. The industry that is most like a sectoral employer for office workers is the finance and insurance sector. Banks and insurance companies have a long tradition of reluctance to work with government or in joint structures with employees, and this makes the industry-specific route unpromising. The other route – the creation of a cross-sector, occupation-based council – has received little support from employers or from government.[23]

Countrywide Occupational Standards

While the Canadian government has not attempted to produce occupational standards for administrative occupations, experiences in other countries indicate reason for caution. The exercise of developing a national standards framework can relieve some frustration with the absence of a training overview, but its translation into a set of accepted standards is enormously labour-intensive and is problematic from the perspective of workers.

In 1998 the US National Skills Standards Board (NSSB) began the process of developing voluntary federal standards for occupations in business and administration services. The difficulties encountered in this complex project are instructive. First, no key group of employers has stepped forward to make the investment in administrative workers that is required by this kind of initiative. Second, it involves merging a tremendous number of existing standards developed by industries, associations, state governments, and public and private training institutions. Representatives of the American Federation of Labor/Congress of Industrial Organizations (AFL/CIO) are involved but have raised significant concerns. They see the possibility that the NSSB process will undermine current union-controlled apprenticeship programs by legitimizing lower-quality alternatives and that workers and unions may be cut out of training definition where apprenticeships don't exist. The system's reliance on the codification of complex jobs into skills or competencies could contribute to deskilling. And finally, they argue, it could entrench a two-tiered postsecondary education system where some workers are tracked into a narrow job-related system with few connections to the public educational system.

Some Conclusions

The changes that are affecting office administration have created challenges for workers struggling to navigate the growing complexity of hype, new tools, and knowledge required in the work and in a much more competitive job market. They challenge trainers to design more useful "ladders" that would:

- prepare workers for the breadth of responsibilities and knowledge required in the current work and prepare them to change quickly as those demands change. This requires meeting knowledge acquisition as well as skill development needs and may require rethinking whether or not office work is an "entry-level" occupation.
- assess whether experienced workers need training or just more useful credentials. This would require more extensive use of prior learning assessment and recognition.
- recognize links to new occupations and areas of knowledge developing in the workplace and facilitate the mobility of experienced workers into these areas.

The proposal to address these challenges by developing either organizational or meta-standards is fraught with difficulties. When the suggestion comes from workers, it usually expresses the hope that standards will make it possible for them to gain some bargaining power with employers. Our review suggests that while the process of developing a meta-standard might create some coherence in the training system, it doesn't necessarily increase workers' bargaining power and, in fact, can open up new, negative consequences for workers. Standards-setting processes that are based on skills and competency descriptions tend to equate the needs of employers and employees, and make it possible for employers to directly negotiate their needs with trainers. This is not an acceptable way to proceed for those in an occupation in which employers consistently fail to recognize the knowledge needed to do the work.

Our review underscores the need for effective organizations of office workers: many existing associations and union bargaining units are not strong enough to challenge training providers and employers in a standards-setting exercise, nor are they prepared to define training needs. Strong worker advocates need to be able to prevent training competency standards from being used to assess individual employee performance and development; to insist on the recognition of, and education for, the broad knowledge required in the new work; and to insist on systems that allow experienced but displaced workers to use their experience to move into other occupations.

The prospect of the development of a meta-standard raises policy-related issues. A meta-standard would provide a mechanism for incorporating private trainers into a publicly sanctioned system of credentials and would consolidate the development of the private training industry. From an industrial policy perspective, the "branding" of standards is an essential step in the process of developing training as a service industry with tradeable commodities and preparing it for inclusion in current international trade negotiations.[24] For US trainers, for instance, the ability to advertise that the credentials they provide meet a US federal standard is likely to provide them with a certain advantage in an international training market.

Meta-standards do not necessarily guarantee higher-quality training. In Aeotearoa/New Zealand and Australia, where national classification and training modularization systems have been implemented, the systems provide little capacity to actually monitor or evaluate local program delivery.[25] And because office workers are constantly working with information and, like other information workers, need a solid academic background in order to understand and work with that information, we share the concern of the AFL/CIO that federal standards in vocational training could increase the distance between skills-based vocational education and knowledge-based academic postsecondary education.

Canada has not yet initiated occupation-based standards projects, except through its human resource sector councils. Even in the context of the negotiations surrounding the Free Trade Agreement of the Americas, the federal government is unlikely to undertake such a project because it has little remaining jurisdiction over training, and there is no sign that the provinces are about to undertake such a complex project. We feel strongly that there are enough concerns about the standards-setting process that labour- and community-based groups should not initiate it. We may have some space in Canada, then, to strengthen office workers' organizations and their approach to training and standards development.

Ladders: Where the Energy Might Be Better Invested

Organizations that represent office workers need to develop stronger policies regarding the training of their members. A large number of workers could be affected by some collaboration between the public and private sector unions that have training clauses in their collective agreements. Collaboration could put unionized workers in a position to identify what kinds of employer-supported training are most useful to their members and to negotiate content and transferability with training providers.

More trainers should offer courses that contribute to certification with the International Association of Administrative Professionals and the Payroll Association. Despite a generally uneasy relationship between associations and unions, both want their members' knowledge and expertise to be recognized by employers; therefore, there may be room for collaboration on the content of training and negotiations with training providers.

If a Canadian proposal for occupational standards emerges, then public sector unions are in a strategic position to respond. Over the last decade they have undertaken a massive project to develop pay-equity job descriptions, through which they have gained considerable expertise in office work classification systems. As we noted earlier, the content of detailed job descriptions is similar to that of training and performance standards: the differences tend to be in how they are used, who controls their use, and how thoroughly they recognize the knowledge required for the work. Public sector unions could pool this expertise and develop a strong challenge to trainers to provide training for their current and future members that enables them to perform and progress in their work. A more proactive step would be for these unions to identify and "capture" the training needed for each job classification and to certify those training providers who could provide members with the needed courses.

The enormous reconfiguration of office work and the explosion in knowledge requirements for office workers show no signs of slowing over the next decade. We have argued that an exercise in setting standards for the occupation – seen by many as the requisite starting-point for a coherent training system – will not only add to the confusion and opacity of training options for individual workers but will also be an instrument to further privatize training and render it a more "profitable" – and hence less accessible – enterprise. It is also clear that the stakes are high for office workers, much higher than our "Snakes and Ladders" title might indicate, given the debt levels workers take on to finance training. We have tried to highlight some of the ladders for the occupation as well as to point out the more worrying snakes. The activism, advocacy, and support of key unions and organizations could produce a truly worker-centred and worker-driven training system as well as begin to eliminate the current confusion, fragmentation, inequities, and ineffectiveness of training for office workers.

Notes

1 The term "office workers" refers to a cluster of over twenty occupations, which include office clerks, receptionists, bookkeepers, secretaries, administrative assistants, data entry clerks, customer service clerks, and production clerks.

2 Twenty-five percent of women in the labour market were clerical workers or secretaries at the time of the census in 1996. See Statistics Canada, *The Nation Series 1996* (Ottawa: Statistics Canada, 1998).

3 At the end of the 1980s, when unionization rates were higher, approximately 72 percent of public sector office workers were unionized, compared to 11.7 percent in the finance sector and 26.2 percent in manufacturing. See Julie White, *Sisters and Solidarity: Women and Unions in Canada* (Toronto: Thompson Educational Publishing, 1993), 173.

4 Alice de Wolff, *Job Loss and Entry Level Information Workers* (Toronto: Metro Toronto Clerical Workers Labour Adjustment Committee, 1995).

5 Job loss among office workers has been particularly dramatic in Toronto. Between 1989

and 1997, 35 percent of clerical jobs were lost in the city (i.e., 92,600 jobs). This is by far the largest job loss of any occupational group in the region. See Pat Bird and Alice de Wolff, *Occupational Analysis: Clerical Occupations in Metropolitan Toronto* (Toronto: Clerical Workers Centre, 1997).
6 de Wolff, *Job Loss,* 1995.
7 Ibid.
8 Alice de Wolff, *The Impact of E-Business on Office Work* (Toronto: Office Workers Career Centre, 2000).
9 Daniel Glenday, Ann Duffy, and Norene Pupo, "Do Unions Make a Difference? Unions and the Introduction of Information Technology into Clerical Occupations." Presented to the Advanced Research Seminar, Women and Unions: Industrial Relations Collective Bargaining and Union Militancy, York University, 24 January 1992. Another study of 1,120 office workers showed that 29 percent had a college or university degree; 53 percent had a college program diploma or courses in high school; 53 percent had taken individual courses; and 73 percent had received training on the job. Diane Moore, "Office Professionals in Transition. Preparing for the Millennium." Presented to the 1999 American Society for Training and Development International Conference, Atlanta, Georgia.
10 Between 1980 and 1985 approximately 60 percent of Canadian employees trained on-the-job for computer technologies were clerical staff, compared to only 20 percent between 1985 and 1991. See Gordon Betcherman, Kathryn McMullen, Norm Leckie, and Christina Caron, *The Canadian Workplace in Transition* (Kingston: Industrial Relations Centre, Queen's University, Kingston, 1994), 39.
11 de Wolff, *Job Loss,* 87.
12 Human Resources Development Canada, *Interactive Training Inventory* (Ottawa: Government of Canada, 1998), <www.trainingiti.com/pls/itiv38/common.opening_screen> (25 November 2002).
13 Ministry of Training Colleges and Universities staff, interview by Alice de Wolff, November 2000, Toronto.
14 J. Wills, *Standards: Making Them Useful and Workable for the Education Enterprise* (Washington, DC: Office of Vocational and Adult Education, US Department of Education, 1997).
15 Director, Toronto-based bank training centre, interview by Alice de Wolff, October 1998, Toronto.
16 All of the approximately thirty Toronto-area MOUS test centres are private institutions.
17 "Minister Announces KPI Launch," *kpi express,* 1, 1 (1998): 1. Ontario Ministry of Education and Training/Association of Colleges of Applied Arts and Technology of Ontario.
18 College program coordinator, interview by Alice de Wolff, February 2000, Toronto.
19 College instructor, interview by Alice de Wolff, January 2000, Toronto.
20 College program director, interview by Alice de Wolff, November 1999, Toronto.
21 Human Resources Development Canada, *Essential Skills* (Ottawa: Government of Canada, 2000).
22 Nancy Jackson and Steven Jordan, *Skills Training: Who Benefits?* (Toronto: York University, Labour Education and Training Research Network, Centre for Research on Work and Society, 2000), 1.
23 The Metro Toronto Clerical Workers Labour Adjustment Committee approached both the CLFDB and the HRDC with the possibility of developing a full occupation-based council in 1996 but found little support.
24 Training and education has been included in Asia-Pacific Economic Cooperation discussions and in the current negotiations for the Free Trade Agreement of the Americas.
25 Space limitations prevent us from providing detailed analyses of these three complex national experiments. See the Business and Administrative Services, *Recommendations to the National Skill Standard Board* (Washington, DC: National Alliance of Business, June 1998); *Registered Apprenticeship and the National Skill Standards System* (Washington, DC: American Federation of Labour/Congress of Industrial Organizations, 2000); and Jackson and Jordon, *Skills Training,* for fuller discussions.

3

The Road to Equity: Training Women and First Nations on the Vancouver Island Highway

Marjorie Griffin Cohen and Kate Braid

There are good reasons to train and employ women and people from minority groups in highway construction. Massive amounts of public money are involved and the employment needs of the projects are large. The overwhelmingly "White, male" face of the workforce in highway building makes this setting an ideal opportunity for equity initiatives, particularly because virtually all governments profess to be committed to equal opportunity in employment. Highway construction jobs are skilled and well-paying, and the exclusion of women or people from minority groups has become increasingly difficult to justify.

Until the building of the Vancouver Island Highway in British Columbia in the mid-1990s, women's work in highway construction in Canada was confined almost exclusively to traffic management. A survey of unionized workers in British Columbia in 1990 indicated that women accounted for less than three-tenths of 1 percent of the province's unionized construction workforce. Aboriginal workers fared slightly better, making up about 1 percent, and the total for visible minorities was 2.67 percent. Workers identified as "equity" workers comprised only 4 percent of the entire unionized construction workforce.[1] No reliable information exists on the employment of equity groups in highway construction, but most analysts assume that the representation of these groups in highway construction is less than it is in building construction.[2]

Integrating the construction trades is notoriously difficult. Even in the United States, where legal requirements and funding for ameliorative programs have been available, not much progress has been made, and women's proportion of construction trades jobs, at 2.4 percent, has increased only one-tenth of 1 percent over the last decade.[3] In an industry where work is always temporary, the continuous process of finding a job is particularly onerous for workers who face a succession of hiring barriers not typical in other discriminatory workplaces.[4] Equity initiatives for the Vancouver Island Highway Project (VIHP) marked the first time equity measures were a specific requirement in a project agreement in highway construction in Canada. This innovative contract was negotiated through a project/labour agreement in which Highway Constructors Ltd. (HCL), a subsidiary of a provincial Crown Corporation, was set up as the exclusive employer for all construction labour used on the highway.[5] HCL provided labour to contractors, and contractors reimbursed HCL for labour costs. HCL's involvement in the hiring process facilitated the initiatives to hire labour from local communities and from targeted equity groups.

The equity component of the project agreement was difficult to negotiate primarily because the major participants to the agreement – the building trade unions and the highway building contractors – were initially opposed to the equity measures, although many individual trade unionists supported them. Despite this start-up handicap, the equity initiatives were surprisingly successful. As seen in Table 3.1, the numbers employed from the equity target groups were much higher on the VIHP than is normally the case for their representation in building construction projects altogether.

As Table 3.1 shows, in each year of the project during the major building years, the proportion of hours worked by members of equity groups increased. "Hours worked" is a better indication of representation of the equity workforce than is a calculation based on the number of individuals working because it more accurately reflects their actual participation in the project.

These figures may appear to be modest, but when compared with the normal numbers, which were virtually zero for each of these groups, they

Table 3.1

Vancouver Island Highway equity groups' proportion of total hours worked

	1994	1995	1996	1997	1998	1999[a]
Women	2. 2	4.0	5.8	6.5	10.3	8.4
Aboriginal	5.3	5.9	7.6	7.5	11.6	8.9
People with disabilities	0.8	1.6	1.2	1.2	0.8	0.8
Visible minorities	0.0	1.8	1.8	2.0	1.5	1.2
Equity as % of total[b]	8.3	12.6	15.5	16.3	22.1	17.8

[a] The figures for 1994-97 are for the full year, while those for 1998-99 are for the construction season. Only the contractors' core labour force would be working throughout the year, a factor that would depress statistics for equity hires.

[b] Total equity is less than the sum of the columns because some people are included in more than one category.

Source: 1994-97 calculated from the Labour Force Report of Highway Constructors Ltd.; 1998-99 information from HCL Payroll Summary, Construction Season 26 April to 7 November, 1998 and 1999.

indicate substantial gains. At various times during the project, particularly during summer months, the number of equity workers hired climbed to over 23 percent, with women representing over 10 percent of the total and First Nations representing 12 percent.[6] The project was also a clear success in its attempt to provide labour for local residents since 93 percent of the workforce was local hire.

Over the course of a year, we conducted extensive interviews with the workers who participated in the equity process. We also interviewed contractors, trainers, trade union representatives, and government personnel responsible for the project at various stages. In total thirty-eight people were interviewed. Other information about the workforce came from unusually detailed bi-weekly labour statistics collected by HCL. This material provides information about the number of people employed, the hours they worked, and the type of job performed, in addition to specifying the equity classification of the employee.

Our assessment is that the HCL model used on the VIHP is an excellent model to use as a generic approach to training and integrating people from traditionally excluded groups into the workforce of large-scale construction projects. The potential for substantial and lucrative work for both trade union members and independent contractors, despite equity hiring, is a powerful incentive to achieving the compliance of these groups. In addition to the very important goal of providing work for women and First Nations, HCL's commitment to equity hiring provided considerable social benefits to both the local community and the culture of the industry. Its success also shows that these results can be obtained within the budgetary constraints of the project.

Project Agreement

Analysts of nontraditional employment in the construction industry identify three key ingredients as essential for establishing a successful equity program. These are: (1) building collaborative relationships between contractors, trade unions, and community-based organizations; (2) establishing a critical mass of specific equity group employees; and (3) creating an atmosphere "characterized by cooperation rather than the demand for 'compliance.'"[7] The challenges encountered during the process of integrating women and Aboriginal people into the HCL workforce were considerable, but these three components were always present, albeit in various degrees.[8] However, the most significant ingredient identified for this project contradicts conventional wisdom; that is, a certain degree of compulsion was essential at the outset because neither the contractors nor the trade unions welcomed equity provisions in the project agreement.

The equity provisions were the result of a top-down decision that was codified both in the collective agreement and in the structure of the project's management. This occurred for several reasons. First, the equity provisions had support at the highest levels, including Glen Clark, the minister under whom it had been initiated who later became premier of the province. Second, they were initiated, monitored, and continuously supported by women's groups and First Nations bands on Vancouver Island.[9] Third, the equity and local hire issues were in some respects tied together so that the VIHP had strong support from the local community. Fourth, there was a model project agreement to follow that, in the past, had worked in other large-scale construction projects.

Traditionally, construction projects are built through a bidding process during which, in a tender document, the owner specifies what work is needed. Each successful bidder can subcontract portions of the work in a similar bidding process. At no time does the initial owner deal directly with workers or labour issues, and when no common collective agreement exists, very disruptive strikes can occur at any point in the process. The first attempt to change this process began with the historic St. Lawrence Seaway Project in the 1950s. The governments involved initiated project/labour agreements in which a single agreement was negotiated for contractors and trade unions. The main point was to eliminate the right to strike for the duration of the project. When trade unions accepted these agreements it was usually because the pay and other conditions were excellent for workers, and contractors agreed to pay relatively high wages because these premium labour costs were covered by the contract price. In British Columbia these types of project/labour agreements were used throughout the great building phases of BC Hydro in the 1960s and 1970s and continue to be used in all new building highway projects.[10] Long-standing familiarity with the idea of a project/labour agreement was a very important first step in getting contractors and trade unions to accept the further step of government intervention in the makeup of the labour force on this project.

Traditional bidding systems encourage large contractors to transport their skilled urban labour forces to remote areas by including pay for workers' travel and housing expenses. As a result, the labour benefits to local communities are minimal. As governments became more conscious of the political efficacy of promoting local employment, the long-standing use of a project/labour agreement was expanded to make provisions for a workforce more reflective of the populations in areas where the work occurred. Including the interests of the First Nations was especially crucial in the VIHP because the highway would cross the land of twelve First Nations, covering areas where major land claim issues were unresolved.

Two important new aspects of the HCL project agreement make it an equity model that is distinct from previous models. First, it is the first major construction project in British Columbia that has included women as a target group for hiring and training.[11] Second, unlike other project agreements that had equity components, this one applies to a labour force specifically associated with road construction. Previous agreements were associated with large, fixed-site, and relatively long-term projects with a labour force that was not as intermittent as is typical in highway construction.

The VIHP was announced in 1994 as a part of the BC government's "BC 21" initiative for economic development through capital spending on large public construction projects.[12] This seven-year project had a budget of $1.2 billion to cover building about 250 kilometres of highway. A new Crown corporation, the BC Transportation Financing Authority (BCTFA) was created to undertake capital spending on transportation building throughout the province, with a subsidiary, HCL, established as sole employer for the VIHP. While HCL was the exclusive employer and it hired, dispatched, and paid for workers, it did not supervise actual highway building; rather, it functioned as a source of employees – a sort of "hiring hall" – for private contractors. This was a major concession from the unions, who were not enthusiastic about giving up traditional hiring hall practices.

Equity in the Contract
Neither private contractors nor trade unions embraced the new hiring arrangement, and they specifically resented the equity and restricted local hire requirements of the contract.[13] The contract language gives hiring preference to local Vancouver Island residents and people from equity groups, although contractors were able to "name-hire" some of their own workforce.

The relationship between equity issues and other preferential hiring provisions was made clear by a specific clause: "Employment Equity hiring shall operate in priority over other preferential hiring processes."[14] This is a strong statement, and it should have made equity hiring fairly straightforward, but various other provisions in the contract lessened its impact.

For example, a provision permitted contractors to specifically identify up to "50 percent of employees, on a one-for-one basis (first dispatched by Union) to a maximum of five (5) "named" employees."[15] This meant that, on a large contract, five of the first ten employees could be the traditional employees of the contractor. In addition, all supervisors could be named directly by the contractor. The ability of contractors to "name-hire" all employees on contracts of $30,000 or less also served as an effective way for some contractors to circumvent the equity hire priority.[16] These concessions for "name-hire," which took priority over equity considerations, were considered necessary in order to make this unusually structured agreement acceptable to contractors.

For the trade unions, a very important advantage of the agreement was the provision that all labour on the project would be union labour. During the 1980s the Social Credit government changed labour legislation in British Columbia and generally promoted an anti-trade union climate that resulted in a dramatic fall-off of union membership. By the 1990s only about 20 percent of building trades workers were unionized. The requirement that all workers employed on the project join a union within thirty days of starting work, even if the contractor was a non-union firm, was a strong feature favouring trade unions.[17] It was also a very controversial feature that was fiercely attacked by some contractors.

The requirement for union membership, combined with the local hire and equity provisions, was also controversial with the members of trade unions. The feeling of many in the construction trades was that, with high unemployment among existing union members throughout the province, the local hire and equity provisions brought new workers into the union, which worked to the detriment of an already underemployed labour force. In the three years immediately preceding the VIHP the unemployment rate for construction workers in British Columbia averaged 16 percent.[18] Another unpopular concession made by the unions was to agree to wage rates at about two dollars per hour lower than the standard rate negotiated for the industry.

Contractors ultimately appreciated the fact that HCL was the employer for all projects. This saved them money on record keeping, payroll, finding employees, and other personnel functions.[19] Another important cost-saving aspect of the contract was the local hire provision, which eliminated the need for providing room and board for out-of-town employees.

Training for Road Construction

Contractors in the road building industry tend not to formally train employees, and no traditional apprenticeship system exists to enable workers to learn a broad range of skills in a systematic way. According to one contractor, "road building is a transient business so there is no major commitment to training in principle."[20] Hiring is done by reputation. Few contractors are willing to risk $500,000 machines on novices or people they do not know, particularly knowing that, once trained, workers are easily poached. As one contractor explained, "preferably, you look for people who are already trained and hire them away from other companies."

The disadvantages of such a system are obvious. The learning process, without any formal component, is haphazard and inconsistent; the quality of training depends on who happens to be around to teach and how skilled they are at both their job and at teaching; and the whole system is largely dependent upon trial and error through on-the-job training. An employer has no easy and reliable way of knowing the skill level or range of ability of someone applying for a job. As one contractor explained, "It's all just what a guy tells you. How do I know he's going to be a good operator? Do I risk this guy wrecking my machine and not producing the work? I wish they had an apprenticeship for operators." The informal training system also makes for a closed system in which just getting experience on a machine requires personal connections or a great deal of assertiveness, something that can disadvantage even White males. It is a particularly effective barrier to First Nations, women, and other nontraditional groups of workers.

Designers of HCL understood that training would be an important part of the whole project mainly because the commitment to equity and to local hire would reduce the pool of qualified workers from which they could hire. Initially it was assumed that this training would be done under the umbrella of the building trades unions and that the length of the project would allow time for traditional four- or five-year apprenticeships. Oddly, it appears that no one at the planning stages had fully realized that 80 percent of highway building is done by three unions, none of which commonly use the formal apprenticeship system practised by other building trades, such as carpenters and plumbers. The three major highway building unions are the Teamsters, who drive heavy trucks; the Construction and Specialized Workers Union (commonly known as Labourers), who do general labour as well as the stake work that estimates how much earth is to be removed to reach engineers' specifications; and the International Union of Operating Engineers, who operate large road building equipment such as bulldozers, excavators, cranes, and compactors. Of these, only the Operating Engineers have formal apprenticeships and then only for crane operators and heavy-duty mechanics. All other positions covered by Operating Engineers and Teamsters measure a person's skill readiness by "hours in the seat"; that is, by how many hours members have spent driving and operating rather than by any specific trades qualification certificate. The building trades that do rely on apprenticeships and trades qualification programs, such as the Ironworkers and Cement Masons, have relatively little to do with highway building.

The only formal training program available for road builders was a seven-week program in Haney, British Columbia, for Operating Engineers; and a training school in Sardis, British Columbia, for Teamsters. The HCL trainees who took these programs liked them, but they taught only the basics of how to operate equipment. As one woman Teamster reported, "It was a good training course in terms of what the equipment could do, but it wasn't practical. I mean, after the first day on the job for HCL I was wondering what I'd gotten myself into! All of a sudden I had six trucks flying at me, two packers running behind me, foremen running around pointing, asking me to do things and excavators swinging behind me – all in a small congested area. I was so unaccustomed to anything like that." Clearly what was needed was a training program that included actual road building, something the HCL program eventually provided.

Recruitment

The equity provisions of the collective agreement opened the door for people from the targeted groups and gave them a chance to gain access to jobs on the highway. However, early on one BCTFA employee reported to the premier of the province that there were virtually no women, First Nations, people of colour, or people with disabilities at work on the new construction jobs. This would not have been a surprising result to the small group of people who deal with integrating women and minorities into nontraditional workforces. Merely supplying an opportunity for employment is not sufficient to overcome the enormous barriers faced by those traditionally excluded from construction jobs.[21] According to one employee, one critical point for a focus on equity came from the minister responsible for BC 21 when he pointedly asked, "How are we doing on the equity and training side?" The initiative also received strong support within Cabinet and was consistent with other attempts to increase the participation of under-represented groups on provincial boards and commissions.[22]

When construction jobs were initially posted very few people from the targeted equity groups applied. Women did apply for clerical work, but few seemed aware of the construction postings. If they did know, they assumed that, as in the past, they would not be welcome. HCL personnel therefore changed focus. First they changed their recruiting sites. They began to actively recruit on First Nations reserves and in women's centres and to seek the help of organizations for Women in Trades, people of colour, and those with disabilities. Second, they adjusted their interview questions. When asked, "Do you have experience in building roads or operating heavy equipment?" people from equity groups generally answered, "No." When asked, "Do you have any experience relevant to building roads," the answer was more likely to be something like, "Yes, I've run my father's skidder." Most applicants assumed that when employers asked about "work experience," they meant paid experience.

These special outreach initiatives were very effective, prompting a large number of applications for road building work from targeted equity groups, with particularly high numbers coming from women and First Nations. For each month during the major intake period between December 1994 and June 1995, equity applications accounted for between 28 percent and 33 percent of all applications. Aboriginal applications constituted 60 percent and women's 40 percent of all applications from equity groups.

About 5 percent of the equity groups' applications came from people with disabilities and about 9 percent came from visible minorities. The major problem, once people applied, was that the vast majority did not have even basic road building skills and the jobs they were applying for did not have apprenticeships that offered entry-level positions. Without skills and "hours in the seat," contractors refused to hire them. It was clear that if the equity initiatives were to work, then applicants would have to be trained.

HCL Training

The most innovative equity training initiative on the project involved on-the-job experience at several locations, the most significant being at Hindoo Creek. This involved the actual construction of a 5.2-kilometre section of the highway in the forest near Union Bay by women and First Nations trainees. Since the training program was not part of the original design of the VIHP, it did not begin until well after a large portion of the labour force was in place. A serious flaw in the whole training process on the project is that a well developed training system was neither in place nor even planned before actual construction on the highway began. Also, the cost of training was not built into the budget, resulting in considerable scrambling to pull together the necessary resources and, ultimately, a drastically underfunded program. Eventually less than two million dollars was committed to all the training schemes, including $900,000 from Skills, Training, and Labour.

In hindsight the lack of planning for specific on-the-job training at the outset seems a serious oversight. However, it needs to be kept in mind that the innovative feature of integrating women and Aboriginal people into highway construction meant that many mistakes would be made. As assessments are made about what worked and what did not in the training process, it should be kept in mind that this was a pioneering effort. The remarkable results of the project, given this late understanding of the importance of creating a training site, indicate that a great deal of what occurred worked extremely well.

Before the training site at Hindoo Creek began, a variety of short introductory training programs were provided to prospective employees. The first was a two-week course designed to familiarize prospective workers with the construction industry. About 200 people were chosen to attend this course in the first year, 127 of whom were from equity groups. It informed applicants about issues of health and safety and the conditions of this work, particularly its seasonal nature; the demand for physical fitness; and the lack of job seniority. It also included some hands-on experience. Only fifteen people left the program after this course. A small proportion (2 percent) of those with sufficient experience went directly to worksites, but most went on to further training conducted in cooperation with the local community college and union training plans. Most of the trainees in these courses were from equity groups. Those in the operating engineers' course had the most difficulty being hired because of the limited nature of the training (which was due to the high cost of heavy equipment).

The first on-the-job training site came about early in the project, when trainees who had completed their courses were given hands-on experience in the form of building a section of road on the Chemainus First Nations Reserve at Shell Beach. Trainees were neither paid for this work nor reimbursed for travel, daycare, or other expenses.[23] At least one trainee was so eager to get work experience that she lived in a car. Two important things happened on this project. First, a First Nations company, Yiasulth Management Corporation (YMC), supplied the machinery used. YMC was set up to create a single entity to speak for the twelve First Nations involved and was designed to serve their long-term construction interests. Second, the experience of training on an actual piece of road building became a distinct and innovative feature of the VIHP. All parties who participated in the Shell Beach experiment, including contractors, unions, and (especially) the trainees, agreed that this was an excellent way to introduce people with no road building experience to actual job conditions. It was the success of this venture that led to the development of the training site at Hindoo Creek.

The alternative to establishing a training site to build a section of highway would have been for contractors to take on trainees before they had specific road building experience and teach them on the job. This did not occur because training was not written into contract documents and, therefore, contractors were reluctant to spend the time and money required. Training for highway building is a particularly expensive business, more onerous than what is involved in other building trades. As one contractor explained: "A trainee gets on your machinery and breaks a centre pin on a D10, that's a $12,000 bill. We pay." He compared this cost to an apprentice carpenter who "cuts the cord, nails the air house to the floor, drops the saw. The difference is that the saw costs $200 but a 330L hoe costs $250,000."

Hindoo Creek

Hindoo Creek[24] was an extraordinary training site, and its existence was the primary reason that equity hiring results for HCL were so impressive. The equity trainees, specifically women and those from First Nations (in about equal proportions) were not only being trained but were also the primary employees on the road site. The contrast with other large-scale projects in Canada, such as the Hibernia Construction Project in Newfoundland, where women made up only 4 percent of all trainees, is dramatic.[25]

Trainees began at Hindoo Creek with a raw site in the forest and – with the exception of logging – performed virtually all work. At the outset the Ministry of Transportation and Highways (MOTH) managed this section of highway with seventeen trainees. During the peak summer seasons, as many as fifty-two trainees were working on two shifts. A trainee was considered to have completed training when s/he had 2,000 hours "in the seat." The 2,000-hour limit appears to have been somewhat arbitrarily chosen, and trainees were often dispatched to other jobs before these hours were reached and, when laid off by a contractor, would resume training in order to accumulate more "seat time." Interviews with both contractors and trainees indicate that the 2,000 measure was not a good indication of a mastery of skills. Contractors would have preferred some detailed "report card" to indicate exactly what skills the trainees had mastered and to what degree – a report card similar to that provided by an apprenticeship training test.

Trainees wanted more variation in training, depending on the piece of equipment. As one noted, "You don't need 2,000 hours to learn a compactor. You're fully qualified after a week." Some equity trainees saw the 2,000-hour figure as a further delay to getting on the job, and only about thirty equity trainees ultimately achieved the 2000-hour goal. The 2000-hour figure was particularly limiting given the late start for the training program, and, as work on the Hindoo Creek site was nearing completion, even fewer trainees worked, which further affected their seat time.

Time spent on the job was focused strictly on actual production. At the students' request, informal lectures were arranged on the training site during lunch breaks, and they focused on subjects such as MOTH specifications on lift thickness, rolling techniques, and ways to provide preventive maintenance on machines. Trainees were generally eager to learn as much as they could. But the main limitation to training was created by funding problems.

There were several instructors at the site over the course of the project. The instructors were skilled drivers and equipment operators, but none had previous training or experience in teaching. Nor did any of them have instruction in issues related to training people from equity groups. Some contractors felt that one particular instructor was not very skilled as an operator, so they had little confidence in the people he trained. In the worst case, early in the project one trainer was said to have sexually harassed some female trainees, and he was removed. Clearly, a more careful selection of instructors with a specific focus on both their skill level and sensitivity to equity issues is important. A strong orientation course for trainers would also be helpful, as would specific training in teaching skills.

One trainer learned the hard way that it was necessary to employ different techniques to teach people who were unfamiliar with the construction culture: "With these folks, it motivates them to give them some strokes once in a while. In the old days it was yelling, screaming, and fist fights with the foreman. That doesn't cut it any more." One important innovation at Hindoo Creek, highly praised by participants, was to employ a First Nations "shadow trainer" who received on-the-job training as an instructor. The job of this individual, who was from a local band, was to oversee the work of the trainees and to assist them when the instructor was unavailable.

In the first year of training, instruction was intensive and required close work with the instructor; however, by the second year, as one instructor explained, "We found we could give instructions in the morning and just periodically check on them." The instructors suggested an instructor/trainee ratio of one to five in the first year – a ratio that could be reduced to one to eight as the trainees gained skills and confidence. At Hindoo Creek the ratio was roughly one to ten, but at times it went as high as one to twenty-five.

A fascinating feature of the Hindoo Creek site was that women and people from First Nations (who were mostly men) were trained together. There was general agreement that the men were more successful in getting access to a wider variety of machines than were the women, which may have been partially due to differences in prior experience with machines. But it was also clear that women were more enthusiastic than were men about taking any training available. One union official noted: "When I'd go down the dispatch list looking for who had a certain training, the women had everything: they had first aid tickets and you name it, everything available." This was something of an exaggeration, but women soon learned that if they acquired some additional skill, then they were more likely to be dispatched. The women, however, felt they were more likely than the men to be trained on smaller trucks, as Teamsters, or on the least challenging piece of heavy equipment (the compacting machine or "packer"). One woman who repeatedly asked to be trained on other machines described the problem: "No offence to packer operators, but I found it extremely boring. Most of the men don't want it either: it's like pushing a rolling pin back and forth all day."

The trainees were extraordinarily enthusiastic about their training. The overridingly positive aspect of the training program at Hindoo Creek, and one to which the trainees, contractors, and HCL repeatedly referred, was the actual work experience of a construction site. "I wasn't just pushing barrels around from one side of a training yard to another," one trainee explained. "I was doing real work. My kids will drive on that section of highway and know their mom built it." Their main complaints about the training centred on its limited resources. As one trainee explained, "Every piece of equipment out there has a person for it so if you break down, you're in trouble. You may as well go sit in a bar because you're not going to work 'til it's fixed." This is the kind of issue that can be eased with more resources.

Dispatch

The method of dispatching workers to a job is critical with regard to placing equity trainees, and no training program can be effective unless there is a clear relationship between training and employment. At the initial training intake, projected labour needs indicated that all the trainees would be employed on the project. However, the combination of the late start of training and significant scaling back in the size of the project after training had begun meant that competition for jobs was greater than anticipated, and it increased as the major phases of building were completed.

Traditionally, unionized building trades and road builders are paid hourly. When a job is finished, the worker returns to the union hall and "signs in" at the bottom of the dispatch list. The next time an employer calls, the qualified person nearest the top of the list is sent, or "dispatched." It is impossible to overestimate how important this system is to the workers affected and how closely they monitor it. The fairness of the dispatch system and the scrupulousness of the dispatcher constitute the difference between working or not working. But dispatch is rarely a simple issue of "who is next on this list"; it involves constant judgment. If an employer calls for an equipment operator skilled in handling a bulldozer under hazardous conditions, then the dispatcher has to determine if that description really applies to the next person on the list or to the one after: if it does not work out, an irate call from the contractor or an on-site accident may follow. Pressure on the other side comes from the employee who demands to work. The dispatcher's position is a pivotal and highly sensitive one, and it is complicated by the fact that employers are not eager to hire unskilled labour. As one contractor noted, "Nobody would ever ask for a trainee."

Dispatch was carried out in a distinct way and involved collaboration between HCL and the unions. A contractor would make a single call to the dispatcher at HCL, requesting a specific type of worker – say, for example, a carpenter experienced at concrete formwork. HCL would, in turn, contact the Carpenter's Union and make the request, preferably for an equity hire. The decision about who to dispatch then depended on some discussion between the union and the HCL dispatcher.

The fact that the equity provisions in dispatch were part of the collective agreement was extremely important. It meant that, since the normal way of dispatching was being bypassed, the union officials who needed to enforce this were, in some respects, not blamed. This evidence of compulsion was important to union officials, who had to be sensitive to membership demands. The fact that equity provisions in the contract had been negotiated meant that they had been discussed and voted on by trade union members, even if equity was a feature they specifically disliked.

Ultimately this system worked, after what one union official described as a period of "some arguing and jockeying and posturing while we all figured out exactly what each position was. If a member came in saying 'I have a problem with this,' I could say, 'it's in the collective agreement.'" Still, hostility to the dispatch of equity personnel could be strong. Upon leaving work, one union official involved with equity hiring is reported to have said, "I hope there isn't a bomb stuck underneath my car when I go home today."

Equity dispatch did not always happen when it should have, especially at the beginning of the project when, as one official confided, "We felt we had to cater to the contractors." The position of dispatcher proved to be crucial. At least one HCL dispatcher was sometimes reluctant to dispatch women, in part responding to the incredulity of contractors at being sent a woman but responding to his own prejudice against giving women physically demanding jobs. Over time and with some changes in personnel, the difficulty of dispatching equity trainees through HCL lessened somewhat. This tension eased as trainees became more qualified, as both unions and contractors were more willing to "take a chance" on trainees, and as dispatchers were more sensitive to equity. The increased hours of work for equity hires over the years reflect this (see Table 3.1).

Despite some problems with dispatch, the contractors grew to appreciate the time and effort it saved in the ongoing hiring process. The fact that HCL was the sole employer took the emotion associated with hiring off the employer. As one contractor explained, "Guys used to knock at my door saying, 'My wife and kids are starving. You have to hire me.' Now I say, 'You have to talk to HCL.' It takes the weight off my conscience."

Construction Work Culture and Trainees' Experiences

Moving from the training site to a job with a contractor was rarely simple for equity trainees. According to one First Nations male, "Anybody in the HCL training programs that went out into the union jobs had a hard time." The normal culture of the construction workforce dictates that bad situations be resolved individually. This trainee told of one incident where a hoe operator referred to him as "'some fucking Indian,' and stuff like that, so I got out and I choked him. He leaves me alone now and it's been worked out."

Women, First Nations, people with disabilities, and people of colour enter a very different culture when they enter a traditional road building or construction workforce. Although it is usually not recognized as such by the men who work within it, it is a culture characterized by aggression, intense competition, and specific types of language and behaviour.[26] The language, for example, is competitive, brief, aimed at humour and, if possible, undermining other workers. The preferred attitude is one of aggression, demanding a brash confidence, no matter how little you know. The unspoken expectation of the construction worker is to tinker until the problem is solved and, when in doubt, use brute strength to get out of trouble. "When in doubt," trades people say, "hit harder." Ignorance is not to be admitted and, above all, workers must not take things personally. In contrast, there are factors that mitigate this culture, factors like the common use of humour, camaraderie, and the satisfaction inherent in building.

The destructive effects of this brutal type of workplace culture on all employees, no matter what their gender or ethnicity, are beginning to be understood, and attempts have been made to bring about changes. For example, a recent management initiative to reduce conflict is under way in the logging industry, where disagreements have "traditionally been settled with a piece of two-by-four," and where techniques to encourage productivity "had been based on screaming."[27]

When the workforce was still entirely White and male, the small jokes and challenges that greeted every new employee were referred to as "testing." Often, equity hires identify it as "harassment." Men on the job call it "tradition" and often can't imagine it being any different. One experienced male operator explained: "Everybody gets harassed. Period. When you walk onto the construction site, you're the new kid on the block and it's your turn. Take it. Get through it." He made a distinction, however, between this traditional type of harassment and that which comes from the real "bad apples," the bullies on the job. Workers should be protected from these bullies by their unions, but few ever complain. If it becomes too difficult, they quit. Not wanting to be perceived as "whiners," they leave without explanation. One male contractor explained that it is not just women who take harassment personally, but the men have learned to hide it: "You may be going through hell inside but you say nothing on the outside."

All construction workers go through some form of initial testing. So when anyone, including equity hires, has experiences that go beyond teasing, it's often difficult for other construction workers to sympathize. Hostility from co-workers can erupt in many ways that undermine the confidence and performance of the equity hire. One contractor reported a First Nations man who had been dispatched as a driver: "If anyone came near him, he was absolutely terrified and he'd start making mistakes. Eventually I found out the man had been terrorized on another site where his co-workers had been trying to get rid of him." As could be expected, the harassment women experienced was specific and sexist. One woman, the first equity trainee dispatched to a job, was immediately asked, "What are you doing here? Why don't you go find some rich sugar daddy?" This woman had considerable experience driving heavy vehicles, but she was "tested," both by the project supervisor and the project manager, "to the nth degree. But I was lucky I had the support of one teamster who just took me under his wing, and of a cat operator who was totally supportive." According to the project manager (one of her original tormentors), she became a highly sought after driver because of her skill. Even off the job equity trainees encountered hostility. In one case, a woman explained: "I walk into my gym and one of the trainers there says, 'Yeah, you've gotta be a goddamn Indian or a woman to work on this highway,' which is not true at all!"

Opposition to the equity hires was often attributed to introducing this new group into a field in which unemployment was high. As one worker put it, "If you were working with a system that had ninety percent employment, the idea of introducing equity would probably work pretty smooth. But when you have a system like the one on Vancouver Island that averages 50 percent unemployment and you introduce 20 percent new people, there are going to be some unhappy campers. The guy who's been around for twenty years is wondering why he isn't working when someone who's been a member for two months is."[28] The fact that trainees came from targeted equity groups created, as one union business agent acknowledged, "animosity. Big time." According to one contractor, "The immediate reaction of 60 percent of the guys on the job when an equity trainee arrived was pure hatred."

A co-worker who wants a trainee to fail could make sure that s/he did. In road building, if everyone does not work together, then the whole job goes badly. When anything starts to go wrong, the tendency is to blame the trainee. Sabotaging a trainee's efforts was not difficult. A contractor explained how it could work:

> A hoe operator might set up a truck driver by putting his bucket in a certain place, then just as the truck is set up to back up to it, the operator moves the bucket slightly. When the supervisor drives up and sees the truck three feet off where it should be, now pulling out to take yet another run at situating itself, you can think it's the truck driver's fault – that damn trainee again – unless you're very conscious of what's going on and who's driving what. Or if the skilled driver is in the truck, he can dump it in such a way that it will be hard for the trainee to get it. Then all of a sudden the dozers are backed up and the whole job is behind schedule and who do you blame? If you're laying off, who do you get rid of?

Knowing how to control this type of behaviour requires specific skills on the part of supervisors. Several factors were in place on the project to help motivate contractors to integrate equity hires into the workplace. One-day (optional) diversity seminars, which HCL provided for contractors and front-line supervisors, seem to have given important skills to those who were not adamantly opposed to equity hires. One contractor explained how, after attending the seminar, he learned of a crew leader who had been harassing a woman under his supervision and knew exactly what to do. He called the supervisor into his office, gave him a copy of the HCL Harassment Policy, and made him attend a diversity seminar. He said this woman experienced no further problems.

The presence of equity hires on the worksite began, in small ways, to change this particular workplace culture. Some contractors liked having women drive their equipment, mainly because they tended to be less aggressive. According to one contractor, "They're easier on it, they don't drive it into the ground." Another noted that women have a better attitude towards their work than men and that they work harder. Others who worked with trainees noted that it was often easier for the women to admit that they did not know something, so it was easier to teach them. Some men learned that skill was not dependent upon sex or race. One contractor admitted: "The best hoe operator I ever had was a woman. Anything she did with a backhoe wasn't just good, it was beautiful. It looked as if someone had been over the ground with a rake. She had the most talent I've ever seen; a real finesse operator."

Many involved in the VIHP felt that the job culture there changed. According to one contractor: "People are getting to be more aware of each other's feelings. As the equity groups get involved ... attitudes are changing. That's a fact." A union business agent concurred and noticed in particular how behaviour at union meetings changed with a woman present. "You'll get a guy swearing and yelling at a meeting, totally out to lunch, when a sister walks in and all of a sudden the same person is very polite. They don't swear. They deal with the issues. And I say, 'Sisters, keep on coming!' This is how the old school changes."

Significance of Equity Officer and Outside Groups

Early in the project, HCL personnel recognized the need for an employment equity coordinator. This person facilitated outreach, recruitment, training, and delivery of services to trainees and was generally a vital advocate for employment equity to all parties. The trainees, unions, and employers all repeatedly mentioned her importance as an invaluable resource for informally resolving difficulties. Most seemed to find traditional union grievance procedures unnecessarily cumbersome and felt that harassment complaints were most effectively dealt with informally through her. Her constant monitoring of the equity initiatives on the project was a critical feature of its success in integrating the labour force.

Shortly after hiring began, local equity groups and First Nations pressed for the formation of the Equity Integration Committee (EIC), which included members of the designated equity groups, HCL, contractors, unions, and government representatives. Of particular importance was the representative from the Ministry of Women's Equality. This group met once a month during the busy seasons and once every other month in winter to examine progress and to make suggestions for changes. An initial request from this committee was for very detailed record keeping so that the monitoring of equity hires could be tracked.[29] In other equity programs in Canada, the lack of reliable, long-term statistics has made it difficult to determine the true effectiveness of equity initiatives. The reliable numbers generated indicated that the equity trainees listed were not token short-term hires but, rather, had significant hours in employment and training. This information was also useful to union business agents, who used it to quell frequent rumours of huge numbers of trainees working while traditional union members were unemployed. The statistics showed that, although the number of equity hires was large by traditional standards, it was still very modest in terms of actual numbers. Knowing the numbers made it easier for traditional members to accept trainees and for union business agents to defend them.

Another benefit of EIC meetings was the regular exchange in information and recommendations for solutions among parties traditionally suspicious of each other. Diversity training for front-line supervisors came initially from an EIC recommendation. All who participated recognized the value of the committee and credit its success to the fact that all members were from local communities and had a stake in the project functioning well.

Conclusions

The most instructive result of the experience of the VIHP is that the mandatory requirement to hire workers from targeted equity groups through a specific negotiated project agreement is essential to the success of the process. While there was no specific numeric target established at the outset, the unofficial goal was to have equity hires constitute 20 percent of the workforce – a figure that was met and surpassed during peak hiring times.[30] Without this element of compulsion in the initial project agreement, the overwhelming obstacles to equity training and hiring would have ensured that yet another equity project failed. As someone from HCL noted, "Given that the walls that equity has to penetrate are made of concrete and reinforced with steel, I think we've done well." The introduction of training on an actual worksite; the existence of an active, community-based advisory committee; and a permanent equity coordinator also made a significant contribution to the success of this project and are features that should be retained in future large highway building projects.

While this study was not designed to present detailed recommendations for future building initiatives, two major recommendations flow from the experiences uncovered. The first involves the establishment of an apprenticeship system in highway construction and the second involves equity provisions in the tendering process.

Establishing an apprenticeship system in highway construction would serve the needs of both employers and workers. The need for contractors to have a clear indication of the kinds and degree of skills achieved was one clear message from employers. Workers, too, expressed the need for entry-level positions and understood the value of practical experience and theoretical knowledge. These features of training could be best provided through a structured apprenticeship system. As one person from HCL noted, "The one thing that would have made life easier for everyone from day one would have been to have entry-level positions for all these trainees." An apprenticeship system is also important for establishing a more integrated workforce because it would provide a clear access point to the industry for workers from equity groups as well as for White males without contacts in the industry.

The second and related recommendation is that the tender documents with individual contractors be more specific about the equity and training provisions required of them. The compulsory equity provision in the HCL collective agreement should extend to all contractors and subcontractors in detailed and specific ways.

This project presented an unusual and effective model for integrating people from targeted equity groups into highway construction. However, throughout the life of the project the government that spearheaded it suffered from repeated criticism – especially from non-union contractors. Criticism focused on the assumption that high wage rates would increase the cost of the project. In fact, the Vancouver Island Highway has come in under budget projections at virtually every stage of construction. This was at least partly because the commitment to providing opportunities for local contractors and for local hire meant that a larger number of smaller contracts than usual were tendered, and room and board costs were eliminated. For each job there were, on average, six bids, as opposed to a provincial average of 3.7 bids.[31]

Despite the general approval of the project from the people closest to it, the government's innovative action with the equity initiatives on the VIHP did not win widespread public praise, and those who opposed both the fact of the union contracts and equity hires spoke loudest when the project was discussed in the media. To many supporters of employment equity, who aim for high proportions, the figures did not seem dramatic. However, to those who understand the complexities of integrating construction workforces the results were extraordinary. Another damper on attempts to replicate the successes of this project relate to the politics of the province. The problems associated with the government's large-scale construction projects, specifically those related to the Pacificat Fast Ferry, has made these more innovative types of initiatives harder to carry out.

The completion of the VIHP was accomplished within the budget and on time, granting bids to local contractors and using Island people for its labour needs. It trained people from targeted equity groups, and it brought the proportion of equity hires to over 22 percent of the total workforce during peak building periods. This was an astonishing improvement on standard rates of employment of equity workers in construction. It is easy, in retrospect, to see how it could have been improved, but this cannot detract from what was accomplished – something that has not occurred previously in highway construction on this scale anywhere in North America.

The epilogue to this successful program in British Columbia is a sad story. With the election of the Liberal government in 2001, the public company that was the heart of the program, Highway Constructors Ltd., was cancelled. This means that equity initiatives are no longer a feature of highway construction in British Columbia.

Source

This chapter was initially published through the Canadian Centre for Policy Alternatives, British Columbia, in 2000. A more detailed version of the training program is available in Cohen and Braid, "Training and Equity Initiatives on the British Columbia Vancouver Island Highway Project: A Model for Large-Scale Construction Projects," *Labor Studies Journal* 25, 3 (Fall 2000): 70-103.

Notes

1 The Amalgamated Construction Association of BC and Employment and Immigration Canada, Women, Native Indians, Visible Minorities, and People with Disabilities Working for Employers (Vancouver: Employment and Immigration Canada, 1990).
2 John Calvert, "Maxamizing Social, Training and Economic Development Spin-Offs from Public Capital Spending: The Experience of the Vancouver Island Highway Project," unpublished paper, 1997.
3 Barbara Byrd, "Women in Carpentry Apprenticeship: A Case Study," *Labor Studies Journal* 24, 3 (Fall 1999): 3-22.
4 For a discussion of this issue, see Andrea W. Gale, "Women in Non-traditional Occupations: The Construction Industry," *Women in Management Review* 9, 2 (1994): 3-14; Susan Eisenberg, *We'll Call You If We Need You: Experiences of Women Working Construction* (Ithaca and London: ILR Press, 1998).
5 HCL is a wholly owned subsidiary of the BC Transportation Financing Authority. This Crown corporation was established through the Build BC Act, 1993.
6 The terms "equity workers" and "equity hires" are used to identify people from groups that had been targeted for special consideration in this project.

7 Sharon Nelson, "Women in Business," *Nation's Business*, October 1991: 41-44.
8 When this study was complete most of the building of the highway had occurred, but some building, involving a much reduced labour force, occurred until the project was completed in 2001.
9 The training focus on First Nations people and women was directly related to the strength of these groups and their lobby efforts during the life of the project. While initially there was an attempt to elicit applications from visible minority and disabled groups, the program did not ultimately focus on them.
10 The first major initiative of this sort that included equity was BC Hydro's agreement, which was negotiated in the early 1990s between Columbia Hydro Contractors (BC Hydro's construction entity) and the Allied Hydro Council (the bargaining group representing the trade unions). The innovative feature of this agreement was that it stipulated provisions for local hire and, specifically, for hiring Aboriginal workers.
11 The BC government has decided to expand the mandate of HCL to provide labour to other new transportation projects. This will allow similar equity targets to be set for large-scale highway building in the future.
12 The Build BC Act created the BC Transportation Financing Authority and set out the policy goals that became known as "BC 21." The purpose of the act includes: "2(b) ensuring that all regions of the Province benefit from economic expansion and diversification; 2(d) promoting training and investment in people as a significant component of public sector investment activity; 2(e) targeting activities under this Act toward traditionally disadvantaged individuals and groups."
13 Many trade union members in other parts of the province were particularly unhappy that they would not be eligible for work on the project through the local hire provisions, which gave preference to residents of Vancouver Island.
14 HCL Contract, Article 6.222.
15 HCL Contract, Article 211b.
16 The original intention of the $30,000 specification was to cover very small, two- to three-day jobs, such as landscaping. But this clause sometimes could be used by contractors who wanted to break larger jobs into several smaller ones in order to keep complete control of their workforce.
17 HCL Contract, Article 6.110.
18 Statistics Canada, *Labour Force Survey* (Ottawa: Statistics Canada, 1999).
19 HCL also has a health and safety program that, for several years running, has resulted in national health and safety awards.
20 Quotations are from VIHP participants interviewed for this study.
21 See especially Sharon R. Goldberg, *Women in Construction: A Report on Access, Training and Retention in the Construction Trade* (Vancouver: Amalgamated Construction Association of BC, 1992); Kate Braid, "Invisible Women in Non-Traditional Occupations in B.C." (MA thesis, Simon Fraser University, 1979); Marcia Braundy, ed., *Surviving and Thriving: Women in Trades and Technology and Employment Equity* (Winlaw, BC: Kootenay Women in Trades and Technology, 1989).
22 It was the equity provisions in the collective agreement that swayed the opinion of many cabinet ministers who had reservations about a union-only project agreement for the VIHP. Trade unions became more helpful on equity issues as they were reminded that the project/labour agreement itself only came about because of the equity provisions.
23 This road was not a VIHP project and, therefore, was not covered by the collective agreement.
24 This name causes considerable discomfort to those involved in equity issues. It is likely from the distant past, although it is still prominent on maps. This site was a 5.2 kilometre section of the highway located in the forest near Union Bay. The two other projects were the Little Qualicum Underpass and Farwell Pit.
25 Brenda Grzetic, Mark Shrimpton, and Sue Skipton, *Women, Employment Equity and the Hibernia Construction Project* (Newfoundland: Women in Trades and Technology, June 1996).
26 See, for example, the BC Council of Human Rights decision on *Karen Burton* v. *Chalifour Bros. Construction Ltd., Thomas Chalifour, and Edward Tai*, Vancouver, 9 March 1994, for a confirmation of the culture of harassment in the construction industry.

27 "I'm a lumberjack and I'm okay," *Globe and Mail*, 17 November 1999, B3.
28 The figures in these quotations are literally figures of speech and are more illustrative of the attitude than the actual situation.
29 This initiative was strongly supported by the HCL board of directors, who wanted accurate records for governance purposes.
30 Hewitt-Ferris and Associates, "A Review of the Equity Component of the Vancouver Island Highway Project," HCL, unpublished paper, May 1997.
31 HCL document, May 1998.

4
Women's Training and Equity on the Hibernia Construction Project
Susan Hart and Mark Shrimpton

The development of the Hibernia offshore oilfield was one of the largest construction projects in Canadian history. It required expenditures of over five billion dollars and was of great significance to the economy of Canada and, in particular, Newfoundland and Labrador. Work developing the Bull Arm construction site, 140 kilometres west of St. John's, started in late 1990. This was where the massive concrete base of the production platform and some of the modules and assemblies for the topsides (the drilling, processing, and accommodations complex that sits on the base) were built, and where the topsides were assembled and mated with the base. The project employed, at peak, nearly 7,000 people, most of them at the construction site. Work at the site ended in the summer of 1997, with the platform being towed out to the oilfield shortly after.

The project would not have proceeded but for major financial support by the federal and provincial governments. The former committed to pay 25 percent of the construction costs to a total of $1.04 billion and provide loan guarantees for 40 percent of these costs to a maximum of $1.66 billion. The main motivation for this was spelled out by the senior federal representative at the 1990 signing ceremony: "The significant financial commitment by the federal government to make Hibernia happen is a clear demonstration of our determination to overcome regional disparities in Atlantic Canada."

Given the size of the project and the levels of government involvement, it is not surprising that the project was used as a test-bed for initiatives in the area of public policy. These included training, hiring, accommodation, and other policies and programs designed to encourage the employment of women in both traditional and male-dominated occupations at the construction site. However, the project was a very challenging environment for such initiatives, bringing together, as it did, the cultures of the oil and construction industries.

While both can claim, with some justification, to have made progress respecting employment equity, both have histories of excluding and marginalizing women. The oil industry largely developed out of the southern United States, and operating and contracting companies have been noted for a culture that is unsupportive of women in male-dominated occupations.[1] Collinson found "the independent male breadwinner and dependent female homemaker ... embedded in many (UK offshore sector) discourses and practices,"[2] and, while a year 2000 survey of 135 oil industry companies in Newfoundland found that "women's participation in oil and gas activities is increasing," they comprised only about 1.5 percent of workers in male-dominated occupations.[3] The construction industry has also been slow in facilitating women working in male-dominated occupations. For example, as of 2001, only 1 percent of the membership of the Newfoundland and Labrador Building and Construction Trades Council, which represents sixteen construction trade unions, were women.

This historical barrier to women's participation in both sectors was acknowledged in the project's regulatory framework, which included equity requirements. However, these formal attempts to integrate women were limited in their scope and implementation, and undermined by informal practices and day-to-day interactions in the workplace. These undervalued women's work and underlay inequitable decisions about training, hiring, advancement, and layoffs. In particular, there was a tendency to upgrade men's qualifications and work histories and, conversely, downgrade (or make invisible) women's. In the end, exclusion from training limited women's job opportunities; inadequate on-the-job training limited their promotion; and lack of promotion in turn led to their experiencing a higher likelihood of layoff. Continually excluded, women were less qualified than men, creating and perpetuating a self-fulfilling prophecy that women just do not belong in construction work. Overall, a study conducted for Women in Trades and Technology (WITT) (Newfoundland and Labrador)[4] found that all parties in the Hibernia construction project – the proponent, contractors, unions, and the federal and provincial governments – bore responsibility for the failure to adequately provide for the training, recruitment, and occupational integration of women.

The chapter will continue with an overview of the equity requirements for the project before moving on to a discussion of the experiences of women with regard to training, hiring, and working on the job.

Hibernia Equity Requirements

A number of agreements and memoranda specified training and hiring policies for the construction project, and they included equity requirements for women. The most important of them were the Project Labour Agreement, the construction contractor's Equitable Hiring Policy, and Human

Resource Development Canada's (HRDC's) corporate Designated Group Policy.

The 1990 Project Labour Agreement between the Oil Development Council of Unions (ODC) and the Hibernia Employers Association stipulated that priority for work be given to members in good standing of the ODC unions prior to July 1990; anyone joining thereafter would not be given priority over a nonmember until two years of seniority was attained, during which time hiring of qualified workers would be on a "first come, first served" basis. As specified in the 1985 federal/provincial Atlantic Accord, Newfoundlanders were to receive preference for employment and project-related training, provided they had kept a principal residence in the province for six months prior to starting employment.

Newfoundland Offshore Development Constructors (NODECO), the main construction contractor, had an equitable hiring policy respecting its own employees. As described in the September 1992 Environmental Protection Plan:

> NODECO will advertise positions that fall outside the scope of the Project Labour Agreement locally and give qualified local residents priority in hiring for them. NODECO will make special efforts to extend full and fair opportunity for qualified members of employment-disadvantaged groups to be employed on the project. It will notify organizations representing such groups of this policy and invite them to encourage their members to seek project employment. NODECO will give hiring priority to qualified individuals who respond.

HRDC's Designated Group Policy seeks to "facilitate adjustments required for the effective functioning of the labour market by eliminating the barriers preventing the full productive contribution of the designated groups." It is important to note this government policy, given that approximately eighteen million dollars of federal funding was allocated for unionized training for Hibernia.

However, although the Project Labour Agreement, NODECO equitable hiring policy, and HRDC Designated Groups Policy provided women with a formal framework for equitable access to training and employment on the Hibernia project, in practice the framework was ineffective. The NODECO equitable hiring policy, promising special efforts to recruit members of employment disadvantaged groups, was inadequately and poorly implemented and, after 1993, ceased to exist. Construction managers were generally not proactive in supporting the occupational integration of women; rather, some managers and supervisors were notably unresponsive to women's concerns about work assignments, training, and harassment. The HRDC Designated Group Policy states that designated groups and their needs must be considered in allocation of funds and in programming content. However, HRDC did not ensure adequate training and recruitment of women or their occupational integration once hired. This lack of monitoring and enforcement has also been highlighted in Riddle's evaluation of the policy.[5]

One explanation for the ineffective implementation of these equity requirements is that the commitments were made during the course of seeking regulatory approval and bidding for the work. With project approval and contract award, new management personnel replaced most of those involved in the approvals and bidding process, and their priority was completing this challenging construction project in time and within budget. They were often unaware of, or placed a lower priority on, equity and other commitments. For example, while a revised Site Environmental Protection Plan, submitted in July 1993 and subsequently approved by the provincial government, indicated that "the Project will give full and fair opportunity for qualified members of employment disadvantaged groups to be employed,"[6] it no longer included the NODECO or any other equitable hiring policy.

One woman with involvement with both the Hibernia and the subsequent Terra Nova project has described how "having worked in this field for a long period of time and being a woman in a male-dominated trade, I could give countless examples of the employment inequity that I have witnessed."[7]

Training Program
In the event, although the program did include an equity initiative, inadequate access to training prevented women's full participation in the project.

In consultation with HRDC, the ODC established a federally funded Oilfield Development Council Coordinating Group (ODCCG) to purchase project-related training on behalf of member unions. The ODCCG actively recruited women for its equity initiative, with an equity promotion coordinator using college and training institution graduation lists to identify potential welders, painters, and sand-blowers. About 350 applied for construction trades training; however, the great majority of this training went to men.

The College of the North Atlantic, Newfoundland's public vocational training college, provided most of the training, although some was delivered directly by the relevant trade unions. As of May 1995 (by which time almost all training had been completed), HRDC had funded 3,127 training seats. Notwithstanding the equity initiative, 2,361 men (96 percent of training participants) held 2,960 seats, while 102 women (4 percent of participants) held 167 seats. These women received training in both female-dominated and male-dominated fields, with 53 trained as camp attendants and food service workers, 48 trained in apprentice rebar, 48 in rebar, 11 as painter/blaster/fireproofers, 5 in warehousing, and 1 each in concrete and diving. Of the 1,909 trainees subsequently gaining project employment, 1,844 (97 percent) were men and 65 (3 percent) were women.[8]

In the WITT Newfoundland and Labrador study,[9] which surveyed women working at the Hibernia site concerning training and other issues, some of the construction workers noted that women had limited access to training. As one woman commented: "At the time of my training there were one hundred men to fifty women. Now the field has already been flooded with men and very few women, and since then there have been 240 more men trained, and as far as I know there have been no more opportunities for women to be trained in this field."

When asked to evaluate the training they received, a slight majority of respondents (nine, or 53 percent) agreed or strongly agreed that it had enhanced their existing skills, but two (12 percent) disagreed; nine (56 percent) agreed or strongly agreed that it had been adequate for the work they had being doing, but three (19 percent), all construction workers, disagreed; and nine (71 percent, but only 40 percent of the construction workers) agreed or strongly agreed that they were doing the work for which they were trained, but two (12 percent) disagreed and three (18 percent) strongly disagreed. For example, one woman noted that the "training ... was for food service work [but] ... I am now employed as a labourer."

As these responses indicate, the research revealed a number of barriers facing women who wanted to train for work on the project, particularly in nontraditional occupations. From the start, the training for women interested in construction jobs was designated as skills-upgrading, with women applicants having to have prior experience in the trade area for which it was being offered. This labelling of training (to the public) as skills upgrading served to inflate men's qualifications versus women's in a continued undervaluing of women's work. For example, the women were interviewed before being accepted into one course, whereas the men were not, despite the fact that the women had similar or better work experience. This contrasted with the apparent irrelevance of men's qualifications, as is shown by the shifting of workers from one union list to another. This saw men transferring from one union to another, in unrelated occupational areas, in order to ensure their access to training for future referral to the site: "The guys had been selected off [one union's] list and when that list was exhausted, they went to [another's] list. The women that were selected all had [trade] experience except one and she had prior construction experience. We found out [during our training program] that we were the only ones interviewed." Moreover, other women in the WITT study reported that men received extra training: "I understand the males participated in two weeks of apprenticeship training. I also learned that some of the men received some training on the Hibernia site. I heard this at the union office. We were supposed to do this but it was cancelled. Well, I felt this locked us out of having the real on-the-job exposure. It locked us out ... and it benefited some men who got it."

Some women experienced tension during their construction trades training. One spoke of male resistance to, and resentment of, her expertise and ability. A male trainee involved the union in this matter, leading to what the woman felt was intimidation by union officials. A man physically assaulted another woman during training, in an occurrence that was observed by a co-participant. Both women were disappointed that this, and two cases of sexual harassment, was not dealt with in a more thorough manner.

A number of respondents applauded the life skills component of courses, which included discussion of harassment, describing it as extremely valuable for women entering male-dominated occupations. However, many men did not receive it: "The rebar apprentice portion for males and females was the same ... [but] the females did ... life skills and harassment [and the] ... males should have been included in this portion but they were not."

Turning to the women in female-dominated occupations, training was not a significant issue for most of the support and clerical workers or for the sole professional included in the study. One support worker felt that she would have a chance if any training was available, although she understood that there had been a problem in some other occupational categories. Another was very pleased with some specialized, mostly voluntary, training she had taken. However, a third support worker regretted that male workers had dissuaded her and another woman from applying for a firefighters' course. Of the clerical interviewees commenting on training, just under half mentioned a lack of it, with a contrast being drawn between that offered to clerical workers and that offered to male-dominated occupational groups: "There's certainly more training for the men, like weeks and weeks long."

Overall, the design and implementation of the training program resulted in the exclusion of many women from important training, which in turn adversely affected their opportunities for work and advancement on the project.

Hiring

Three main companies (PCL Aker Stord Steen and Becker [PASSB], NODECO, and Major Offshore Catering) employed 88 percent of the project's unionized workforce at peak levels of activity. Women accounted for only 6 percent of these workers. Individually, NODECO was the largest employer, with 2,695 workers, of whom 101 (4 percent) were women. Of these, 40 were in male-dominated occupations (e.g., ironworkers, rebar workers, labourers, and operating engineers) while the other 61 were secretaries, clerical workers, or caterers/camp attendants. PASSB employed 835 workers, of whom the 33 women (4 percent) were mostly in secretarial positions. Unsurprisingly, given the nature of its work, 78 (43 percent) of the 191 Major Offshore Catering employees were women, almost all in female-dominated occupations.

Reflecting past practice on unionized construction sites, the Project Labour Agreement granted control over training and hiring to the building trades unions. Although efforts had been made to train women, many found it difficult to get work afterwards. They reported bias in hiring, based on gender as well as on family and friendship networks. This is not surprising, given that other studies identify it as part of a systemic process.[10] It is also clear that gender identity is caught up in the definition of "men's work," "women's work," and "skill," which is in turn part of the process of excluding women from skilled work.[11] To illustrate the connections between value of work, clear separation of "men's work" and "women's work," and gender identity (notions of masculinity and femininity), one woman spoke of her experience on the site: "A number of foremen treated me with reference to my size and sex ... One foreman in particular followed me everywhere and gave me 'little jobs' which angered and insulted me. I did not feel part of the crew ... [The men] would be responsible for heavy lifting. I had great difficulty trying, well, actually, being allowed, to prove myself in this area. I found that it was not macho for a six-foot male to have a fifty-four-inch, 120-pound female on the opposite end of an eleven-metre bar."

Given the beliefs still associated with women's roles in the home and the workplace, the undervaluation of women's work is increased when they are attempting to enter male-dominated occupations.[12] It is therefore not surprising that it was the women in construction who had the most difficulties. Some of these women reported that, while they were promised work upon successful completion of their Hibernia training course in June 1993, "When the training ended we were told to go home and wait by the telephone ... I didn't know that I would be waiting until 1995 by the telephone." One interviewee told of men hired ahead of equally or more qualified women:

The eleven months were a complete nightmare. We had to wait and wait and then we started to realize that the women weren't going like the men ... When I first applied to the ODCCG I had three years of [specific trade] experience and by the time I got there I had reached journey level. I saw the men go there and I knew that some of them weren't senior union members. I knew they had done the training when I did it. I knew that some of the men who were called to work had no [trade] experience whatsoever ... I also saw how guys pressured the union to be referred to the site, then, when we pressured them, it turned into something ugly ... I really didn't think we would be treated so unfairly.

The union involved used a separate hiring list for women, ostensibly to aid the implementation of equity guidelines; however, in practice it served as an exclusionary mechanism. Notably, the women saw its operation as unfair:

They have all us women on separate hiring lists. And they feel that's OK because they say we don't have early application dates. This is false. We do have the early application dates and they never should have been allowed to make that separate hiring list ... I'm home trying to raise two children on Social Assistance, trying to beat the system, with a full background, stuck on some female hiring list, and the 102 males who trained with us are just going to work.

In August 1993 a number of women met to discuss what they saw as the unfair hiring of men. They were told that they had to wait for jobs in cage fabrication because that was what they were trained for, although during their course they had been told that this was just one of a number of areas for which the training would qualify them. In the words of one woman: "I didn't understand why I had to wait for cage manufacturing. I had an application date to the project in 1992. I perceived cage manufacturing to be segregation because it seemed like they made it a 'female's job'... Males were going to work. We were not going to work and I just didn't see this as fair ... We had a really strong feeling that we were being discriminated against ... Males with less experience were getting the jobs."

In late 1993 most of the women who had trained as rebar apprentices filed complaints with the Human Rights Commission, claiming discrimination by all parties involved in hiring. The government's investigation concluded that the hiring procedures had been fair, based on the requirements of the Special Project Agreement, and that reasonable attempts had been made to recruit and train women.[13] The report justified the small number of women hired by their comparative lack of qualifications and by the earlier date of the men's job applications.

Three women who were trained to do rebar work wrote a rebuttal of this report.[14] They disagreed with the statement that the men had earlier applications than the women, arguing that many of the latter had applied to do project rebar work as early as 1991. As for qualifications, they emphasized that:

There were many women who completed rebar training whose skills could have been considered transferable for the rebar work ... [They were] mechanical; technical; steel inspection; welding; knowledge of concrete and reinforcement; residential construction; construction safety; marine safety; marine construction; blueprinting; warehousing; high tool skills etc. These skills have been viewed as not relevant to the specific job. Males with similar skills (e.g. residential construction) have had their skill viewed as being related ... This has greatly reduced many of the opportunities for women with accessing employment on the Hibernia project.

Despite formal equity requirements, the job statistics and women's experiences of the hiring procedures for the project clearly indicate an exclusionary process in practice, whether intentional or not.

Experiences on the Job
The WITT study[15] also investigated women's experiences of working on the Hibernia project. They were generally both excited by, and pleased with, the work: when asked how, overall, they felt about their job, 93 percent of questionnaire respondents said they were satisfied or very satisfied, with interviewees from all occupational groups expressing pride at being part of the project. However, they also had some serious concerns, although those women in female-dominated occupations – such as clerical and support work – generally had fewer problems and were more content than were those in construction.

The following section describes how the few construction women who gained employment on the site often experienced exclusion, with consequences for both success on the job and their quality of life.

Advancement
Women in construction often had problems gaining access to on-the-job training, which adversely affected their position with regard to advancement, layoff, and recall. Indeed, some women saw trades enhancement courses as exclusionary because they were reserved for workers with prior experience and journeypersons: "Women out there do not have enough work experience to get in ... they know they're cutting out the women by having it set up this way."

Twelve percent of the questionnaire respondents, including 25 percent of the construction workers, reported that they had at some time not been given an on-the-job training assignment because they were female. In the interviews, two-thirds of the construction women referred to exclusionary treatment at work. For example, one described how, despite being journey-level and company-trained for a specific task (with a 100 percent mark in the examination), she was assigned "apprentices' work ... While I was doing all the cleaning, they were training three guys in [a specific job] ... At one point the boys actually called me Molly [Molly Maid]. They still call me that once in a while, just joking. I think it's terrible. If I were a man with those qualifications, I'd be given the opportunity to learn other things ... I enjoy the work immensely. I'd like to be able to do quality control. I feel though [that] my opportunity for advancement is nil."

Other women described how different criteria were used in classifying men's versus women's jobs, thus impeding women's advancement. For example: "There is this superintendent out there who had never done some of this work and he's only done entry-level work in other places. I [have prior experience as] an inspector and ... the union kept me as an apprentice. It's not a certified trade, and if you're with the union you can become a journeyperson in two weeks, four weeks, four months ... but I'll guarantee that I will do the full two years before I get journeyperson."

Layoffs and Recall

Just under half of the construction workers expressed concern at the way layoffs were handled. One was laid off after only seventeen days, while a male co-worker with no more experience in her trade was kept on. She said he had been on a higher than entry-level training course, to which none of the women was able to gain access.

Other women construction workers were laid off despite a Human Rights Commission settlement that guaranteed work and union membership. Immediately before these layoffs, a foreman told one woman that she was an excellent worker and would be retained. He subsequently told her that his superintendent had overruled him. These women filed a new complaint with the commission, arguing that the signatories to the settlement had reneged on their agreement.

Shortly afterwards, these and other women and men were called back to work. However, on their first day back they were told that journeypersons, not apprentices, had been requested, and one man and all the women were sent home. An interviewee noted that one of the men who was kept on had been marked up to a journeyperson just prior to being called back, even though he had less experience, less seniority, and fewer qualifications than some of the women.

Harassment

As was noted above, many of the women, but few of the men, discussed harassment as part of the life skills component of their training. Various policies and initiatives sought to address it at the construction site. For example, the ODC introduced a discrimination and harassment policy in May 1992. It instructed forepersons, shop stewards, site representatives, business managers, and medical workers to always be available to discuss, and to fully investigate, harassment claims. All incidents were to undergo prompt investigation, including notification of the appropriate union business manager. The punishment for harassment ranged from a written reprimand to mandatory counselling to dismissal. In 1994, the Hibernia Management and Development Company (HMDC) and the major site contractors introduced their own policy and instituted courses on sexual harassment, in part in response to having received six to eight complaints during the previous year. Under the policy, workers were required to report harassment to their department manager, superintendent or union, or the labour relations department. The GBS Management Team committed to investigate all such complaints and threatened automatic dismissal of those found guilty.[16]

The WITT survey found that 46 percent of all the respondents, including 61 percent of those in construction, had experienced harassment. For most, it had occurred "occasionally," but three women reported that it happened "once a week or so" or "most days." Many women reported that, while they had worked with men in the past, they were not prepared for the comments made by some men at the Hibernia construction site. Three women in construction had at some time stayed away from work because of harassment.

In one example, two drunken workers accosted and demanded a kiss from a woman working in the dining hall. One of them grabbed her before another male worker intervened and called security. One of those accused received a letter of reprimand, while the other, who had already been reprimanded after another offence, lost his camp privileges for thirty days. In another case, a male worker was disciplined twice for indecent exposure. In the first case, he was suspended from work and lost camp privileges for a week. When he reoffended, he lost camp privileges indefinitely and was threatened with job termination.[17]

In the WITT study, one woman commented that the situation improved over time as a result of anti-harassment pamphlets and training, not least due to the increased awareness of the threat of dismissal. However, one limitation of the policies was that complaints often involved one union member accusing another, putting the union in a position of having to mediate between two of its members. When asked if they thought a complaint would resolve a harassment situation to their satisfaction, most female construction workers thought that it would not. One reported that "women report incidents and are disciplined themselves as a result ... I would be very wary of reporting an incident on site." Another reported that, because of "the nature of the work and the camp and how quickly things travel, there are a lot of repercussions that can happen that will make just living and working there much more challenging and difficult if you were to take things the formal route."

One construction worker who experienced harassment from her crew with the apparent collusion of her foreman elaborated on how she was sent back to work with the same crew after reporting this problem to management. Her account illustrated the complexity of harassment, its connection with exclusion from work for which she was qualified, and the potential for reprisal. When she had repeatedly pointed out her need to be allowed to do heavier work, she described how eventually, and without any easing into heavy work, her foreman forced her to lift reinforcing bars heavier than her own body weight at an unreasonable pace and with no break between lifts: "When I was on the bars I worked really hard ... My arms would be vibrating from the work, they'd be literally moving on their own so at times I wouldn't even eat my lunch ... and I really wanted to work. I said [to my foreman] that I was scared that I might drop the bar and hit somebody with it."

Other female rebar workers had similar experiences, including one who quit after being assigned nothing but lifting vertical bars for ten consecutive nights. Apart from undermining these women's (and their co-workers') safety, the cumulative effect was ultimately exclusionary – a self-fulfilling prophecy that women just could not do the heavy work.

Life in the Work Camp

Life in the work camp provided further disincentives to women working on the project. While attempts were made to accommodate women, management and unions were slow to recognize and address the particular difficulties of being a woman in a social environment dominated by male construction workers. As a result, good though the camp facilities were, many women were unable to gain access to and benefit from them, and they found the social environment at work and in the camp a source of stress. While it seems likely that most men were largely oblivious to "gender issues" in the camp, supported as they were by the culture of the male majority, these were a matter of constant concern for many women. This had implications for their mental and physical health, productivity, safety, absenteeism, turnover, and all aspects of employment equity.

The 3,500-room camp was free to all workers normally living more than fifty kilometres away. It provided single-occupancy rooms with communal washroom facilities in each building, and it had a large dining hall, tavern, clinic, swimming pool, and other recreation facilities. There was a women's dormitory, and 58 percent of the women surveyed in the WITT study lived at the camp.

When asked whether, "all things considered," they enjoyed living there, 10 percent strongly agreed and a further 41 percent agreed. However, a full one-third did not like living in the camp. Many found it a difficult and potentially threatening environment, especially in terms of interactions with men, who made up the great majority of residents. The threat related both to the maintenance of acceptable social relationships and to physical safety. In the former case, many women felt they had to constantly monitor and manage their behaviour within an environment that was dominated by men and their culture.

Life in the camp could be a minefield, especially when first starting work. Respondents expressed a large range of gender-related concerns, communicating a sense of constantly having their work-related performance and social behaviour watched, although a number of the comments suggest some women "got used to" the situation.

When asked how they relax in camp, the great majority said they relied on personal pursuits in their rooms, social relationships with other women, and contacts with their families. One respondent, when asked how to improve the camp and camp life had as her first priority "more women!" However, there was concern that even the dormitory was not totally private or safe. Contrary to camp regulations, men came into it to visit women, while male security and maintenance personnel entered as part of their work. In the words of one interviewee: "It's good that we have our own rooms where we can relax. [But] I put on pajamas and go down the hall to the washroom and run into a male security guard or male maintenance worker. The men wander in and do room checks ... it's men that do that and they don't even knock on the door."

Women were particularly reliant upon the dormitory because the number of men affected their use of the recreation and leisure facilities. When asked how often they used such facilities, the gym was the most popular, being used daily by 17 percent of respondents and at least weekly by a further 34 percent. However, 87 percent never used the TV room, followed in declining order by the games room (70 percent never used it), sauna (56 percent), outdoor facilities (52 percent), swimming pool (54 percent), library (44 percent), gym (29 percent), and tavern (19 percent). Furthermore, more than half (54 percent) of these women did not believe these facilities contributed to their relaxation.

It is clear that it was the predominance and behaviour of men that limited women's use of, and benefit from, these facilities. For one interviewee the swimming pool was "a fishbowl. Everywhere you go someone is watching you ... I'd like to see times at the pool just for us. A lot of people say, 'You're looking for special treatment,' but no, I'd love to go swimming but I'm not going to go over there with a bunch of men staring at me. I don't want ... to be put on display."

It should be noted that, for many women, this was more than a relaxation and leisure issue. Given the physical requirements of some of the work, and some men's questioning of women's physical strength in the workplace, it was important for them to have easy access to these facilities.

Men's behaviour also limited women's use of the tavern; one intervie-wee commented that "a game of pool in the recreation area became a kind of show instead of a relaxing game ... The ogling is incredible." Similarly, some women found the dining hall very intimidating, one noting that walking into it was

> one of the most daunting experiences I've ever had ... You're walking in there with generally a thousand men sitting there and you have to walk up to line up ... I don't know that I ever really did adjust to it. It's like the longest mile ... you could hear the cover being placed on the plate just so they could have a good gander. I used to say, "My God, where do they come from?" I mean, they have been locked up for the last six months and haven't seen a woman for six months. I think it's construction site men-tality; all of a sudden they start thinking like Tarzan.

Conclusion

As noted in the introduction, the Hibernia construction project was to be a test-bed for public policy initiatives to encourage the employment of women and the development of their skills in the industry. The material presented above indicates that these initiatives were largely ineffective, and this may have set the model for Newfoundland's second offshore oil-field development project, which saw Bull Arm used to fabricate and install the topsides for Petro-Canada's Terra Nova floating production ves-sel. This work lasted from May 2000 until July 2001, with a peak employ-ment of 2,400 workers. Given the smaller numbers of workers, no use was made of a work camp. While there has been no research into women's employment on Terra Nova construction, such evidence as is available suggests it was otherwise little different from what occurred in Hibernia. Men made up the great majority of the workforce, with many of the same factors limiting women's involvement.

Bearing these problems in mind, it is clearly important that the propo-nents of future construction projects, and the main contractors and unions involved in them, jointly develop and implement comprehensive employment equity plans.[18] These should promote the parties' commit-ment to equality and occupational integration, and they should include: clear routes from training to recruitment, jobs, advancement and promo-tion; retention methods; statistical tracking of women proactively hired, trained, and promoted; and consultative monitoring mechanisms.

In this context, it is a positive sign that Husky Energy, the proponent of Newfoundland's third offshore oilfield project, has a history of being proactive in employment equity. It is the only oil company to have won HRDC's Vision Award, honouring companies governed by the Employ-ment Equity Act, and it has a corporate and business unit designed to assist individuals in attaining the minimum job requirements for male-dominated employment.

The White Rose construction project commenced in early 2002 and will be completed in 2004, with employment levels similar to the Terra Nova project. Husky has expressed a broad commitment to employment equity on the project, and it has been working with local women's groups in the planning of equity initiatives.[19] In developing policies in respect to construction activity, it has recognized the importance of the work environment and, drawing on the Vancouver Island Highway Project, has committed to such activities as workplace assessments, diversity awareness education, and anti-harassment training.[20]

However, there will always be challenges associated with ensuring that such approvals-process commitments are carried through to construction as well as ensuring that they are adopted and implemented by the large number of contractors and subcontractors working on such projects. The slippage between pre-construction commitments and the corporate and other actions during construction has already been noted with regard to the Hibernia project. Carrying such commitment through the project requires considerable rigour and dedication on the part of the most senior levels of management.

The second major challenge, and one that also applies with respect to safety and local benefits concerns, is to ensure that the proponent's corporate commitment is reflected in the actions of the myriad contractors and subcontractors responsible for the great majority of the work. However committed the proponent's senior management is to employment equity, this will have little effect unless it can ensure similar commitment on the part of other companies in the construction value-chain. This requires that there be a clear, formal, and unambiguous communication of the commitment to equity, specific implementation requirements, a regular monitoring of performance, clear sanctions in the case of nonperformance, and a willingness to implement these sanctions.

In any case, governments also need to be more proactive. Especially when public funding is allocated for training women for male-dominated occupations, they must build in monitoring and enforcement mechanisms to ensure equitable access. In particular, any training funding has to be conditional upon the demonstration of proactive equity planning and implementation.

Acknowledgment
We would like to thank Brenda Grzetic for her leadership in the original WITT study of this topic. See B. Grzetic, M. Shrimpton, and S. Skipton, *Women, Employment Equity and the Hibernia Construction Project* (St. John's, Newfoundland and Labrador: Women in Trades and Technology, 1996). We would also like to thank her for her input into this chapter.

Notes

1 J. Lewis, M. Porter, and M. Shrimpton, eds., *Women, Work and Family in the British, Canadian and Norwegian Offshore Oilfields* (London: Macmillan, 1988).

2 D.L. Collinson, "Shift-ing Lives: Work-Home Pressures in the North Sea Oil Industry," *Canadian Review of Sociology and Anthropology* 35 (1998): 301-24.

3 Women in Resource Development Committee, *Where Are the Women?* (St. John's: Women in Resource Development Committee, 2001).

4 B. Grzetic, M. Shrimpton, and S. Skipton, *Women, Employment Equity and the Hibernia Construction Project* (St. John's, Newfoundland and Labrador: Women in Trades and Technology, 1996).

5 D. Riddle, *Assessment of HRDC's Designated Group Policy* (Ottawa: Government of Canada, 1995).

6 Hibernia Construction Sites Environmental Management Committee, *Socio-Economic Review Hibernia Development Project* (St. John's: Government of Newfoundland and Labrador, 1995).

7 P. Murphy, submission to the White Rose Public Review Commission, Submission MR-087 (St. John's, 2001).

8 Government of Newfoundland and Labrador, Investigative Summary: Complaints Received Regarding Hibernia Referral and Hiring Procedures Related to Women (unpublished report, St. John's, 1994).

9 Grzetic, Shrimpton, and Skipton, *Hibernia Construction Project.*

10 See, for example, J. Acker, *Doing Comparable Worth: Gender, Class and Pay Equity* (Philadelphia: Temple University Press, 1989); and J. Fudge and P. McDermott, eds., *Just Wages: A Feminist Assessment of Pay Equity* (Toronto: University of Toronto Press, 1991).

11 C. Cockburn, *Brothers: Male Dominance and Technological Change* (London: Pluto Press, 1983); C. Cockburn, *In the Way of Women: Men's Resistance to Sex Equality in Organizations* (London: Macmillan, 1991); J. Gaskell, "Conceptions of Skill and the Work of Women: Some Historical and Political Issues," in *Politics of Diversity*, ed. M. Barrett and R. Hamilton (London: Verso Editions, 1986); A. Phillips and B. Taylor, "Sex and Skill: Notes Towards a Feminist Economics," *Feminist Review* 6 (1980): 79-88.

12 D. Rhode, *Justice and Gender: Sex Discrimination and the Law* (Cambridge: Harvard University Press, 1989).

13 Government of Newfoundland and Labrador, Investigative Summary, 1994.

14 P. Frangos, S. Gardias, and C. Hookey, Response to the Findings of the Investigation into Women's Concerns about Hiring Practices on the Hibernia Construction Project (unpublished report, St. John's, 1994).

15 Grzetic, Shrimpton, and Skipton, *Hibernia Construction Project.*

16 We would like to thank Michelle McBride for use of this material, which forms part of the research for her PhD dissertation (in progress).

17 Ibid.

18 The problems described in this chapter are not limited to oil industry projects. For example, the construction of the Confederation Bridge between Prince Edward Island and New Brunswick saw the use of the same training model as was used for Hibernia, with similar results. See B. Grzetic, *Women in Technical Work in Atlantic Canada* (St. John's, Newfoundland and Labrador: Women in Trades and Technology, 1998).

19 Husky Oil, *White Rose Oilfield Development Application*, vol. 1: *Canada-Newfoundland Benefits Plan* (St. John's: Husky Oil Operations Ltd., 2001).

20 Husky Oil, *White Rose Oilfield Development Application: Response to Additional Requests from the White Rose Public Review Commission* (St. John's: Husky Oil Operations Ltd., 2001).

5

The Culture of Construction: Or, Etiquette for the Nontraditional

Kate Braid

Both of my aunts worked in wartime industry, one as an inspector in aircraft construction and the other making ammunition. But in 1977, when I got my first job in construction in British Columbia as a labourer – apart from my aunts (and stories of other "Rosies" in the Second World War) – I had never heard of women in traditionally male-dominated jobs in construction. I had certainly never met one, and for good reason. I would later find out that in 1977 women were less than 3 percent of the nontraditional workforce.[1]

In the ensuing twenty-five years, numerous women – including me – achieved their skilled trades qualifications to become journey "women,"[2] and support services have bloomed. We have seen studies, reports, conferences, and courses to introduce women to trades work. Provincial trades training schools have made specific commitments to train women,[3] organizations have been formed for and by women in trades, there are summer go-cart building camps for girls, occasional commitments to affirmative action, and role models galore.

And still the number of women in trades remains stuck at around 3 percent.[4] The obvious question is "Why?"

Speculation abounds. Tradeswomen's organizations, word of mouth, and some trades schools have affirmed that the numbers of women entering skilled blue collar work – the recruitment aspect of trades – has increased. Yet with roughly the same number of women in trades today as existed twenty-five years ago, we have failed miserably at retention – at keeping them there. Why?

After fifteen years as a construction labourer, apprentice, journey carpenter, union member, trade school instructor, researcher, and owner/operator of my own construction business, I have become convinced that the answer is not simply in the obvious – in pervasive sexual harassment by male members of the trade. The answer is more complex. One woman describing her decision to leave the trades said to me: "It's a whirlpool. There are so many intricate little things happening around the edges yet there's no conspicuous core problem, no single thing that's happening." Although harassment is certainly a factor, I would argue that the key to the lack of retention of women in trades lies in all those "little things happening around the edges," in what might be summarized as the "culture" of the construction trades.

Culture?

Just as, over time, any country evolves distinctive ways of speaking, dress, and codes of behaviour and values, so over hundreds of years in the exclusive presence of men, the all-male worksite has evolved a culture that is distinctively male and therefore "foreign" to most women.[5] I would argue that, when a woman (usually the first and often the only one on the job) walks onto an all-male worksite, she has entered a foreign country where, like an immigrant, she must learn and adapt to local ways. However, unlike most immigrants travelling to a different country, women entering the trades are not prepared for a different culture only a few blocks from home – and not knowing is like running full speed into a brick wall.

Most of the current training for women going into trades work says nothing of culture.[6] We are given the same trade skills as men, of course, which is vital. In addition, we may be prepared with extra physical strength training and preparation for dealing with harassment (such as confidence building and assertiveness training); all of these are important. But when a woman, new on the job, works her butt off, waiting for someone to say, "Good job!" and it never comes; when her partner insists on carrying her lumber in the face of the increasing fury of the foreman; when she responds to all teasing as if it were intended as harassment and then can't understand why she is shunned by the rest of the crew; then she is missing something that is vital to her success and to her survival – her retention – on the job: information about the culture.

After a certain amount of time, even women who have earned their journey tickets and know how to get along, how to "speak the language," get tired of being "a foreigner" and drop out, "go home" to some other job where they feel more welcome or at least more comfortable as women.

To understand construction culture, it is first necessary to understand at least one key difference in the socialization of men and women. Deborah Tannen, a linguist who bases her observations on research into the differences in men's and women's speaking styles, points out that most North American men engage in the world "as an individual in a hierarchical social order" in which they are either "one-up or one-down." For most men, "conversations are negotiations in which people try to achieve and maintain the upper hand if they can, and protect themselves from others' attempts to put them down and push them around. Life, then, is a contest, a struggle to preserve independence and avoid failure."[7]

On the other hand, her studies show that most North American women engage in the world "as an individual in a network of connections." For most women, conversations are "negotiations for closeness in which people try to seek and give confirmation and support, and to reach consensus." For most women, she continues, life "is a community, a struggle to preserve intimacy and avoid isolation." Hierarchies tend to be "hierarchies more of friendship than of power and accomplishment."[8]

Examining the construction site in light of this basic difference gives some invaluable insight into what occurs on a construction site when the first woman comes to work. What a difference it might make to retention rates if we could offer women a guidebook to the culture of construction, a sort of "Ms Manners for the Nontraditional" that might read like this:

The Mega-Muscled, the Mighty, and the Rest of Us: Strength

How do most women respond when asked to lift something heavy? We ask for help. It's heavy – we might hurt ourselves.
How do most men respond when asked to lift something heavy? They lift it, even if it kills them.

The most frequently heard excuse not to hire women for blue collar work used to be, "They aren't strong enough." It's heard less often now because so many women are actually doing the work and employers know it's against the law to refuse a woman a job based on the fact of her sex.

In two trips across Canada from the Yukon to Nova Scotia, during which I interviewed women miners, carpenters, electricians, welders, boilermakers, machinists, heavy equipment operators, labourers, and others, I didn't meet a single woman who had a physical problem she couldn't handle. It's just that most of us handle the physical challenges differently from men.

Kinesiology experts say that if you take "averages," then the "average" man is stronger than the "average" woman.[9] However, strength varies so greatly between individuals that the generalization is almost useless. An inch of muscle is an inch of muscle, so some women are stronger than some men because they have more muscle, and no one can generalize that "all women are weaker than all men."

The difference that makes a big difference is in the quantity *and location* of muscle. Men tend to be physically larger than women, and their strength (their muscle) tends to be concentrated in their upper body (shoulders, arms, and back), while women's strength tends to be greater in our lower body (hips and legs). One of the advantages is that our centre of gravity is lower, which may contribute to better balance. (For other reasons, mostly to do with more body fat, women also tend to have better endurance to cold.)

If you're a small woman, or not yet in shape, don't be discouraged by the fact that many men have greater upper body strength. There are many ways to compensate, including:

Physical conditioning
Everybody who starts this work, male and female, has blisters and is sore and tired for the first few weeks. You'll get stronger; strength is one of the most trainable of physical attributes.

Endurance
Aerobic endurance, the ability to tolerate prolonged periods of work, is also trainable and, with practice, improves dramatically.

Technique
The proper use of balance and leverage will let you carry heavier and more awkward loads with grace and genuine ease. You'll also be working more safely. Remember that our bodies are different from those of men. It's part of the culture that men will use upper body strength to throw the eighty-pound sack of cement over their shoulders. If this is difficult, use your greater lower body strength to hug the sack close and carry it balanced on your hips like a baby.

Note that, for some men, carrying a load "differently" counts as not carrying the load at all. Don't be intimidated. All the foreman cares about is that the cement gets from A to B as fast as possible.

Motivation
Attitude is everything. Ask any boss: women who are strongly committed, reliable, and hard working – even if they need training – are almost always more desirable than someone physically stronger or more skilled but with a big chip on his shoulder.

Finally, remember strength isn't always the answer. Because strength alone so often works for them (at least until their backs give out) there is a tendency among men to assume that strength is the first (and often the only) solution to every problem. In fact, it is a hidden "strength" of women that, if muscle doesn't immediately work, we tend to more quickly consider alternatives. If all else fails, ask for help. Two people carrying drywall up a staircase can do more than twice the work of two people working separately, and they can do it with less strain.

Health and Safety and Danger Pay

> *How dangerous are jobs traditionally done by women?* They have their
> dangers but they don't usually involve blood or severed limbs.
> Jobs such as clerk, secretary, and waitress may lead to physical
> disabilities that aren't visible but are still debilitating, such as
> carpal tunnel syndrome, bad backs, and so on.
> *How dangerous are jobs traditionally done by men?* Just as dangerous
> but more dramatic.

If you are working on scaffolding, a single backward step can shorten your
life. One careless moment when using the skill saw can result in blood – yours.
Be vigilant – every second. Every time you use a power saw in one hand,
check to see what all five fingers of the other hand are doing. Every time.

Nice and Neat

> *How do most women wash dishes or vacuum?* Neatly, systematically,
> in rows.
> *How do most men wash dishes or vacuum?* Not neatly. But notice
> how they cut the lawn.

Women tend to be "perfectionists," to perform each job carefully and
thoroughly, but in most trades jobs the focus is on speed. The faster you
work, the happier the foreman will be to get this job finished, collect the
money, and move on to the next. Don't be shocked if he continually
pushes you to go faster! faster! and your partner tells you not to be so
"picky." "It's not a piano," someone will say as you struggle for yet another
perfect fit. As you gain skills you'll find a pace and a level of care you can
feel comfortable with and that still gets the job done in decent time.

A good boss will acknowledge that, if you're just learning the job, it's
more important to go slowly and learn to do it right. "Speed will come
later," they'll usually say. But there will always be pressure to go faster.
Watch what the people around you do. Find a balance.

The Clothes

> *What did you used to wear to work in the office?* High heels, the latest
> fashions, hot colours, and makeup.
> *What will you wear on a construction site?* Steel-toed boots, blue
> jeans, and at least one hot colour: your day-glow orange, gorilla-
> sized rain gear.

As the only woman, you are instantly conspicuous. Spend a few days, weeks, however long it takes, getting comfortable before you decide whether or not to express your individuality with spray paint and sparkles. Some men will assume you are there just for sexual partners. If you wear tight clothes, heavy makeup, and no bra, they'll be certain of it and may make your life a lot harder. Then they'll say you asked for it.

Dress practically. You can buy workclothes – T-shirts, shirts and jeans, even coveralls – cheaply at recycled clothing stores. In the men's section the clothes will be looser, better made, and cheaper. Wear layers. The plaid jackets and vests you see in men's workwear stores are light, warm, loose, and comfortable. They keep you warm, don't bind free movement, and, if the weather changes, are quickly pulled on and off. (In construction, time is almost everything.)

Food

> *What do women in offices eat for lunch and how do they carry it?* We eat celery sticks carried in pretty bags.
>
> *What do men on construction sites eat for lunch and how do they carry it?* They eat a white bread sandwich with one slice of baloney and an Oh Henry! chocolate bar, washed down with a thermos of black coffee, all carried in a tin lunch bucket.

The good news is that you're now going to be burning a lot of calories so you don't have to worry about exercise. Carry a substantial lunch and eat healthily to keep your energy up. I always packed the biggest lunch on the crew and usually it was the only one with any fruit in it. On a large job there may be a coffee truck that comes round at breaks to sell sandwiches, drinks, and chocolate bars, but the time you spend waiting in line is time off your ten-minute break. (Did I mention that when the boss says "ten minutes" he doesn't mean eleven? What are you doing still sitting there?)

At first, you may find you're more thirsty than hungry. Drink plenty of liquids; you'll be sweating. There's some controversy about salt tablets, but a mixture of juice and mineral water will help replace the sugars and salts lost in sweating. Legally, water must be provided on the job for drinking, but it is rarely (if ever) available for washing.

The Talk

> *How do most women carry on a conversation?* We start at the beginning and go to the end. We talk about relationships and personal things.
>
> *How do trades men carry on a conversation?* In one-liners that are

meant to be funny and, preferably, put the other guy down. They talk about sports and impersonal things. If she is referred to at all, even "the wife" is talked about impersonally.

The first time you hear lunchtime conversation on a construction job is the first time you realize you really are in a foreign country, only this one sells no postcards. Most of the talk will be in the form of a shorthand that makes no sense, as in:

"Last night, eh?"
"Yeah, twelve!" followed by much laughter.

Don't worry; this is normal. Eventually you'll learn the language. It is based on a complicated system of hierarchy regarding who can be the funniest and quickest in repartee. The guys will put each other down a lot – in fun. If they do this with you, and they've been doing it to each other, it's probably meant to include you and make you feel like one of the crew. Take it as a compliment and try to quip back. If you're not good at comebacks, just smile. It's amazing how much you can get away with, and what you can say, if you just smile while you're doing it.[10]

Conversation is a key to the cultural differences between men and women on a construction site. As linguists such as Tannen, Lakoff, and Spender have pointed out,[11] relationships for women are held together by talk, while relationships for men are held together by activity, then talking about that activity. Men talk when they need to impress or when their status is in question. So when women talk, we're usually asking, "Do you like me?" While the men are asking, "Do you respect me?"[12]

You'll see this when the foreman asks if someone can do a certain job. No matter what the job, a man won't hesitate. "Sure," he'll say. "No problem!" While the woman says, "Well, I ... Maybe ... that is, I took a course once but ... I'm not sure."

So guess who gets the job? And you can bet on it, nine times out of ten, the man hasn't done it or taken a course in it – ever – but he's not going to let you know that! And the woman just didn't want to boast about how she actually topped the class.

This sort of "faking it" plus practical joking and funny one-liners are seen by the men as a sign of being in control, one-up. So if someone is giving you a hard time and you're not good at snappy comebacks, ask a friend to help you think up a few lines. Use one the next time the slightest opportunity comes up. The guys will love it. Now you're learning the lingo. In the competitive culture of the trades, you have just "one-upped" somebody. Most guys love to laugh at anyone else who's been "one-upped." It's even better if it's in public with lots of other guys around to see it.

Swearing, or The Part You Won't Want to Tell Your Mother

How do nice men talk when they're with women? Nicely (most of the time).
How does this change when they're at work with (mostly) men? They leave you amazed at their creativity, for example about a man who is overly pleasant to the boss, "He's up the boss's ass so high you can't see his ankles."
How do nice girls talk when they're with women? Nicely.
How does this change when they're with (mostly) men? They talk even more nicely.

Swearing is not uncommon in trades work, but often, when a woman comes on the job, the men stop swearing because there is a "lady" present. This is meant to be respectful but soon they resent you for making them stop swearing. If you (the "lady") start swearing to make them feel more relaxed, they resent you because "ladies don't swear."

This is a contradiction in which you're damned if you do and damned if you don't, and there's no way out as long as the men think (and you expect that) they will treat you like a "lady." You are now a tradesperson, making as much money, and expected to do the same work, as they are, and it's important that you impress them with your focus on the job rather than having to be treated as someone to be "protected." If someone says something about a "lady" being present, you might want to remind them there are only "tradespeople" here. This is not to deny you are a woman, only that you do not need any special treatment.

Of course, the men are struggling to deal with these changes too. The first time I swore on a construction job where no one had ever worked with a woman before there was a shocked silence until one of the men said, "Shush, there are men present!" And we all laughed as a potentially uncomfortable moment passed.

Some women prefer to swear. When the first woman mechanic in a motorcycle shop was being interviewed for the local newspaper, the journalist asked, "Do you mind the swearing?" One of the men yelled over, "No, we don't mind it when she swears!" Sometimes this can be a defence. This woman told me, "I didn't want them to be uncomfortable around me, so I swore first."

"Ladies and Gentlemen"

What do most men do when they have a heavy load to move when they're alone? They move it.
When there's another man around? They move it.
When there's a woman around? They rush over to move it for her.

Men who have never worked with women in construction are often confused as to how they should behave. They thought this was "men's work" so what does it say about them, or about women, when a woman comes on the job? They see themselves as gentlemen off the job so some will adopt a "gentlemanly" behaviour, as in the example of swearing, above. But it's another of those no-win situations: a woman assumes, often as the first woman, that she must work hard to please the boss. (Sometimes she's overtly told this.) She knows she's being watched as a representative of her entire sex and that if she doesn't do well it might be a long time before another woman is hired. (Often she's told this, too.) So she works very hard to prove herself capable. And the harder she works, the more she rouses the resentment of the men for "showing them up."

Another example of "ladies and gentlemen" is the issue of weight. A man unsure about his role with a woman on his job site may feel obliged to offer to help "the little lady" carry her materials. If she allows this, she is inevitably resented; she's being paid the same as him, so why should he do her work and his too?

But here's the bind: if the woman says, "No, thank you," and politely insists on doing her own work, often the "gentleman" feels she's trying to show him up.

Be assertive. When a man offers help, assume he is trying to be helpful. Smile and say, "Thanks. I appreciate the offer but I can do it myself." This is valuable information for him (and all the other guys who will instantly hear about it) for the next time. It's important they know you want to do your share of the work: this earns big points in respect.

As long as women and men play "ladies and gentlemen" on the construction site, there will be dissatisfaction – and confusion – on both sides. When women begin to do work that has traditionally been done only by men, new roles are called for, along with new definitions of feminine and masculine.

Feminine and Masculine

What makes a man masculine – a real man? Doing men's work.
What makes a girl feminine? Sugar and spice? A shiny new pair of steel-toed boots? Help!

Traditionally in North America – especially before the latest wave of feminism – a desirable woman was "feminine"; that is, physically weak, mechanically ignorant, and physically beautiful. "Beautiful" meant thin-bodied and big-breasted as revealed by short skirts, low necklines, and high heels. Helplessness was a definite plus.

Women who enjoy physical work, especially women who practise a trade, soon become physically strong, mechanically competent, assertive, and – in order to work effectively – wear loose shirts, blue jeans, hard hats, and steel-toed boots. If there's something they don't like, they speak up – definitely no daisies. Does this make us less feminine? When we were first getting into construction, we joked about meeting each other on Saturday mornings at the second-hand store, looking for black silk lingerie to reassure ourselves in the old-fashioned way that we really were "feminine" – whatever that was.

On the other hand, the men we'd been working with who defined themselves as masculine by virtue of doing dirty, physically difficult "men's work" were suddenly shaken. What did that make them? One day a fellow carpenter, a man, approached me with a sexual offer. "Not interested," I told him. The next day he showed me a tiny cut on his finger and wanted me to fix it. "I'm not your mother," I said, "and the First Aid shack is over there." On the third day he said to me, "You're not my girlfriend, you're not my mother, you're my ... my..." "Your sister?" I suggested, picking up on the union idea that all of us, as members, called each other "brother and sister." "Yes!" he said, relieved to find a category. "You're my sister!"

Men and women working together for the first time in construction must also work to make new definitions work between us, as men and women in offices have been doing for years.

A Voice, a Mighty Voice

> *How are women encouraged to talk?* In little quiet voices that rise up with a question mark at the end, as in, "My name is Kate?"
> *How do men in trades talk?* In big loud voices that carry over the noise of saws and machinery.

When all around you big deep voices are calling for materials and yelling orders and one small voice squeaks out like a single soprano violin over all those bass drums, "More studs?" you may not get much response. (In fact, one tradeswoman who did exactly that got a labourer asking, "Will I do?") Practise lowering your voice. Project from your chest. Talk from your whole body.

"One of the Boys": Just Testing

When you start a new job, especially if you're a rookie at construction, you'll be tested. Everyone in construction gets tested. It's nothing personal, as the men would say, just a way of seeing how you fit into the hierarchy, how good a sport you can be. If someone asks you for a yard of shoreline, or a skyhook, or a left-handed hammer, joke along. Even better, ask them first. Now you're starting to fit in!

Sometimes women are deliberately asked to handle heavy weights, just to test us. Know your limits and make your own decision as to how far you're willing to push them.

Sometimes, while "just testing," men will push a bit too hard, get a bit nasty. Take every assertiveness course you can and don't get angry, don't get scared: this is all part of the culture. Just smile and push right back. Stand your ground, say what you think, and if you possibly can, say it with humour. Nine times out of ten that guy will turn out to be your best friend, "just testing." A guy likes to know where you stand.

The tenth time may be a case of genuine harassment, but you won't know that until you've tried the assertiveness test on him first. Never assume harassment.

Yes, Virginia, There Is Harassment

As one male construction worker succinctly put it, "When you walk onto the construction site, you're the new kid on the block and it's your turn. Take it. Get through it." That's "testing." But there's a difference between this and what comes from the real "bad apples," the bullies on the job. This is harassment, and men as well as women have the stories to prove it – stories of co-workers and bosses who just didn't want them there and were determined to get rid of them in any way they could, not excluding violence. Men who get this extreme treatment don't like it any more than we women do, but most men have learned to hide it. As one male heavy-duty equipment operator told me, "You may be going through hell inside but you say nothing on the outside."

If someone is being harassed, everyone on the job knows it but almost no one ever speaks up against it. In many cultures – not just that of gender – it takes courage to speak up when someone else is being unfairly treated. In the trades, women call it the "pack mentality" and interpret it as unwillingness to break an unspoken male bond and criticize the behaviour of another man.

The best explanation I've heard for this was from a high school industrial arts instructor. When I asked why he thought men say nothing when they see a woman harassed, he said, "Perhaps it's because the men don't want to insult her by stepping in. It would imply she can't look after herself." This is consistent with Tannen's description of male patterns of communication, where "sympathy potentially condescends."[13]

Whatever the reason, if you've tried assertiveness and the man (or men) hasn't backed off, it's time to up the ante. Go beyond assertive; get aggressive. Saying, "Fuck off, asshole!" two inches from someone's face is often successful. If you can do it with a smile, he'll be so confused he probably won't even get mad.

Don't be afraid to ask for help: talk to your union job steward and/or other men on the job who might be allies. It took me years to learn that if someone is being a jerk, he's not just a jerk to you, he's a jerk to everyone. He may be picking on you because you're a woman, on someone else because they're Muslim, and on a third because they're short. But the problem is him, not you! Never fall into thinking of yourself as a victim.

The Porn

Pin-ups seem to be the single most emotional issue on a job, and some men take them very, very personally. One researcher has called them "totems," evoking "a kind of worship,"[14] and asking for them to be removed guarantees strong resistance. For this reason, many tradeswomen have learned to ignore them. We sit with our backs to them, we eat in another lunch shack, we go out of our way to avoid them.

Sometimes countering female pin-ups by putting up male ones will prompt the men to take down *all* pin-ups – male and female. One woman I heard of who had no success with this tactic realized that most of the men on her job were devout Roman Catholics. She put up a postcard of the Virgin Mary, and by noon the walls of that shack were virgin pure.

Again, it's hard for many of us to understand why. One man explained to me he had a right to have "beauty" in his life. I offered him flowers, a picture of a beautiful landscape, but it was the pin-up he thought of as beautiful. It was another man who explained it. "In the hard, dirty world of construction," he said, "a woman's body represents one of the few soft, really beautiful things he knows."

Another man persuaded a male co-worker to take down his pin-up with this explanation: "If I put up a picture of a guy with a twelve inch, steel-hard penis, you'd feel bad. And when a woman sees that poster," he said, "with its forty-four inch bust, she feels just as bad."[15] Most women find this reasoning ludicrous, but it worked for that guy; another example of some of the deep differences in our two cultures.

If You're a Tradeswoman, You Must Be a Lesbian

It's clear by now that some men feel threatened by women who step outside traditional "feminine" boundaries and that they may respond by looking for ways to tag you. One of these tags could be that you're a lesbian – especially if you just rejected his sexual advances. He (and some women, too) may be assuming lesbians "just want to be men" and therefore only lesbians want to do "men's" work. Or he assumes only lesbians would want to work with their bodies.

Don't be intimidated, and don't let your own fear of other's assumptions separate you from other women who might be allies on the job, regardless of their (or your) sexual preferences. The real message behind this tag is that you're rocking the boat. They'll just have to get used to it.

In Praise of Work: Taking It Personally

> *How does a woman tell you the work you've just done is not OK?* She says, "That was a good effort but next time you might try harder." The next time you do something well she will make an admiring comment.
>
> *How does the foreman tell you the work you've just done is not OK?* He yells, "Call yourself a carpenter? Tear it out!"

One hour later he will ask in a genuinely friendly manner if you want to join him and the rest of the crew for a beer after work. He will be surprised when you act hurt and wonder why you take everything so personally. You will think he is an insensitive boor and hates you.

The focus in trades work is entirely on getting the job done, preferably as quickly (and, incidentally, as well) as possible. Any comments made in the process of getting the job done quickly are not intended personally. The boss isn't yelling at you, he's yelling at what you did; it's important that you see the difference. Over and over, women hear, "Don't take it so personally!" It's a thing that, in our upbringing as women, we've been specifically encouraged to do – to take things personally, to empathize with others, to be concerned about how the other feels.

But in the trades culture you get no points for "sensitive." There are, on the other hand, lots of points for getting the job done fast; and there are even more points if you also do it well. Don't look for approval or back patting. Assume that, if they're not yelling at you, you're doing a good job.

This useful lesson can also be applied in other parts of our lives as women. You can learn from construction to be selectively tough, to let comments slide off your back when you know they weren't meant personally, or when there's a job to be done. Focus on the work and process feelings later. Now you have two skills, two potential responses, not just one. You're becoming "bilingual."

Making Mistakes

> *How does a tradesman react when he makes a mistake?* He grins and says, "It's not a mistake if I caught it." Or, "A good tradesperson is known by how they fix their mistakes."
>
> *How do many tradeswomen react when we make a mistake?* We think we're a bad person. We can't do this. It's because we're women.

Don't take it personally. When the nail bends, I could tell myself it's because I'm a woman – or I could notice there's a knot right there and the wood is too hard. If anyone else notices, I could tell them (like the guys do) it's because there's a heavy wind.

Everyone in the trades makes mistakes on a regular basis. Stay alert and catch them before they're permanent and have to be torn out. Learn from them. Mistakes make you a better tradesperson. You may not be perfect, but it's OK to be merely excellent.

How to Pee Politely

> *How do men look after their bodily functions on a construction site?* They use the Porta-Toilet and don't tell anyone how much they hate it. They forget to lock the door.
> *How do women look after their bodily functions in an office?* We carefully lock the door behind us and don't shake it furiously, assuming it's just stuck, if we find it locked. We keep spray bottles of "Mango Freshener" handy and use the tampon dispenser on the wall.

Nobody likes Porta-Toilets. They are cramped, the seats are built to the height of giants, and often they are not kept clean. Porta-Toilets aren't built with women in mind. They're not built with men in mind either, but the men put up with them because it's sissy to complain. (Remember the "real man" part of the culture?) Putting up with inconvenience is part of being "tough." Real men don't complain about toilets.

Your first visit to the Porta-Toilet will be one of the olfactory highlights of the job. Contrary to your first impression, the small trough inside with the moth ball in it is not a sink; it is not a moth ball. The Porta-Toilet does not boast a tampon dispenser on the wall. Women have to make do, although if you're on a large site with plumbers around, you might ask the foreman if the plumbers can't hook up a flush toilet. Coming from a woman, the foreman will probably take the request seriously. Phrase it as a challenge – "I bet the plumbers couldn't fix up a flush toilet on this site if they tried." When they do, the men will appreciate it as much as you, though they'll never admit it.

Every woman deals with the issue of menstrual periods and Porta-Toilets differently. I used to carry a plastic bag and take the used tampons home to dispose of because my worst nightmare was of some guy staring down into the liquid tank, watching my used tampon bob about. Be creative, especially when it's raining or freezing cold and you have to take off not only your raingear but several layers of clothes in the two-foot-six-inch space. There are companies that make coveralls with a back flap.

Never be caught without toilet tissue. On some jobs, you may have to use the bushes along with the guys. The men will be extremely self-conscious and wish as heartily as you for a real toilet. These times make the Porta-Toilets look good. On one job in the middle of the city, a cheap foreman didn't want to pay for Porta-Toilets on the job. He also thought it might be a handy way to get rid of the first woman the union had sent him. The woman just said, "Fine. I'll just go around the corner with the guys," and the toilet was there within an hour. (Notice how she knew enough about the culture to take on his dare.)

Granted, Porta-Toilets aren't the Ritz, but don't go for an entire day at work without using one. This is not good for your health. You're a tradesperson now: use the Porta-Toilet like everyone else.

The Big "L": Lay-Off

> *What do men do when they get laid off at the end of a job?* They pick up their toolbox and go straight to the union hall to sign up for another job. If they're not in a union, they head out the next morning to look for work.
>
> *What do women do when we're laid off?* Cry. Worry. It's because we're no good. Worry so much about what we'll tell our next boss about why we were laid off that we're afraid to apply for another job.

It's an unfortunate aspect of building houses or bridges or highways that eventually the job comes to an end. Sometimes, before this, your boss will move you to the next job, sometimes there is no next job and he or she simply lets you know there's no more work. If this is a union job, the foreman will approach you at afternoon coffee, one hour before quitting time, and give you the infamous "pink slip" that says you're laid off. You will be paid for the next hour but you won't work it: instead, you'll pick up your toolbox and, with the other(s) who may be laid off with you, trudge out of the lunch shack towards the union hall to sign in for the next job.

Every tradesperson knows layoff. It's no fun, and no one ever gets used to it, even the old-timers who've been through it many times. The fellow workers who were your best buddies at lunch time suddenly won't look at you, even to say good-bye, as if you have a terrible disease, as if "layoff" is catching.

If you feel you were laid off unfairly, talk to your business agent. The only difference on a non-union job is that there's no one-hour pay and no appeal. On both union and non-union construction jobs, there is no seniority. If the boss likes you, you stay; if he (or she) doesn't, you go. Period.

Don't take it personally. Go home, have a good cry, then either go directly to the union hall to sign the dispatch list or prepare to go job hunting tomorrow morning. Enjoy your time off.

The Paycheque

What does a woman say when she receives her paycheque? She says, "Oh thank you!"
What does a tradesman say? He says, "Is that all?"

If you work for the union, the rule is that everyone gets the same hourly rate of pay: the rate negotiated in the contract between union and employer. On non-union jobs, each worker negotiates her/his own rate with the boss. This is usually considerably lower than the union rate. Non-union workers rarely show their paycheques to each other; union workers often do. In fact, there's usually a regular (voluntary) betting pool that requires showing each other the cheque number (and, incidentally, all the other information on the cheque).

Generally, the hourly rates of pay in the trades – union or non-union – are better than most women have ever seen. Some employers like hiring women because, even when they pay us less than men for doing the same job, we're grateful; it's still more money than we've ever been paid in our lives. But if the men on the job find out we're working for less, they may be resentful; if a woman works for less, maybe the boss will offer less to the men. Don't be guilty of this. Find out (if you can) what men doing the same work as you are being paid and demand the same. You owe it to your fellow workers. You owe it to the women who come after you. You owe it to yourself to be paid what you're worth. You're in a new ball park now: play ball!

Acknowledgment
My thanks to the British Columbia Institute of Technology's Trades Discovery for Women Program for permission to use this material, which was first developed for them.

Notes
1 From the beginning, it has been notoriously difficult to find reliable statistics on numbers of women in trades and blue collar work. The 3 percent figure is the result of a culling of data, both published and taken from direct inquiries of major employers. Its trail can be followed in Kate Braid, "Invisible Women: Women in Non-Traditional Occupations in B.C." (MA thesis, Simon Fraser University, Department of Communication, 1979). "Non-traditional" is defined as being less than one-third of the work force.
2 By "trade" I mean a skilled craft such as carpenter, plumber, electrician, boilermaker, welder, and so on. Most of them require a combination of theory and on-the-job apprenticeship training that leads to a certification called a "journey" ticket.
3 For example, in 1991 the British Columbia Institute of Technology, British Columbia's largest trades training school, made a commitment to achieving 20 percent women in its trades and technology programs.

4 Statistics Canada, 1996.
5 This culture is also distinctly European and working-class, and the impact of these aspects I leave to others. Here, I will concentrate solely on gender.
6 One significant exception is the "Bridges" program developed by Susan Booth and published as *Bridges to Equity* (Toronto: 1991).
7 Deborah Tannen, *You Just Don't Understand: Women and Men in Conversation* (NY: William Morrow, 1990), 24-25.
8 Ibid., 25.
9 Thanks to Stephen Brown, kinesiologist and ergonomist at Simon Fraser University, Burnaby, British Columbia, for technical advice and assistance on strength. See also Karen Messing, *One-Eyed Science: Occupational Health and Women Workers* (Philadelphia: Temple University Press, 1998).
10 I have always been grateful for this survival tip from Marcia Braundy, journey carpenter.
11 See, for example, Tannen, *You Just Don't Understand*, 1990; Robin Lakoff, *Language and Women's Place* (NY: Harper Colophon, 1975); and Dale Spender, *Man Made Language* (Boston: Routledge and Kegan Paul, 1980).
12 Tannen, *You Just Don't Understand*, 47.
13 Ibid., 61.
14 Marie-Josée Legault, "Workers' Resistance to Women in Non-Traditional Sectors of Employment and the Role of Unions" (unpublished) (Université du Québec à Montréal, 2001), 14.
15 Thanks to Marcia Braundy for this anecdote.

6

Hammering Their Way through the Barriers: Low-Income Women Retrain to Be Carpenters

Margaret Little

Every workday for five years low-income women picked up their hammers and began to build a new life for themselves as they participated in the Women's Work Training Program in Regina, Saskatchewan. This was a unique retraining program that was the brainchild of Valerie Overend and Denise Needham, two women who had become carpenters in order to become self-sufficient. Valerie, a single mother, has an extensive background in community development and is an influential member of the national organization Women in Trades and Technology. Denise created her own carpentry company in Regina and received the YWCA Women of Distinction Award for her business acumen. Together these two women fully understood the need to provide nontraditional skills training within a women-only environment that would be free from harassment. They appreciated the need to establish a long-term program that would include a life skills component. They understood that women required flexibility in order to juggle their retraining program with their heavy domestic demands.

The program was unique in a number of important ways. Established in 1995, it was intensive, being five years in length. Rarely do retraining programs for low-income women extend beyond six to twelve months. Women were expected to be in the retraining program five days a week for five years. Women who were underemployed or without paid work, Saskatchewan residents, had Grade 10 math, and were physically able were eligible to apply to the program. Sixty-four women were accepted over a three-year period. Almost three-quarters of the women were on welfare and 20 percent were on Employment Insurance (EI) when they began the program. Initially, the women received an income from one of these two funding sources. However, after the first year of the program the Regina Women's Construction Co-operative was formed and women could apply to become members. If accepted women received a co-op wage based on seniority and job performance. The co-op was a unique experiment that permitted its members to continue their training with some financial security, a women's-only work environment, and an opportunity to develop business skills alongside their growing carpentry knowledge. If women were able to maintain their commitment to the program throughout the five years, then they could receive their Level 4 in carpentry and write the provincial examination to receive their licence. Funding for this unique program involved a complex web of commitments from federal and provincial government levels as well as from the Women and Economic Development Consortium.[1]

One of the unique features of the program was its flexibility, which permitted women to leave the program for a few days or a few months when life crises struck. If the participant needed a day or two off she was expected to call in and to inform one of the staff. If more time was required, then a participant could request a leave of absence for several months. Some participants did this in order to enter alcohol and drug rehabilitation programs, to leave the city to work on a construction program, to have surgery, or to stay at home with a child who was going through a difficult period.[2] Most of the women who left the program for an extended period chose to leave at the end of a specific learning phase. Creating this amount of flexibility within the retraining program was always challenging. If a participant was missing several days the staff or the co-op board would address the issue and insist that she renew her commitment to the program. Similarly, participants who left the program for an extended time were expected to renew their commitment through daily attendance following their return.

For many, personal difficulties did not allow them to pursue the program full-time for five years. Of the sixty-four women who started the program, sixteen left within the first week or month because they quickly realized that they were not in a position to commit to it.[3] Other women took extended leaves when a crisis arose. These women who took time off work to deal with personal challenges did receive recognition for their accomplishments to date. A total of forty-two women completed Level 1 carpentry and wrote the Level 1 provincial exam. Twenty-eight were registered as apprentices and continued working and training as carpenters. And four women have completed their requirements for Level 4, have passed their final level exams, and are hoping to write their interprovincial exams. The others are at various stages in their careers; some choosing to work full-time at carpentry and others choosing to do a mixture of work and schooling to upgrade their skills.[4]

The purpose of this chapter is to explore the barriers that affect low-income women's participation in retraining programs. I will also briefly outline how this program specifically attempted to address these barriers. During interviews with thirty women participants over a three-year period it became evident that most of the retraining programs and the retraining literature have underestimated the significant barriers faced by low-income women.[5] These barriers cannot be exaggerated as they are simply colossal. The fact that any low-income woman continued to return to the Regina shop and pick up her hammer week after week is nothing short of a miracle. Against all odds, these women continued to be a part of this program. While there are many barriers to low-income women's participation in retraining programs, there are five in particular that have deeply affected these women's life choices: race, motherhood, violence, lack of experience as paid workers, and poverty.

Race

It is impossible to spend time with the participants of the Women's Work Training Program without noticing how profoundly their racial identity has affected all aspects of their lives. Two-thirds of the women participants interviewed are Native, seventeen are status, three are Métis, and ten are White.[6] For the Native women in the program it is profoundly obvious that their daily lives, from childhood through adulthood, have been deeply marked by the devastating impact of centuries of colonization. I will not deal with the race factor in isolation; instead, during a discussion of the other five barriers to low-income women's participation in this retraining program, I will address how race has affected each of these other barriers. Even though White and Native women shared all five of the following barriers, the latter experienced them to a much greater degree than did the former.

Motherhood

One crucial barrier in these women's lives is also their greatest source of pride and identity: motherhood. Twenty-four of the thirty women interviewed are mothers, twelve of them are single mothers, and seven of them are raising children other than their own.[7] During the program these thirty women were caring for and financially responsible for sixty children. This does not include grown children who are financially independent or children who live with relatives or in foster care. Even with these figures it is difficult to capture the magnitude of this mothering responsibility, which is compounded by the fact that these women are low-income and have few economic resources to draw upon. Quality childcare, restaurant meals, and laundry services are all luxuries that low-income mothers cannot afford, even though they would significantly help them juggle their paid work and mothering responsibilities.

Motherhood has greatly affected these low-income women's life stories. Many of these women left high school as a result of teen pregnancies. Their later attempts to upgrade their education were often interrupted by other pregnancies. And, as a consequence of their intensive mothering responsibilities, their employment history tends to be sporadic and short-term.

Colonization has created further anxiety for Native mothers. If Native women were considered to be poor mothers, then this provided an excuse for the state to remove Native children and place them in residential schools and foster homes. Many of the Native women interviewed spoke about how their mothering was their most important responsibility. Those who had experienced neglectful childhoods were even more adamant that they would be exceedingly attentive to their children's needs. While low-income mothers are often criticized for their parenting abilities, this is even more the case for Aboriginal mothers. There is a long colonial history that makes it very apparent why the Aboriginal mothers interviewed were particularly concerned to prove that they were good mothers and why they vowed that the needs of their children came before their own.

Motherhood, for Native women, is more demanding than it is for White women partly because they have more children requiring love and attention. As studies have documented, the Aboriginal communities in Canada have the highest rate of population growth. As Aboriginal scholar Kim Anderson explains, in Native cultures new life was always considered precious: "Children were always welcome, and because women were esteemed for having children, pregnancy was a natural part of the sexual cycle."[8] Given this cultural heritage it is not surprising that, of the women interviewed, the Native women bore and raised more children than did the White women. On average, the Native mothers interviewed had 2.6 children, with one woman having raised eight children and two women having raised five children. In comparison, the White mothers interviewed on average had 1.8 children, ranging from five children to none. What is perhaps more telling is the number of White women that remained childless. Forty percent (or for of ten) of the White women in the program did not have children at all, whereas only 15 percent (or three of twenty) of the Native women did not have children.

Many of the Native mothers are raising not only their own children but also often extended family members. Cheryl, a status Indian, recalls her early mothering years when she raised six children. She remembers all too vividly the death of one of her babies. She also recalls another time when she and her children were homeless and sleeping outside. Cheryl is adamant that none of her children will ever be homeless, and her current living arrangements attest to this: "I live in a tiny little two-bedroom house. And I've got my son and my daughter-in-law, my other grandchild and my other son and my other grandchild came and camped last night. And I have my daughter-in-law's brother and his baby there."[9] Rhonda M., also a status Indian, explained that there are seventeen people who are financially dependent upon her. She and her partner support two houses side by side on the reserve. Some of her children live with her and some of them live next door.[10]

These extended family ties create a number of demands that interfere with women's participation in the retraining program. For instance, one week when I interviewed Rhonda she had a very small paycheque, and this concerned her. "I need all the money I can get for my family," she said. But she had missed two days' pay that week because she had taken her grandson to the Saskatchewan Penitentiary to visit his mother. "She [the boy's mother] has been away from him for four years so every chance we get I like them to be together. I couldn't find anyone else to take him because it takes three months for the security clearance."[11]

At other times extended family members were a tremendous help to the women in the program. Some women relied upon their sisters and mothers as pinch-hit babysitters when their regular babysitter could not be at their home. Others had their young children move in with other family members, especially during the summer months when the children were home from school and their mothers continued to be in the program.

It is a tremendous achievement to juggle this intensive retraining program with the extensive demands of mothering. Many of the participants spoke about their elaborate organizational schemes to keep the home fires burning while training to be carpenters. One single mother with two children explained what has to happen every evening in order to make the morning rush possible: "When I come home I make supper, clean the house at the same time, and usually try to get my youngest to sit at the table and practise her alphabet or numbers or something. After supper is homework and then they must get their clothes all laid out for school tomorrow and then story time and bedtime. Then I make the lunches, tidy up and do my own homework."[12] Rhonda H. lives forty minutes away in Vybank with her partner and four children. In order for her to be at work on time she rises at 5:30 AM and she drops the children off at the daycare at 6:30 AM before heading into town. "Yes it's a big rush and it's a fight in the morning with the girls," she says. But the biggest challenge is making certain that the children get picked up by 6 PM when the daycare closes. "Many days we have meetings or we're working late or whatever and my mom picks them up."[13]

Many single mothers worry about their children's school attendance while they are at work. One single mother with five children is particularly concerned about her fifteen-year-old son. "He's got like a 50 percent school attendance. When I have to be at the worksite at 7:00 AM I can only hope he goes to school. When we move to another jobsite and I don't have to be at work until 8:00 AM I'm hoping that then I'll be able to keep an eye on him."[14]

Some women have quit, or temporarily withdrew from, the training program because of their mothering responsibilities. For instance, Evelyn, a mother raising four children and one grandchild, withdrew briefly from the program when her teenage children began to experiment with drugs. "My sixteen-year-old has a little girl. But it took something in her life to make her straighten out ... She landed in the hospital, she was really sick from taking drugs ... It was very stressful." Evelyn didn't feel she had her children's support for this retraining program, and this added to her stress: "I was trying and trying [in this program] and the children weren't trying and I felt like I was doing it all for nothing. And then I remembered that I'm doing it for myself; they don't want to be a part of the way I'm going and they can do what they want and find out the hard way the way I did. So I just said I'm just going to go to work and forget about everything until I get home and deal with it, and that's what I did."[15] Eventually Evelyn left the program for a second time because she found it impossible to juggle the stress of her rebellious teenage children with her intensive retraining program.

This retraining program has deeply affected the women's home lives. In some cases male partners have increased their domestic responsibilities in the home so that the women can participate in this training program. This is the case for Shelley, who describes her own childhood as difficult. Because her parents were deeply traumatized by the residential schools they were forced to enter, they turned to alcohol for relief. Her parents were rarely home to attend to her needs, and it was Shelley's grandmother who generally stepped in to care for her. She is adamant that her own children will never be neglected by their parents. Consequently, she and her husband Dion have promised that one of them will be home full-time with the children until they attend school. So in order for Shelley to participate in the program Dion has to be a full-time parent: "Childcare is number one. If I didn't have Dion I wouldn't be here, plain and simple, because I'm so protective of my kids. I figure if I can't watch them, the only other person I trust to watch them would be Dion. And he has lovingly given up his career temporarily while I start mine."[16] Shelley explained in detail their new domestic arrangement: "He does the sheets, I do the clothes, but he does everything else, he pays the bills, he does errands, grocery shops, he's great. I come home to a beautiful clean house, supper. Yes, if I need anything I ask him and he's wonderful."[17]

Given the demands of motherhood and the training program a number of the women have complained about difficulties with their boyfriends or partners. One single mother said she broke up with her boyfriend because there simply was no time for him. "We just didn't have time for each other. He was busy and whenever he had time I was busy ... It was high maintenance to take care of that relationship, and I just couldn't do it anymore," she explained.[18]

Another mother explained that she and her husband split up for a month because she was in the retraining program. "He was feeling low self-esteem because I'm making money and he's not."[19] To add to her anxiety this mother's husband did not want to look for a job because he didn't want to leave the children with a babysitter. This made the woman feel quite guilty about the retraining program. Eventually the tension between the two parents was too great and they separated. This separation caused financial worries for the mother as the father had left her with the phone bill and other debts that she could not afford to pay. She was terribly distraught about all of this, and she took an extended leave from the program to get her home in order.

Violence

Up until recently domestic violence has rarely been connected to issues of poverty and retraining. There is very little scholarship on low-income women, retraining, and violence in Canada.[20] However, the extensive American research has shown, in study after study, that low-income women experience significantly higher levels of violence than do more privileged women.[21]

The experiences of the women interviewed reflect similar findings about low-income and Aboriginal women's experiences of violence. The women interviewed had experienced verbal, physical, sexual, and psychological abuse. They had been raped at gunpoint, thrown down stairs, and had feared for their lives. They spoke about the violence they had experienced as little girls and as adult women. The Aboriginal women talked about the violence they experienced from White culture, which was a daily part of their lives. They also spoke of how centuries of oppression and forced assimilation had promoted violence within their communities. During the three years in which I interviewed the participants, one woman's brother committed suicide, two women's sister-in-law died when she fell out of a speeding truck, and others have dealt with their own or other family members' alcoholism and the abuse/violence associated with it. In sum, violence is an integral part of these women's lives. With the exception of three women (two White and one Métis), all the others interviewed had experienced significant levels of violence in their lives.

The violence from White culture that Native women in this program experience each and every day of their life creates further inequities for them. During the interviews Native women spoke about how they have been harassed and how they have endured catcalls as they walked to or from job sites. On the job site more than one White customer accused the Native women of stealing. What this speaks to is the many ways that Native women are considered guilty and sexually available simply because they are Native. The White women interviewed never encountered any of these experiences of violence, harassment, or suspicion during their time in the program.

As a result of colonization, violence is epidemic in Native communities both on and off the reserve. Colonization in and of itself is a violent process. The federal government and church policies instilled violence into Native children who were placed in residential schools and foster homes where they were deprived of love and were abused physically, sexually, and psychologically. Abused Native boys and girls grew into adults who abused or who accepted abuse as a part of a relationship. This violence has destabilized and destroyed homes, families, and communities.

Certainly the Aboriginal women in this retraining program have witnessed and experienced significant levels of violence within their homes, their families, and their communities. This violence, which is part of Native urban and reserve life, has made Native women more transient than White women. In their attempts to protect their children from violence, many have been forced to leave their communities.

Childhood experiences of abuse and neglect were rampant among the women participants in this retraining program. Forty-three percent of the women participants who responded to the anonymous violence survey said that they had been sexually abused as children. One Native woman describes her childhood on the reserve: "I was molested as a child. And I had a pretty rough life with my mother, too. I looked after all my siblings. My mother would leave me on a Sunday night and she'd come back Friday. I used to haul water, wash diapers, cook and clean. If the house wasn't clean Friday night, I'd get a licking. I never had very much of a life."[22]

Sharon Murray, who was hired as a forewoman for the program, is well known and liked by the participants. She has visited their homes, met their families, and been a confidante to many. When interviewed, Sharon estimated that every single Native woman in the program, with the exception of one, was dealing with an abusive relationship.[23] Certainly the anonymous violence survey supports Sharon's belief that the vast majority of the participants have experienced abusive relationships. According to the survey, more than half of the women had partners who destroyed or took their possessions and prevented them from seeing their friends or families. And more than 70 percent of those who responded to the questionnaire said that they were verbally and physically abused by their partners. The severity of the violence experienced is also worth noting. More than half said they had been cut, bruised, choked, or seriously harmed by a partner. And more than one-third said a partner had used a gun, knife, or other sharp object to threaten them.

In many ways both previous and current experiences of violence affected the women's ability to fully participate in the program. Violent traumas can cause depression, low self-esteem, and health problems. In the United States abused women have been found to have higher rates of depression and drug or alcohol abuse than do non-abused women.[24] The women in this retraining program reflect many of the findings of earlier studies about health and violence. According to the anonymous violence survey administered to these women, 22 percent said they felt depressed daily or once a week, and 36 percent said they had no energy daily or once a week. Of the thirty women interviewed over a three-year period, seven said they had dealt with, or continue to deal with, long-term alcohol and drug abuse issues. All seven of these women had experienced significant abuse as children and/or as adults.

This experience of violence can interfere with a woman's ability to participate in retraining programs or paid work. American studies have shown that as many as 40 percent of currently abused women are prevented from participating in education and training by their abusive partners. It is not surprising that low-income women in abusive relationships in the United States have reported higher spells of unemployment, more job turnover, more absenteeism, and more reliance upon welfare than have non-abused low-income women.[25] Certainly the Regina women's experiences support this finding. According to the anonymous violence survey 14 percent had been harassed by their partners at work during their participation in this retraining program. Twenty-one percent said that their partners were jealous and were afraid that they might meet someone new at work (even though these women seldom worked with men). And 14 percent said that their partners were worried that they might become lesbians because they work in a women-only environment.

Certainly, for many women in the program, violence and abuse have interfered with their ability to concentrate and to participate. Some of the women mentioned that flashbacks continue to be a problem for them, disrupting their sleep and sometimes interfering with their ability to work. According to the anonymous violence survey, 29 percent of the respondents said that they had intrusive memories while they were at work, while 14 percent said that they had trouble concentrating at work because of stress at home. "Flashbacks are a big part of my life," explained one woman. "When they happen sometimes I have to go, I have to leave and I have to cry and there is no way around it. You can't do that in front of customers. But I just go off in a corner and I'm OK. Other women in the program, I know they have to stay home when they can't cope."[26]

There is now some evidence that low-income women experience increased levels of violence when they attempt to work or to participate in retraining programs. Often, low-income women's partners are also poor and their self-esteem fragile. These male partners may be threatened by women earning an income and having a social life outside the home. This was the case for one woman in the program. After several months she left the program because her partner felt threatened. When things calmed down on the home front she returned, but again her partner became difficult.

"He calls the women I work with dykes. He's jealous of them and he's jealous because I like this work," she explains. "I tried to fix the fence at home but he [her partner] said it was a man thing. He got mad because the neighbours might see me doing a man's job."[27] Other women in the program said they were worried about her and witnessed her coming to work bruised after a weekend at home with her partner. Although she turned to the coordinators and the other women in the program for support, she eventually left the program for a second time because she simply could not handle the increased conflict in her life.

Other women reported that their partners were jealous of the training program and the friends they were making. The men seemed particularly upset about the women getting together for a drink after work on Friday nights. "She [one woman in the program] said I can't go with you for a drink 'cause my husband will come and he'll hit you," explained one woman.[28] Another woman said that her partner hid her second-year carpentry apprenticeship card when it came in the mail. "I was so excited and proud. I was flashing it around in front of him, showing it off so he hid it on me because I was getting carried away."[29]

Many women spoke about how their participation in the retraining program helped to break the isolation they felt when dealing with an abusive partner. Some of the women confide in each other about these difficulties, and a number of them create safe houses for each other – allowing a workmate to secretly stay at their house for a while so that her abusive partner cannot find her.

Previous Employment
Another barrier to women's participation in the retraining program is their limited experience as paid workers. For seven of the thirty women interviewed the retraining program was their first job ever. Most of them left school around Grade 11 and have since been trying to complete their high school education. Eleven of the thirty women interviewed were on welfare all their adult lives; however, the majority of them had scattered careers of short-term employment interrupted from time to time by the birth of a child.

For the most part, these women's job experiences have given them little hope of climbing out of poverty. The vast majority of their employment was short-term service sector work (e.g., secretarial, receptionist, and waitressing jobs). As with most service sector work, this employment was minimum wage, often part-time, and offered no hope of advancement or job benefits. Only two of the women described their previous employment experiences as in any way self-fulfilling. The rest had been harassed at work, forced to work for low pay, and had virtually no support from their co-workers.

Postsecondary education was simply impossible for most of these women. A number of them never went to high school, and many have juggled young children and endured poverty while attempting to return to school to get their high school diplomas. The horrors of residential school left one woman with little desire to go to high school: "I just never went to high school. I got out of that residential school as fast as I could – after Grade 5." Out of school at thirteen years old she moved off the reserve and into Regina to live with her mother and care for the younger children. "I was 13 when I went to visit her and then I got raped and then I had my own baby nine months later." Two weeks after the baby was born she was kicked out of her mother's house and had to fend for herself. "I did odd jobs like house cleaning, babysitting – anything to feed the baby. And I got welfare."[30]

Many of the women straddled the divide between welfare and paid employment. It was often very difficult to trace the employment history of the women participants. They were very much a reserve army of labour, working when childcare arrangements and a job were available and then falling back on welfare when a baby was born or their job disappeared. They had absolutely no job security. Delphine accurately described her employment history as follows: "It's always been a job, unemployment, a job, unemployment, just back and forth, back and forth."[31]

These women often complained that welfare regulations made it difficult to pursue training or paid employment. As one single mother explained, "Welfare didn't really help me ... Every little job, even babysitting, I would claim it and I was using the money to go for computer classes at school and the more I tried to get off of welfare, the deeper I got dragged in ... By the time I paid my transportation and daycare and everything I was in the hole."[32] Another woman was frustrated that welfare wouldn't let her retrain: "I wanted to upgrade but they [welfare] wouldn't let me. As long as I had a job they were happy and they'd subsidize the wages but absolutely no chance to upgrade."[33]

Their employment history was also deeply affected by personal tragedy. One woman stopped working and started drinking when her baby died of crib death. Another gave up her job when her husband was murdered and returned with her three-year-old twins to Regina, where her family lived.

More than one-third of the women had no paid employment experience and had been on welfare all their lives. The majority of these women were Aboriginal single mothers with virtually no resources, little education, and few family contacts that would help them enter the workforce. With children to raise they had previously viewed paid work as impossible.

Money, Debts, and Grinding Poverty

Another significant barrier to participation in a retraining program is the grinding poverty faced by most of these women in their daily lives. Almost all of the women in the program know what it is like to live without food at the end of the month, to not be able to pay the regular bills, to be anxious about money on a daily basis. This is the reality of low-income women's lives. Some of the women in the program do not have phones; some have insecure housing that changes frequently; the majority do not own a vehicle; and most are very anxious about outstanding bills.

Native identity has also deeply affected the amount and types of resources available to the women participants. As a result, the Aboriginal women in this retraining program have fewer resources to draw upon than do the White women participants. Of the ten White women interviewed, two had received financial help from their parents and one from her grandparents. As a result, one of these White women was debt-free, two were paying cheap rent, and one had been given a second-hand truck by her family. None of the Aboriginal women had family members with such economic resources; rather, they were viewed by their families as the ones with the economic resources because they had a steady (albeit minimal) income. Consequently, these women spoke of the constant requests from family members for money and food.

This grinding poverty can leave one feeling helpless and hopeless. Combined with a childhood of abuse it is little wonder that drugs and alcohol have been a way of coping for many women. One Aboriginal woman explained her hard economic times: "I completely gave up on everything ... I was right down to nothing, me and my husband were getting a divorce. It was a really bad year for my family ... I lost a lot of people in our family that year ... That's when I went back to drugs and alcohol."[34] Another woman recalled her experiences of homelessness: "Back then I had no place to stay. Welfare wouldn't put me up any place. They said they wouldn't give me my cheque for my rent because they said that I wasn't looking for work. So me and my son and my cousin had to sleep out on 13th Avenue where there's a bowling lane. That's where we slept, and it was cold." This single mother finally found work as a chambermaid and waitress, and then another crisis befell her: "I had my third baby. She would have been 18 now but I lost that baby. She was 2½ months old when she died of crib death. And then I sort of just went really crazy and started drinking a lot."[35] A White single mother explained her past: "I've been through my addiction with drugs. I have had my house burn down twice. I have had my kids go with their father. I have had to move many, many times because I couldn't afford the rent. My twenties was one battle after another."[36] Still another recalled her hard times: "I just saw no way forward. I stopped working and I starting doing crime – B and Es [break and enter], stealing cars, drinking, not caring about nobody or nothing, not having a place to sleep and not worrying about it." When she became pregnant at twenty-three she changed her life, went to Alcoholics Anonymous, and began to care about herself. This retraining program has given her another reason to change her life: "I just love carpentry and I love the learning – this gives me another reason to stay away from the bottle."[37]

Many of the women entered the program with significant levels of debt. With relatively low wages they were often unable to get a handle on their debt. Coordinator Denise Needham recalled debt collectors and landlords calling the shop demanding money from the women: "I've had guys [debt collectors] come by and sit in their car for hours waiting to see a particular woman and serve her with papers for the money she owed." One woman who led a fast life and was a cocaine user had a debt load of more than $250,000 and was terrified that someone would cause her physical harm. She recalled her enormous anxiety about her debt: "It was a lot of money. That is money that I didn't even know existed and there I was sniffing it into my lungs and my head." She was relieved when she was able to reach a private agreement regarding her drug debt and publicly declare bankruptcy. Now she no longer associates with "the fast crowd," and her wages are garnisheed to reduce her debt. "After a long time I am no longer afraid for my safety. I am learning to save for the first time. Now things are really working out."[38]

A number of the women who have attempted to get training or education have student loans hanging over their heads. According to Denise: "The minute any of our women start working, start trying to change their lives, the student loan people are harassing them for money." One woman spoke about how frustrating it was to have a debt that she could not erase: "You would like to pay it off quicker. I mean, instead of the $4,500 debt I will pay back something like $7,500. It is good that I don't have to pay it back tomorrow, but I mean you can't help but think about what you could have done with an extra $3,000."[39]

Almost all of the women interviewed have debts. While these debts range from as high as $250,000 to as little as $1,700, the majority have debts hovering around $15,000. This is a constant noise in the background – an anxiety that they can do little to ameliorate on a retraining income that is just slightly above minimum wage.

Conclusion

Each of these barriers was an enormous challenge to the continued participation of these low-income women in the Women's Work Training Program. In a number of ways the program attempted to address these barriers. For example, the mothering responsibilities of the participants have been addressed wherever possible. While the program does not provide childcare, the instructors have discussed childcare arrangements with each of the participants. And the program's flexibility has permitted women to take time off to take care of their children's needs. Violence was also a barrier that the program attempted to address. Life skills workshops dealt with abuse issues and made the women aware of available community supports. And the program's flexibility allowed women to leave for extended periods when they needed to deal with the violence in their lives. The long-term nature of the program stood in stark contrast to the nature of the women's previous employment history. For some, it was their first paid work experience; for most, it was the first job in which they felt empowered. The program attempted to work with the participants and to help them to develop responsible work behaviour.

The program was less able to cope with the grinding poverty that these women experienced. Women, when they entered the program, began at minimum wage ($5.60/hour), and it was hoped that this would increase by two dollars per hour per year as members were promoted through peer evaluations.[40] But the program was never financially sound enough to meet these wage expectations, and the women's wages remained significantly below what they would have received had they worked in the construction industry. However, at the same time, the women received leniencies, such as days off to care for their sick children or time out to recover from personal problems, which they would never have received in the construction industry. Still, given that these women continue to live below the poverty line and have many who depend upon them, these low wages were always a problem.

The barrier that received the least attention in this retraining program was that of race. Racism faced by Native women in western Canada is so pervasive that it is virtually a part of the landscape. White women, as a rule, rarely appreciate the intensity of this ongoing legacy of colonialism, which Aboriginal women experience every day of their lives. This ignorance was noticeable in the Regina program, in which the majority of the instructors were White and the majority of the participants were Aboriginal. Upon reflection, Valerie Overend wished that an Aboriginal instructor had been a permanent fixture of the program and that an elder had been there to play a role in the continued mentorship of the Aboriginal women.[41] This would have greatly helped to ensure that the program met the specific needs of the Native women and that it was sensitive to cultural differences among the participants.

Any one of these barriers would create a huge obstacle to a low-income woman's participation in this retraining program: together, they were almost insurmountable. It was the combination of the unique nature of the program and the sheer determination of the participants that enabled the program to work. The two coordinators, Valerie and Denise, attempted to build a program that was shaped by the everyday needs and realities of low-income women. As the women negotiated with abusive partners, managed childcare arrangements, dealt with angry bill collectors, struggled with their history of drug and alcohol abuse, somehow they still arrived at the shop each workday to learn more about carpentry. They continued, day after day, hammering their way through these barriers so that they could become carpenters.

Acknowledgment

This chapter is dedicated to the participants in the Women's Work Training Program, Regina. I am grateful for the help I received from Valerie Overend, Denise Needham, Bonita Lawrence, and Diane Kearnan.

Notes

1 For further details of the program, see: Valerie Overend, *Foundation for Success: The Story of the Women's Work Training Program in Saskatchewan* (Regina: Saskatchewan Women in Trades and Technology, 2000). I am currently writing a book about this retraining program entitled *If I Had a Hammer: Retraining That Really Works*. In this book I explore more fully these barriers, but I also address the design of this particular program, retention factors, and the challenges it meets. And I suggest new ways to develop retraining programs and to measure their success.

2 For instance, one participant went to Nova Scotia to work on building a church, another left the country to work on a straw-bale house community.

3 Overend, *Foundation for Success*, 29.

4 Ibid., 91. For a fuller discussion of tracking the women through the program and evaluating their achievements, see Little, *If I Had a Hammer*, chap. 5.

5 Because I interviewed the women over a three-year period I was able to follow them throughout different stages of the program. I interviewed every woman participant that was present at the worksite during my four visits over a three-year period. Each interview was taped, and the women later edited the transcript for errors and omissions. During the three years of interviews each woman was given several opportunities to decide whether she wanted to be named or anonymous. They completed a written survey about violence, in which all were anonymous. I have followed their wishes with the following exception: I have chosen to make some of the more intimate details of their lives anonymous even when they did not request this. Above all, I did not want to do anything that might have harmed the tremendous trust they had placed in me.

6 Please note that I generally refer to status and mixed-race women as "Native" because that is the term they themselves most commonly use. I use "Aboriginal" occasionally to avoid constant repetition. When appropriate I specify "status" or "Métis" to differentiate between these two groups. I am grateful for discussions with Bonita Lawrence and for her research on mixed-race Aboriginal men and women. See Bonita Lawrence, "'Real' Indians and Others: Mixed-Race Urban Native People, The Indian Act, and the Rebuilding of Indigenous Nations" (PhD diss., Ontario Institute for Studies in Education, 1999); Bonita Lawrence, "Mixed-Race Urban Native Identity: Surviving a Legacy of Genocide," *Kinesis*, Native Women's Issue, December 1999/January 2000, 15, 18.

7 I define a single mother as anyone who was a single parent during at least one year in which they participated in the retraining program.

8 Kim Anderson, *A Recognition of Being: Reconstructing Native Womanhood* (Toronto: Second Story Press, 2000), 86.

9 Interview with Cheryl Sanguais, Regina, October 1998.

10 Interview with Rhonda McKay, May 1998.

11 Ibid., October 1998.

12 Interview with Tanya Bear, Regina, May 1998.

13 Interview with Rhonda Harrison, October 1998.

14 Interview with anonymous interviewee no. 6, Regina, October 1998.

15 Interview with Evelyn Bitternose, Regina, July 1999.

16 Interview with Shelley Favel, October 1998.

17 Ibid., July 1999.

18 Interview with Pat Fayant, December 1999.

19 Interview with anonymous interviewee no. 5, October 1998.

20 While violence and retraining has yet to be explored within the Canadian context, there are a few studies of violence and low-income women, most notably Janet Mosher, "Managing the Disentitlement of Women: Glorified Markets, the Idealized Family and the Undeserving Other," in *Restructuring Caring Labour: Discourse, State Practice, and Everyday Life*, ed. Sheila M. Neysmith (Toronto: Oxford University Press, 2000), 30-51; Ontario Association of Interval and Transition Houses (OAITH), *Locked In, Left Out* (Toronto: OAITH, 1996); OAITH, *Some Impacts of the Ontario Works Act on Survivors of Violence against Women* (Toronto: OAITH, Standing Committee on Social Development, 1997); Margaret Little, "A Litmus Test for Democracy: The Impact of Ontario Welfare Changes on Single Mothers," *Studies in Political Economy*, forthcoming.

21 Among the most important American literature on the topic is: M.A. Allard, R. Albelba, M.E. Colten, and C. Cosenza, *In Harm's Way? Domestic Violence, AFDC Receipt, and Welfare Reform in Massachusetts* (Boston: University of Massachusetts, McCormack Institute, Centre for Survey Research, 1997); Jodi Raphael and Richard Tolman, eds. *Trapped by Poverty, Trapped by Abuse* (Michigan: Taylor Institute and the University of Michigan Research Development Centre on Poverty Risk and Mental Health, 1997).

22 Interview with anonymous interviewee no. 2, October 1998.

23 Interview with Sharon Murray, July 1999.

24 Eleanor Lyon, "Poverty, Welfare and Battered Women: What Does the Research Tell Us?" (Welfare and Domestic Violence Technical Assistance Initiative. National Resource Centre on Domestic Violence), <www.vaw.umn.edu/vawnet/welfare.htm> (December 2002).

25 Ibid., 5.

26 Interview with anonymous interviewee no. 5, July 1999.

27 Ibid., no. 12, October 1998.

28 Interview with Reagan Haus, July 1999.

29 Interview with anonymous interviewee no. 10, December 1999.

30 Ibid., no. 9, May 1998.

31 Interview with Delphine Bitternose, May 1998.

32 Interview with anonymous interviewee no. 6, October 1998.

33 Ibid., no. 11, May 1998.

34 Interview with Evelyn Bitternose, July 1999.

35 Interview with anonymous interviewee no. 2, October 1998.

36 Ibid., no. 11, May 1998.

37 Ibid., no. 3, October 1998.

38 Ibid., no. 5, July 1999.

39 Ibid., no. 7, December 1999.

40 Women's Work Training Project, "Proposal for Women and Economic Development Consortium," 6.

41 There was one life skills instructor who was Aboriginal, but she only stayed for a few months because she preferred full-time employment. To Valerie's knowledge there is no Aboriginal woman who has a carpentry licence in western Canada. See Overend, *Foundation for Success*, 40.

7

Training and Retraining Health Workers amid Health Care Restructuring, Downsizing, and Rationalization: The Case of Health Care Aides

Larry Haiven and Liz Quinlan

This study of one vocational training program in a small province is set against the backdrop of the increasing privatization and deregulation of such training. In the encounter between public ordering and private ordering, those two initiatives work together intimately. The issue is not just whether the provision of vocational training will be conducted by public or private institutions but also how the delivery of training will be regulated (i.e., who will act as the arbiter of the "public interest").

Public training may never totally disappear in the face of an onslaught of private institutions. However, the future role of the public sector in vocational training is certainly in dispute. Three possible roles (not necessarily mutually exclusive) are emerging for the public sector:

1   *provider* of training (actually developing and delivering its own curriculum);
2   *"broker"* of training (opportunistically buying training programs from many external sources, both public and private, and delivering them); and
3   *regulator* of training (acting as arbiter or quality assurance watchdog over a variety of competing programs as well as a champion of credit transfer and prior learning assessment and recognition [PLAR]).

Vocational training has now largely devolved from the federal government to the provinces,[1] so the ideological approach of different provincial governments is a key factor. Particularly interesting is the approach of the Saskatchewan NDP government, which is rooted in a social democratic political culture within an increasingly neoliberal world.

Since the Second World War the Canadian political economy has experienced three regimes,[2] as has the training that has occurred within it. First was the Keynesian regime, which dominated the first four decades but has now largely dissolved. In it, governments saw state involvement in education and training as providing a public good. However, for the most part, Keynesianism used macroeconomic demand-management policy to ensure full employment. Training – especially in Canada, with its ready supply of immigrants – was a rudimentary program. Since the demise of Keynesianism, the post-Keynesian and the neoliberal regimes have battled it out for supremacy.

The "post-Keynesian" regime sees government involved in training to the extent of using trained workers as a supply-side inducement to greater economic productivity: "train them and prosperity will come," seems to have been the watchword. The neoliberal regime abandons any important government role in training, turning it almost entirely into a private matter. The goal is to free up the market, to concentrate supply-side solutions not on providing training but on weakening labour laws, unemployment insurance, and collective bargaining in order to give employers an edge over foreign competitors. Training, for the most part, is to be left in the hands of individual employers; and the provision of training, for the most part, is to be left to private institutions.

Under the NDP, Saskatchewan appears to have been caught between the post-Keynesian and the neoliberal regimes. This study illustrates a government and a province torn between a traditional devotion to public initiative and public enterprise on the one hand and the tremendous pressures from neoliberalism in other provinces and from the business community on the other.

Another important factor in this study is the role of Aboriginal peoples and their training institutions. These institutions are neither exactly public nor exactly private. The determination of Aboriginals to provide their own training arises, in part, from their drive for self-government. It also arises from a deficiency in the public system, a certain lack of responsiveness to Aboriginal peoples' training needs, which might, paradoxically, be the price paid for the success of that very system.

Training in Saskatchewan: Changing Roles for Private and Public Trainers

Historically, public, private, and Aboriginal trainers have provided vocational training in Saskatchewan. The public trainers consist of four urban campuses of the Saskatchewan Institute of Applied Sciences and Technology (SIAST) and eight regional colleges that service the rural areas.

SIAST, founded in 1987 from the amalgamation of four, much older, technical colleges, performs all three of the roles mentioned above: provider, broker, and regulator. However, SIAST's high level administrators appear to wish to see it expand its capacity as regulator, partly in response to the general move within the training field towards portability of certification.[3] For reasons that will become clear below, this move is being opposed by several department heads and by the instructors' union.

The regional colleges were established in 1972. Rather than investing in bricks and mortar, their philosophy is to provide training programs to a small but extremely dispersed population by making use of existing community resources and delivering courses (in such places as hospitals and nursing homes) in response to locally identified needs. Generally, the colleges do not develop their own programs nor do they award credits; instead, they "broker," or purchase, programs from SIAST and from private and out-of-province trainers who, in turn, issue the credits.

The Saskatchewan Indian Institute of Technology (SIIT) offers a wide range of programs in the urban centres, targeting the needs of the First Nations community (e.g., basic education, management studies, community services, trades, and technology). First Nations governed, SIIT used to partner with SIAST and rely upon the latter for program certification; recently, however, it has been empowered by the province to certify its own programs.

Finally, there is the small but growing array of private trainers. They have traditionally been modestly sized, locally owned businesses offering basic education, cosmetology, massage, basic computer skills, and secretarial and other office support skills. Most of these programs require only low capital investment. However, the new face of private training involves large chain colleges (e.g., De Vry and the CDI Institute), and this reflects a growing trend towards consolidation in private training. Because of greater access to capital, these trainers are able to deliver the more technical, higher-level computer software development, systems management, and computer repair programs. Recently, the small private trainers, unable to compete with the large franchised trainers, have been looking for alternative training programs to deliver. Thus, a number of small private trainers have entered into types of training that traditionally they have not delivered. Their recent incursion into training of health aides will be discussed below.

In the past, the relationship between private and public trainers was that of peaceful coexistence: the private trainers sought market niches that were not being met by the public institutions. It seems that now the coexistence is far from peaceful. The public institutions are increasingly financially strapped and are finding it difficult to respond to all the labour market needs, and the private trainers have access to a greater array of funding programs. This has resulted in a change in the traditional boundaries between the public and private trainers – a change exacerbated by the government's own lack of clarity concerning that boundary.

Restructuring of Health Care

Even before this decade's restructuring, the battle for status, position, and resources among the health care occupations was intense. Health care consumes the largest proportion of provincial budgets and is highly labour-intensive. Much of the work performed is considered "essential" to human life and well-being. There is an incredibly complex array of professions, semi-professions, and special occupations. The structure of interest representation and collective bargaining among these groups is complex and volatile.

The occupational politics of health care have intensified over the past decade as governments have pursued radical restructuring of the sector. Mhatre and Deber have summarized common themes in health care reform across the country:

1 Broadening the definition of health with the collaboration of multiple sectors.
2 Shifting emphasis from curing illness to promoting health and preventing disease.
3 Shifting focus to community-based rather than institution-based care.
4 Providing more opportunity for individuals to participate with service providers in making decisions on health choices and policies.
5 Devolution or decentralization of the provincial systems to some form of regional authorities.[4]

The mid-1990s saw a substantial downsizing of the personnel-to-patient ratio in acute care institutions in Saskatchewan. Though health care spending has risen in recent years and the community sector has grown, the old ratios have not been reinstated.

The division of labour is changing. Not only have the number of jobs in institutions like hospitals been reduced, some of those jobs have been reincarnated elsewhere – but often in different forms.

Four main subsectors in health care can be distinguished (see Figure 7.1). Most immediate treatment takes place in the *acute care* subsector. Where institutionalization is required, patients with chronic problems, the elderly, and the disabled use the *long-term care* subsector. Patients who require some care but who do not need to be in an institution are in the *home care* subsector. Prevention, inspection, and wellness programs are delivered in the *public health* subsector.[5]

In Saskatchewan in 1993, authority for health care management underwent a simultaneous decentralization (downward from province to regional health authority) and centralization (upward from individual institution to regional health authority). The four subsectors and their institutions, which formerly comprised over 400 separate corporate entities, were merged into thirty-one regional health authorities or health districts. Now there is a single regional health care authority in a geographic area, and most of the employees of these organizations now have a single employer.[6] As well, several health care functions previously centralized in the provincial department of health or its agencies were devolved downward to the regional authorities.

One of the key features of health care restructuring has been moving the emphasis away from acute care and towards the "community" aspect of health care. Before reform, patients would enter hospitals earlier for pre-treatment, would receive treatment, and would spend the post-treatment period in hospital recovering and rehabilitating. Now, hospitals cut as much as possible from either end of this continuum. Patients receive pretreatment as outpatients; their stay in hospital is shorter; and they are released post-treatment "quicker and sicker."[7] Their post-hospital care is consigned to lower-intensity locations, either long-term care institutions or home care.

Division of Labour in Nursing

In the key area of nursing, these developments have hastened the evolution of a hierarchy of nursing occupations. As in other industries, management achieves efficiencies by dividing up the work into swaths according to the skill and degree of need involved. "Higher-end" work is assigned to a diminishing coterie of credentialed and relatively well paid workers, and the remainder is relegated to occupations with lower levels of training, responsibility, and compensation. This process often continues in several iterations, resulting in a kind of "salami-slicing" of the internal labour market. The resulting occupational groups often engage in boundary-definition exercises (or "turf wars"), vying for status and resources. For the division of labour in nursing, see Figure 7.2.

Figure 7.1

Health care subsectors

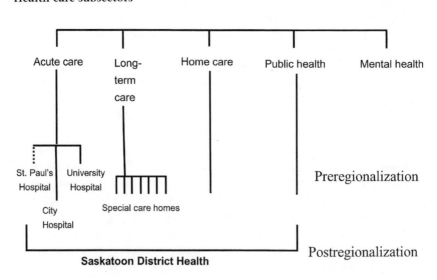

Initially, nursing care was offered largely by registered nurses (who were less well paid than they are now and performed a wider variety of tasks). For a quarter of a century, however, registered nurses have aggressively pursued advancement through unionization (seeking higher compensation) and professionalization (seeking enhanced credentials and status), and they have been quite successful. Nurses in Canada can earn between twenty-five and thirty dollars per hour, and a four-year baccalaureate will soon be the minimum requirement for new practitioners.

As this happened, a new tier of nursing workers – licensed practical nurses (LPNs) – grew in importance. Part of the health care team for at least forty years, their proportion among nursing employees has gradually increased. Trained in SIAST programs lasting about fifty-seven weeks, LPNs work under the direction of a registered nurse (RN) and perform personal care tasks. Recently, several provinces have broadened the scope of LPN practice, encroaching upon traditional RN territory (e.g., catheterization, distribution of medications, suture/staple removal, wound packing, and wound irrigation). Neither the nurses' union nor the nurses' professional society are pleased with this move, and brush fires in a turf war have broken out, with warnings and counter-denunciations and lawsuits.

Like nurses, LPNs have pursued both unionization and professionalization with some success. An LPN with seniority makes over sixteen dollars per hour in Saskatchewan, and possession of a certificate in administering medication nets an extra seventy-five cents per hour. Employers have

Figure 7.2

Nursing division of labour

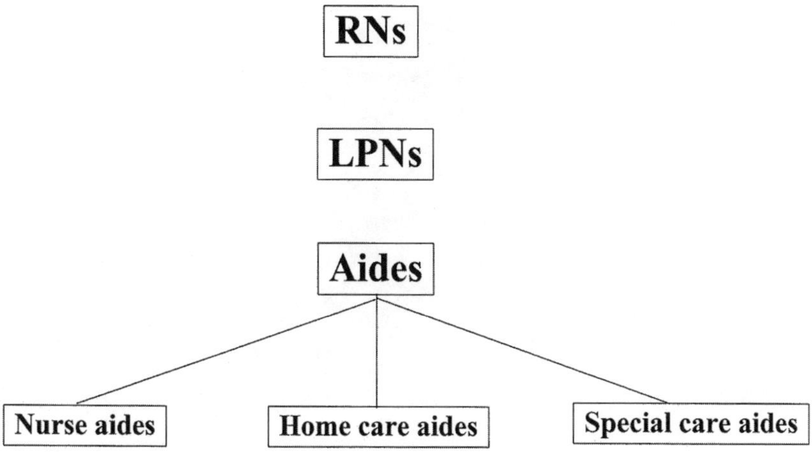

responded by creating yet another, lower, tier of nursing worker – the health care aide. In acute care they are often called "nursing aides"; in long-term care they are called "special care aides"; and in home care they are called "home care aides." The second two are expected to have completed either a thirty-week college program with a practicum or the equivalent in on-the-job training and study modules in a classroom/correspondence course. In its present form the occupation has approximately a twenty-year history.

In the division of labour between RNs and LPNs in acute care hospitals, two models have emerged. Some hospitals follow an "RN-only model," assigning registered nurses a continuum of care from personal bedside attendance to the more clinical specialties. Other institutions follow a "segmented care model," where the work is divided among RNs and LPNs and, in some cases, aides. However, as the level of patient acuity rises, so does the intensity of nursing care, and this is often exacerbated by a shortage of RNs. This, combined with budget restraint, creates pressure to follow the latter model.

Outside of acute care, to which "not-so-sick" patients are discharged, the segmentation model has become well established. In long-term and home care, a relatively small group of RNs act as assessors, treatment directors, and supervisors and there is a much larger contingent of LPNs and aides.

The figures below show employment in nursing and adjunct nursing

Figure 7.3

Nursing and adjunct nursing FTEs as a percentage of total health care FTEs: Saskatchewan, 1999

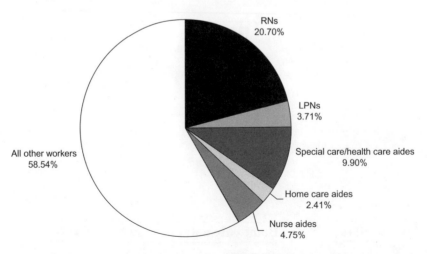

RNs
20.70%

LPNs
3.71%

All other workers
58.54%

Special care/health care aides
9.90%

Home care aides
2.41%

Nurse aides
4.75%

occupations in Saskatchewan as a proportion of total health care employment (Figure 7.3) and as a proportion of employment in nursing (Figure 7.4).

Demand for Health Care Aides

Notwithstanding differences in the division of nursing labour, across
Canada there has been an upsurge in demand for health care aides. A market research report commissioned by one of the private Saskatchewan institutions interested in training aides suggests that two-thirds of the health
care institutions in the province perceive a high current demand for such
workers. Eighty-seven percent had hired such workers in the past year. And
69 percent of the institutions estimated an increase in demand of between
20 percent and 40 percent over the next five to ten years. According to the
1997 Saskatchewan Health Employer Survey,[8] employers of these workers
confirm these statistics. Thirty-seven percent reported difficulty in attracting aides, and the same proportion reported a shortage of personnel in
these occupations.

Yet, there is controversy over the exact nature of this shortage. Private
trainers and some health district managers in Saskatchewan insist the main
problem is that not enough trained aides are graduating from the public
training programs to fill the need in the labour market (a need, they say,

Figure 7.4

**FTEs in various nursing occupations as a percentage of total nursing
FTEs: Saskatchewan, 1999**

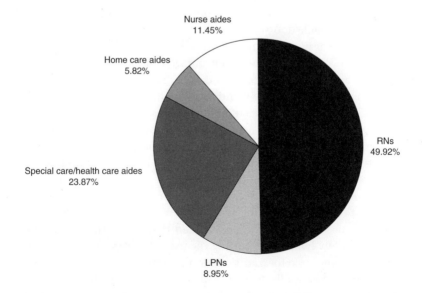

Nurse aides
11.45%

Home care aides
5.82%

RNs
49.92%

Special care/health care aides
23.87%

LPNs
8.95%

that could be met by allowing private trainers into the field). Some in the public training sector insist that the employers and private trainers are exaggerating and that the larger problem is retention. They point to the aides' irregular schedules and poor working conditions, and suggest that many are dropping out of the occupation. Pouring more graduates into a system that leaks, they say, is a waste of valuable public resources.

There is evidence that retention is indeed a problem. Provincial data collected from health care employers by the provincial Department of Health[9] indicate a relatively low vacancy rate for aides (Figure 7.5). Yet, the turnover rate is high for the three types of health care aide. For any occupation, the vacancy rate is the number of positions for which personnel are actively being recruited by a reporting date as a proportion of the total number of full-time equivalents (FTEs). The turnover rate is the number of employees leaving employment in the year before the reporting date as a proportion of all FTEs. The low vacancy rate for all three aide classifications from 1993 to 1997 (seldom more than 1 percent) could mean that employers are having little trouble filling jobs. But the high turnover rate indicates that hirees are not staying, a fact confirmed in interviews with health employers, aides, and their unions. In the Saskatoon health district the situation is similar (see Figure 7.6). The turnover rate dropped by 1999, perhaps due to efforts by Saskatoon District Health to improve hours and other conditions.

The high turnover rate of health care aides is likely linked to their difficult working conditions.[10] Aides of all kinds perform personal care tasks of the most intimate kind, like toileting, suctioning, feeding, bathing, and lifting.

Among aides, the group with the lowest turnover is nurse aides who work in hospitals, where the layout is purpose-built for the efficient handling of patients (e.g., wide doorways, high mechanical beds), with a high staff-patient ratio, clear lines of authority, greater routine, mechanical aids, and other staff for companionship and encouragement.

Turnover among special care aides is high. They work in long-term care institutions, where the above-mentioned amenities are in shorter supply, though at least the companionship of colleagues is available.

The highest turnover exists among home care aides, who work alone and unsupervised in clients' homes and have few, if any, mechanical aids (e.g., to lift patients out of beds and baths). Private homes are an ergonomic nightmare and injuries abound. According to one home care manager, "[Home care aides] are given clear instructions on what to do and what not to do, but they succumb to the pressure of not being able to say no to a client. They need much more training than they are getting to deal with the client politely [while] not putting themselves in danger."

Although reimbursed for transportation expenses, many home care aides find it difficult financially to maintain a suitable automobile to drive to appointments. They have a schedule of clients to visit in a work day and must budget their time strictly. In this limited time, aides are not always able to provide for the patient's "psychosocial needs" (as one job description reads). There is a growing literature on the "emotional labour"[11] performed by nursing staff and the toll it can take on the provider. And this toll is considerably higher in home care, where aides confront patients in isolation.

Contingent employment is likely another reason for the high turnover. Across the province, over 40 percent of aides worked part-time or casual hours in 1997.[12] While a high proportion of RNs and LPNs also work non-standard hours, for aides this drawback may well combine with other discontents to cause incumbents to quit the occupation early. Ironically, as with other nursing occupations, contingent work coincides with massive amounts of overtime so that many part-timers and casuals work more hours than do full-timers.

There are several reasons why contingent employment has persisted into the new century. In the recession of the early 1990s opportunistic employers used contingent employment to gain both numerical flexibility (ability

Figure 7.5

Vacancy rates for aides, 1993-99; turnover rates 1997, 1999 (Saskatchewan-wide)

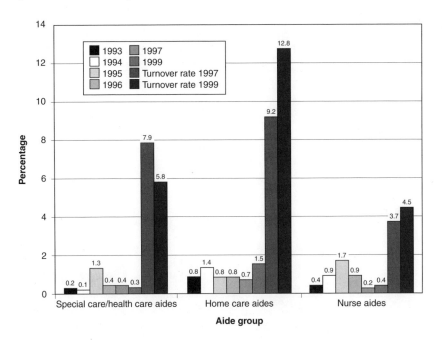

to expand and contract their workforce) and functional flexibility (ability to deploy their workforce in different institutions across the health districts).[13] Employees who had worked in fixed locations and fixed jobs for years were now moved around at will.

Half a decade later, in a tighter labour market, it was time for employees to be opportunistic. Employers had produced a workforce that had little institutional loyalty. In response, unions had negotiated global bidding rights within health districts. The result was that workers bid opportunistically and went to the jobs with the best conditions. Thus, when employers were finally cajoled by governments into providing more full-time jobs, employers did not find a readily available supply of aides to fill these positions. Employees would choose full-time work only if the sum of all conditions made that work more attractive than part-time work. Moreover, in home care, scheduling problems bedevil attempts to create full-time jobs. What is best for clients is not always best for employees.

Figure 7.6

Vacancy and turnover rates, 1997 and 1999, Saskatoon District Health

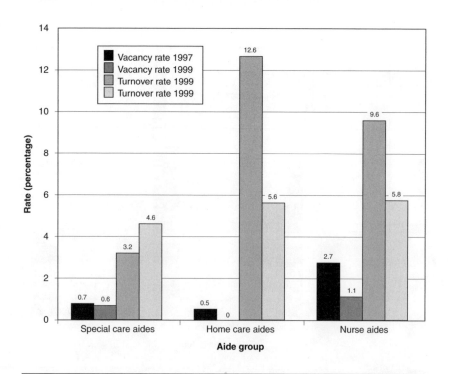

Also, it should not be forgotten that, unlike RNs and LPNs, aides are "unlicensed." Although their unions fight for better wages and have some success, aides have no professional society or regulatory agency to go to bat for their occupational status as a palliative to their often unpleasant work. One could argue, with Wilensky,[14] that such status envy is part of an annoying trend towards "the professionalization of everyone." However, in the nursing field, where professional rivalry is intense, the hidden injuries of class are manifest.

Up until 1999 home care aides were paid five dollars less than were special care aides. This was rectified in that year's collective bargaining so that all aides in Saskatchewan make between $13.13 and $13.91 per hour. This may decelerate the turnover among home care aides. Yet despite a raise that makes them among the better-paid aides in the country, there is still a shortage of appropriately trained health care aides who are prepared to fill the positions open for them.

Parties Involved in Health Care Training and Their Interests
At this point it is necessary to specify some of the more salient conflicts of interest both between and within the parties involved in this narrative.

Government
The government, in its various capacities, serves several functions in the intersection between health care and vocational training. First, the government supports public education by setting training and labour market development policy and providing funding to public institutions and students. Second, the government supports labour market development by providing funds to industry sectors in order to determine their specific training needs and to purchase, adapt, or develop curricula. Third, the government is a health provider as it creates and funds the regional health districts. Finally, in its role as regulator, the government carries out several roles: as guardian of the public purse, it sets the guidelines for compensation of all public service workers, including health care workers and education workers; as consumer protection custodian, it monitors both the public and private sectors; and it also attempts to protect health care users by specifying minimum levels of training for groups of health care workers.

Employers

Health care
By far the largest employer of aides in Saskatchewan are the thirty-one health districts, which are vitally concerned with getting a ready supply of aides. However, they have a dilemma.

Public health care institutions want to provide high-quality staff to care for patients/clients. Yet, subject to severe budget limitations, they want to employ no more staff (of any degree of quality) than is absolutely necessary. One step towards this goal involves the delegation of subordinate nursing tasks to lower-ranked and lower-paid personnel such as aides and others (who have even less training and skill). To do this, the health districts must ensure that even the lowest-ranked staff members are competent to do the work required and to maintain the health of the patients/clients and, indeed, the staff itself. Thus a carefully considered scope of practice must be set out, standards of care established, competencies instituted, and a program to teach all of the foregoing maintained. Yet employers also created the aide occupation to save money, and *too much* training can raise the aspirations and demands of the trained.

Vocational Training
The public training institutions are the primary employers of training personnel. What are their interests as employers? They must fulfill the immediate needs of two sets of clients – students and the employers of those students. And they must be able to respond quickly to changes in those needs. However, they must also have an eye on long-term labour market changes and use their privileged position as public institutions to weather the fluctuations in the economy and labour market demand. For example, in the early 1990s the labour market demand for nurses and registered technologists dwindled as many public training institutions downsized or even eliminated their training programs for these workers. But that labour market demand surged back in the late 1990s. Public institutions that acted hastily found themselves unable to gear up to that new demand. The opposite also sometimes prevails. Employers unable to recruit or retain enough staff in particular occupations put pressure on the public training institutions to churn out as many people as possible in as little time as possible, with corresponding problems in the quality of graduates.

As far as their faculty is concerned, public training institutions are also trying to reconcile high quality with the search for maximum flexibility (by using part-time, casual, temporary, and limited-term appointments). Many of their faculty feel that this is a threat to the quality and quantity of their jobs.

If public training institutions cannot achieve such flexibility through their own faculty, then another avenue to this goal is through "outsourcing" (i.e., getting out of direct provision of a particular program entirely). Health care aide is one occupation around which just such a battle is taking shape.

Employees and Their Organizations

Health Care

Employees in health care find themselves in a highly politicized environment where many groups of workers vie with each other for status and pay. Many of them pursue a joint strategy of unionization and professionalization in order to achieve these ends.[15] Parkin may distinguish between "exclusionary" strategies (professionalization) and "usurpationary" strategies (unionization),[16] but Larson's simpler characterization of the entire process as one of "market control" is more germane to the discussion of these workers.[17] One of the features that distinguish groups with more labour market power from those with less is the degree to which their work can be rationalized and routinized. Generally, the lower the skill involved, the more conducive the occupation is to specification, codification, subdivision, mechanization, cybernetic control, subdivision, and (ultimately) Taylorization. A logical end to this process is the absence of any semblance of professionalism.

The more practitioners can portray their occupation as an "art" or a "science," the greater their potential for market control. The more their work involves the unpredictability and unknowability of human disease, and the more invasive it is of the human body, the greater their potential for market control. Hence, the drive for longer and longer programs of training. The tug-of-war between these two tendencies among nursing and adjunct nursing occupations is especially acute. The hierarchy is clearly established: physicians deal with new and emergent situations; nurses provide prescribed treatments and monitor for emergent situations; the subordinate and adjunct nursing occupations deal with a decreasing rank of instability and unpredictability.

Vocational Training

The other relevant group of employees in this study includes the curriculum developers and instructors at SIAST, who are represented by the Saskatchewan Government Employees' Union (SGEU). This group is alarmed at the perceived erosion of programs of public vocational training and, especially, at SIAST's role as a vendor of curricula that many of them have developed. As long as SIAST alone delivered these programs, the instructors' function and career were clear. With the increasing "marketization" of programs, however, their function is in upheaval. Through collective bargaining, the instructors are attempting to maintain control over the fruits of their labour and their ability to teach students face-to-face. The dispute over ownership puts them in something of a dilemma. On the one hand, it forces them to define their output as an atomized product and to fight for the right to exploit it themselves rather than to allow a third party to do so; on the other hand, what most college instructors really want is not to be independent entrepreneurs but, rather, to maintain a *career*, with the satisfaction, human interaction, and employment security that this entails.

These, then, are the contending interests of the complex interweave of parties.

Delivery of Health Care Aide Training

As with most emergent health care occupations, aide training was originally conducted on the job by the health care institutions employing aides. After 1980 the institutions reluctantly[18] handed the responsibility over to the public vocational training institution, one of the four technical institutions prior to their amalgamation into SIAST. The college program was developed according to an established curriculum development process, known as DACUM (Develop A CurriculUM), a process which is now used throughout SIAST to create new programs and to modify existing ones. Stakeholders, employers, and employees in the health care field were gathered together to identify and and place in order of priority the skills required by graduates.

At its inception, one of the important priorities of the aide training program was to reach students in the rural areas. Television satellite broadcasting was introduced in 1984 and video correspondence courses were soon to follow. Agreements were made with the regional colleges to deliver modules of the program. Also early in its development, the First Nations community was involved in decisions on curricula and delivery. A working partnership and a number of agreements were struck between the institution and First Nations communities so that modules of the program were delivered on the reserves. The strong distance education aspect of the aide program allowed students living in remote areas to enrol in the program part-time, working towards certification while employed in the field.

Today in Saskatchewan it is possible to get recognized health care aide (home care and special care aide) training through six vehicles (see Figure 7.7).

Quality control and updating of these programs is ultimately the responsibility of SIAST. All of the above delivery vehicles together produce approximately 700 graduates each year. That these training programs are "recognized" by SIAST allows graduates to be hired at the "trained" rate of pay, according to their collective agreements with the health districts.

Enter the Private Trainers

In recent times private trainers have begun to provide the training of health care aides. Because of the low overhead required, these programs are attractive to small private trainers. Critics (such as the SIAST instructors' union) point to the emergence of private trainers of health care aides as the slippery slope to the privatization of health care training. In response to this criticism, the private trainers point out that their aide training programs are supplying only one small slice of the health care labour market. As one private trainer of aides says, "We are not in the business of providing the rocket science of health care." Because of the requirement of higher capital investment for other health care training, it is likely that, for the short term, the role of the private trainers will continue to be restricted to training for only this one end of the continuum of health care workers.

Moreover, Aboriginal trainers have recently entered the fray. Over the past several years, the First Nations communities have grown increasingly disenchanted with their partnership with SIAST when it comes to health care training. Despite the fact that many individual Aboriginal SIAST graduates have had no complaints about that institution, representatives of SIIT have expressed dissatisfaction with the learning, evaluation, and student management approaches of the SIAST program. It became increasingly difficult for the SIAST program heads and SIIT representatives to establish mutually agreed upon academic standards. Eventually, on the issue of aide training, the relationship between the two institutions broke down completely.

Figure 7.7

Health care aide training market

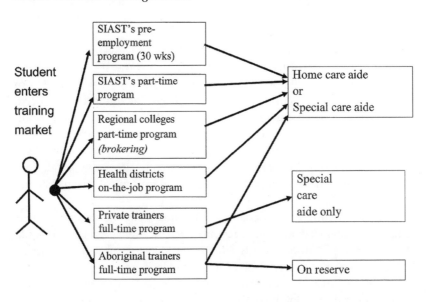

Driven by the need for health care aides on the reserves, SIIT is delivering a redesigned SIAST program. While some SIAST staff are still not satisfied with the quality of SIIT's program, SIAST has recently granted it equivalency.

By venturing, for the first time, into the training of aides, both Aboriginal and private trainers are now in direct competition with the public training programs. However, there are two significant barriers to their graduates actually obtaining jobs in the health districts.

First there is the policy of the Department of Health, one of whose roles is protector of the public interest in health care. This policy states that no health district can employ people as fully fledged *home care* aides who are not graduates of the SIAST program (delivered through any of the four above vehicles) or its equivalent. Part of the policy, as it stands right now, is to give SIAST the power to determine whether or not an outside program is equivalent to its own. The Department of Health's policy is specific to home care aides only. Because of the isolated nature of the work, the lack of supervision, and the safety hazards of private homes, the department feels that adequate training is more essential for home care aides than it is for special care aides.

The second barrier lies in the collective agreements covering aides, which permit union members to be paid at the home care aide or special care aide salary *only* if they are graduates of the SIAST aide program or its equivalent.

In light of the above barriers and the health districts' difficulties recruiting and retaining aides, the government and the districts have turned to SIAST to authorize curricula developed by the private trainers as SIAST-equivalent. The SIAST aide training program faculty are reluctant. Due to perceived inadequacies, SIAST has denied equivalency status of the private trainers' programs on a number of occasions.

The denial of equivalency has raised the ire of the private training institutions, of several health district managers, and of the SIAST administration. Some suggest that SIAST is in a conflict of interest: that it should not be both a provider of curriculum and the arbiter of equivalency. Indeed, there is the shadow of a suggestion that SIAST should get out of aide training entirely and act merely as a regulator/arbiter. Regardless of the validity of these suggestions, every application for equivalency rejected by SIAST must be accompanied by a reason. And eventually either the private programs will meet the criteria or the pressure to grant equivalency will be too powerful to resist.

As of the writing of this chapter, programs from the private trainers remain unrecognized, and the issue of equivalency remains at a stand-still. However, the Saskatoon Health District decided to consider the private training programs to be equivalent to the public ones and is hiring graduates from the private schools. So as not to defy the Department of Health's policy, this authorization is conditional: the graduates are restricted to work in the long-term care facilities only, and they are not considered for full-fledged home care aide positions.

As for the provincial Department of Health, it is currently considering three alternatives to this problem:

1   The department will continue to allow SIAST to make the determination of equivalency.
2   The department will set up a separate mechanism outside of SIAST to review equivalency. The arbiter of equivalency could be the department itself, or the Department of Post-Secondary Education and Skills Training (now named Saskatchewan Learning), or the Saskatchewan Association of Health Care Organizations (SAHO – the umbrella organization to which all districts are affiliated).
3   The department could get out of regulating the setting of standards entirely and leave it to the employer health districts to ensure they have appropriate staff with appropriate training.

The problem with Alternative 1 is that SIAST (and especially the program directors of the relevant programs) are seen by some parties as having a conflict of interest in being both curriculum provider and regulator. The problem with Alternative 2 is that no organization other than SIAST has the resources, the expertise, or the will to do this job. The problem with Alternative 3 is that it could lead to an assortment of different standards for aide training across the thirty-one health districts, with the almost inevitable erosion of training as employers rush to fill positions. Indeed, if SIAST is perceived to have a conflict of interest, then certainly health districts, which are desperate to recruit aides quickly, have an even greater conflict of interest.

While this decision may be merely one small step for a government department, it may prove to be a very giant step for the future of public training.

Conclusions
Just like the debate on private versus public health care currently raging through the country, the future of the public provision of vocational training depends to a large extent on how the public system is perceived by users, who, in this case, are employers and students. As long as users perceive that they can receive no better product on the market, then they will continue to support the public offering.[19] On the other hand, when resources are withheld from the public institutions or are not increased commensurate with demand, the users begin to lose faith in the public provision of service.

There is evidence that the government may not be increasing the resources of the public training system so as to keep pace with the needs of its users.[20] Clearly, there is a great and increasing need for the delivery of home care and long-term care. Clearly, employers are finding it hard to fill the aide positions on more than a short-term basis.

It is also clear that employers of aides in the health districts are beginning to lose faith in the ability of the public training system to meet their needs. Indeed, we met with one health care manager who expressed strong allegiance to the governing NDP and the Saskatchewan tradition of public enterprise in health care and education, a loyalty inherited from and shared by the manager's family. Yet, at the same time, this manager expressed dismay at the perceived failures of the public training system and expressed strong support for private institutions as the solution to problems in maintaining an adequate cadre of health care aides. If even NDP supporters are growing frustrated at the public system, then it may be insecure indeed.

Faced with resources that are not keeping up with demand, SIAST's own administrators also appear to be displaying less than a full commitment to delivering programs (such as the health care aide program) that they consider peripheral because they can be delivered by the private market. Understandably, the administrators would rather conserve scarce resources so as to be able to better deliver other programs.

If that is the case, then to what extent is SIAST the author of some of its own misfortunes? In order to efficiently deliver an abundance of programs and serve the maximum number of people, institutions must be bureaucratic. However, bureaucracy always runs the risk of overlooking the needs and interests of smaller groups and of individuals. The dispute with SIIT is an example of this. The inability to satisfy the Aboriginal community may have as much to do with Aboriginal intransigence and the politics of self-determination as it does with SIAST's insensitivity. But SIAST's very size and efficiency as a public institution may have provoked the split. And the Aboriginal institutions may, despite their good intentions, play the spoiler.

As for whether supply or turnover is the root cause of the shortage of aides, it may well be that SIAST program managers have a strong case for turnover. But appearances are often as important as is reality. The more SIAST appears to be insensitive to the needs of its clients, users, and the public, even if the reason for this is lack of resources, the more it will contribute to a vicious circle that will harm the long-term interests of public training.

This dilemma has led to sharp differences of opinion within different levels and units in SIAST as well as between the employer and its academic staff union, and it has resulted in some punitive measures by management. These disputes can spiral out of control as the internal parties fail to see the larger picture and the long-term interests of the institution.

What is SIAST's role anyway? To deliver whatever its client industries want, when they want it? Or is it to make some sort of judgment call that balances the longer-term needs of industry with the needs of instructors and the needs of students who may find they are being trained as cannon fodder for bad jobs (and who need some assurance that they will not be in oversupply, leading to employment insecurity down the line)? And what of the public interest in ensuring that those who deliver health care are reasonably happy workers and that the institutions are neither under- nor oversupplying the labour market? In other words, is it not in SIAST's interest to make some long-term labour market decisions about supply and quality of work?

While the government's official role is to support the public institutions and to regulate the private trainers in the interests of protecting the students as consumers, the funding changes amount to a set of "push-me-pull-me" policies. Funding to private trainers is more readily available, but it is also more diversified and complicated. Only the private training institutions that have a strong capacity to adapt to the changes in the funding programs have managed to survive, albeit barely. While SIAST has maintained its credit-granting capacity,[21] in recent years its funding has been limited. To the public institutions, the government's historical commitment to public education and training seems to be ringing more and more hollow.

In the end, the danger comes not from those small private trainers purporting to enter an attractive niche in aide training: in and of themselves, they are small threats. The larger threats may be the large private colleges standing right behind these small businesses, casting their shadows over the entire playing field.

Notes

1 See Stephen McBride, "The Political Economy of Training in Canada," in *Training Matters: Working Paper Series 98-07* (Toronto, Labour Education and Training Research Network, Centre for Research on Work and Society, York University, 1998); Thomas Dunk, Stephen McBride, and Randle Nelsen, eds., *The Training Trap* (Halifax: Fernwood, 1996).

2 McBride, "Political Economy of Training," 1998.

3 Prior Learning Assessment and Recognition (PLAR) is one popular method of determining equivalencies. For more information on PLAR, see Canadian Association for Prior Learning Assessment, *A Slice of the Iceberg: Cross-Canada Study on Prior Learning Assessment and Recognition* (Ottawa: CAPLA, 1999).

4 S.L. Mhatre and R.B. Deber, "From Equal Access to Health Care to Equitable Access to Health: A Review of Canadian Provincial Health Commissions and Reports," *International Journal of Health Services* 22, 4 (1992): 645-68. These authors reviewed the reports of health care commissions in the early 1990s in Alberta, Saskatchewan, Quebec, New Brunswick, Nova Scotia, and Ontario. Additional reports, emphasizing similar themes, were issued by Prince Edward Island and British Columbia.

5 To date, mental health, a fifth subsector, has resisted regionalization in most provinces.

6 In some instances, health care institutions were allowed to affiliate with a health district rather than be subsumed within it. This was the case for many denominational hospitals and some private nursing homes. So, while attached to the health district, they are legally independent organizations and employers.

7 See Pat Armstrong, Hugh Armstrong, Ivy Bourgeault, Jacqueline Choiniere, Eric Mykha-lovskiy, and Jerry P. White, *Heal Thyself: Managing Health Care Reform* (Aurora, ON: Gara-mond, 2000).
8 Saskatchewan Health Employer Survey Summary Report (Regina: Policy and Planning Branch, Saskatchewan Health, 1997).
9 Saskatchewan Health Employer Survey Summary Report (Regina: Policy and Planning Branch, Saskatchewan Health, 1994-1999).
10 Health districts and provincial health care officials are reported to be initiating a study of the causes of turnover.
11 N. James, "Emotional Labour: Skill and Work in the Social Regulation of Feelings," *Sociological Review* 37, 1 (1989): 15-32.
12 Saskatchewan Health Employer Survey Summary Report 1997.
13 John Atkinson, "Manpower Strategies for Flexible Organisations," *Personnel Management,* August 1984, 28-30.
14 Harold Wilensky, "The Professionalisation of Everyone," *American Journal of Sociology* 70 (1964): 137-58.
15 Larry Haiven, "Professionalization and Unionization among Paramedical Occupations: National Regulation and the Challenge of Globalization." Paper delivered at Canadian Industrial Relations Association Conference, June 1998.
16 Frank Parkin, *Marxism and Class Theory: A Bourgeois Critique* (New York: Columbia University Press, 1979).
17 Magali S. Larson, *The Rise of Professionalism: A Sociological Analysis* (Berkeley, CA: University of California Press, 1977).
18 The employers know they must hand training over to a college because the occupation in question and its syllabus has grown too large for individual employers to handle. Even though employers still have a say in the design of the course, they are reluctant to hand over training because they lose some control over it.
19 Gøsta Esping-Anderson, *The Three Worlds of Welfare Capitalism* (Princeton, NJ: Princeton University Press, 1990).
20 SIAST annual reports show that, between 1990 and 2000, SIAST's grants fell by 12 percent in real terms. This figure understates the shortfall in funding as it does not take into account the rise in demand for SIAST's course offerings, which top administrators say grew strongly over the decade.
21 Although the Aboriginal training institution now has this authority as well.

8
Community Skills Training by and for Immigrant Women
Margaret Manery and Marjorie Griffin Cohen

Training programs that originate within communities can be enormously successful when the needs of the people in the community are the focus for the development of the program and the programs are developed and run by the community itself. Examples of how well community-based training can work are best illustrated from programs established by two distinct women's groups in 1978 and 1984 in Toronto – training programs that still exist today. The insight into the needs of immigrant women, the shaping of training programs to meet these needs, and the ability to adapt to changing economic and political circumstances have allowed these programs not only to continue for a long period of time but also to remain successful. This does not mean, however, that these programs have not experienced considerable stress as the funding nature of training has changed. The dramatic downsizing of federal government involvement in providing direct funding for training has forced these groups to shift their focus to who can be served. This has been done in order to accommodate the different and changing priorities of provincial and local governments as well as the dictates of a more market-based approach to training.

Need for Specialized Programs
The distinct problems that immigrant women face when they come to Canada, particularly those from war-torn or politically and economically stressed countries, are fairly well documented today.[1] However, when the Working Women Community Centre in Toronto began dealing with immigrant women from Spanish- and Portuguese-speaking countries in the mid-1970s, the magnitude of issues that needed to be addressed was only beginning to be understood and documented and certainly had not been addressed by government.[2] While this community centre could provide a community base and some aid to women in coping with life in Canada, the women at the centre recognized that a community centre's programs alone could not address the enormous barriers these women

faced. Immigrant women needed help getting jobs, and for this they needed literacy skills in English, job training, and skills that would enable them both to understand the specifics of employers' expectations in Canada and to function well in a very different culture. For the latter, they needed a set of skills known by the term "employment preparation."[3]

The barriers to a successful life for immigrant women in Canada usually centred on issues related to poverty: having an adequate income was the crucial issue. Related to this was their ability to function in English or French: immigrant women as a whole were not treated to the types of language and skills training that immigrant men could receive. Although immigrant "heads of households" (men) were entitled to substantial language training while receiving government income support, immigrant women's language training was mainly limited to night classes in local schools.[4] Most significantly, they could receive no income support while taking this training. For many women, this was an impossible route for learning English because their time was amply filled with low-waged work and caring for children: few had extra time or energy for night classes. The cycle of dependency on their "sponsors," and their isolation from the society at large, was ensured by their lack of English language skills.

When these women looked for work the best they could do would be to work either at a perpetual round of minimum wage jobs in small-scale factories where they were grouped together with other people from the same language backgrounds or as cleaners in homes or offices where they were even more isolated. But even this work was hard to find without a certain level of English language competency. Getting decent work in Canada was almost impossible without Canadian experience, and even when women did have substantial education, training, and experience in their home countries, the inability to have this recognized as significant in Canada placed insurmountable barriers to their changing the outlook for a future that looked dismal and mean.

The underlying notion of the nature of government language and skills training programs for immigrants was that sponsored immigrant women were either not to be destined for the labour market or would not, at any time, be suited for anything other than very low-wage jobs that would require few language or recognized work skills.[5] Interviews with women who came through the Working Women Community Centre document the truly frustrating experiences of those who attempted to receive training.[6] One Chilean woman who tried to enrol in an English course was told that she would not be eligible until after she had lived in Toronto for six months. The Manpower officer sent her to a hotel for a job as a maid, which she held for the requisite six months.[7] When she returned to Manpower to apply for language training, she was told that she was not eligible for the English course because she was working and obviously did not need to learn English for her job. By the time she came to the centre she had been working at the same hotel for three and a half years, never making more than the minimum wage.

Another Chilean woman who held an honours BA and was a high school teacher was ineligible for English classes because her husband was employed and he had sponsored her. She worked as a domestic cleaner and attended night classes run by volunteer ESL teachers because she had been told by Manpower that her English was not sufficient to enable her to enter skills-training programs. Ultimately, she purchased an advanced English course at the University of Toronto, although the family was living on a very low income. After these efforts she became proficient at English, but when she attempted to get into government-sponsored skills training classes she was told that Manpower was not an education centre and that she could not expect help from it.

These stories were typical of the experiences immigrant women encountered whenever they tried to improve their employability. The government's profound rejection of the legitimacy of their claims was rooted in a very male-oriented notion of what constituted significant and important work and what women's contribution to their families should be. These were assumptions that the immigrant women's community would not accept. Their mission was to find a way to provide crucial language and skills training to women despite the problems inherent in the existing programs. Establishing an independent training program that gave language instruction, job training, and job experience in Canada would give these women a chance at finding decent, reasonably well-paid, and interesting work. Combining this training with "life skills" training that also gave considerable attention to the process of finding work and keeping a job would round out the program. They understood that only by themselves creating programs that provided this holistic, or integrated, approach to skills development was this likely to happen.

Fortunately the late 1970s, a time when the federal government appeared more committed to social development and improving programs for immigrants, was more conducive than is the current political climate to creative approaches to training. It was a time that allowed space for the development of integrated, community-based training programs. In 1976 the Canadian Immigration Act broke new ground by delineating the principles of Canadian immigration policy and by imposing on the government the responsibility to plan immigration for the future, to create a separate class for refugees, and to enter into agreements with provinces for implementing policies for immigrants.[8] At the same time, according to one federal government caseworker involved in immigrant training, the atmosphere created by the Trudeau years was a time "when there was an emphasis on social development and when there was still a belief that social development was a role of government."[9] It was an era when local initiatives of many types were encouraged and funded, and it was aided by the fact that many people in government departments responsible for the programs came out of the Company of Young Canadians and had been influenced by the vision of a just and equitable society. While creating employable people was a goal of programs for immigrants, equally, if not more, important was the need to "provide them with accessibility to Canadian society." The way to do that was through "language training, support, community building and exposure to the standards of Canadian work places."[10]

The late 1970s was also a time when the power of feminism was beginning to be taken seriously. Feminist groups in the Toronto area had been active in public policy issues for most of the decade, and immigrant women's groups were beginning to have their voices heard as well. This was aided considerably by the Liberal Party's recognition that immigrants were future voters and an important constituency in many Toronto ridings. Organizations like the Working Women Community Centre, which was run by and for women in the Latin American and Portuguese women's community, received government funding to aid immigrant women in finding jobs. But the programs it could provide related more to giving advice and providing a supportive community: it did not have the resources to provide the direct job-ready training that the women really needed. The combination of the recognition of a real need by this community-based organization and the increased availability of government funding for local initiatives led the Working Women Community Centre to try to initiate the first Toronto-area program specifically aimed at job training for immigrant women within their own community – the Working Skills Centre.

Working Skills Centre
The relative openness of the federal government to community development and training for immigrant women did not mean, however, that the programs through which this could occur were truly adequate or that they were well funded. When the Working Skills Centre (WSC) was created in 1978 to provide an integrated training program for Portuguese and Latin American immigrant women, the criteria under which it could receive government funding was strict, and the funding was limited. The main constraints were a short initial training period of sixteen weeks, very little money for capital equipment for training, and the requirement that the training program create a commercial enterprise that would not only provide on-the-job training for women but would also generate an income to partially cover the expenses of the program. The creation of a viable business was further handicapped by the requirement that it not compete directly with private enterprise.

These parameters were difficult and strict and not very promising: the original creators of the WSC understood that meaningful language and skills training could not be achieved with so few resources and such limited time for skills and language training. Nevertheless, the sheer ability to allow women some access to training while they received a modest income, to a supportive community, and to job-related English language training made trying to do the almost impossible a worthwhile effort. The hope was that, over time and with some successful outcomes, the government would commit more resources, extend the training period, and relax the requirements for income generation through the business. The initial funding constraints and short training period meant that the actual nature of job training would produce a relatively slight "skill," but the hope was that the accompanying support and encouragement with language would allow the women to be placed in jobs that were better than those from which they came.

This proved to be a good strategy, and the dedication, experience, and planning of the immigrant community responsible for the centre generated an extraordinarily successful program. In fact, it was so successful that it became a model for other programs. This success allowed the program to expand its length of training time, engage in a more capital-intensive training program, and pursue a wider variety of skills training. In the initial years of the program the skills training and business was related to bulk mailing. This was something that could be learned in a few weeks, and it gave the WSC an opportunity to place its trainees in the mailing departments of non-profit and charitable corporations; that is, it combined the requirements of generating an income-earning business with on-the-job training and job-related language skills.

One crucial aspect of the training period involved treating the women as employees and paying them wages rather than training allowances.[11] Being treated as an employee imposed a specific work discipline that was part of the training process. The trainees learned what was involved in paid employment, starting with checking in on time, making arrangements for time spent away from work, and generally participating in the business environment as an employee. The pay was at the minimum wage level, but it was able to help offset expenses incurred from training (such as transportation costs and childcare). It also helped ease the burden for families that had to rely upon a sole income earner while the women were involved in their training program.[12]

The successes of the training scheme were considerable, and the WSC continued to be funded through various iterations of federal government programs.[13] The number of women who were placed in jobs, and the number who continued to be employed after training, defined these successes.[14] In fact, WSC had one of the best records of any training program and became a model for other programs starting up. As the original founder of the program, Eugenia Valenzuela, noted, the value of the training was not simply the acquiring of English language and job-related skills, although these were important, but, rather, the job placement experience and aid in finding permanent jobs, which were essential features of the system. Most significant was the fact that the program was located within the immigrant women's community itself. This aspect of the training "provided opportunities for women who were isolated, and often depressed, to meet friends and find support and counselling, if necessary. Access to education was their only means of social mobility and they appreciated the opportunity to move from working as cleaners in office buildings, often at night when they would be isolated and at risk of sexual harassment, to working in businesses that offered opportunities for advancement into other jobs."[15]

Over time and through creative initiatives on the part of the staff at WSC, government funding expanded to allow more extensive training as well as an expansion of the job-skills component beyond what was needed for bulk mailing. Interestingly, when the program was first envisioned the feminists involved in securing the initial funding were particularly interested in training the women in some type of work that was sex-atypical and not specifically seen as women's work. This notion was ultimately rejected for two reasons: (1) the capital start-up costs for any type of trades training were much greater than could be obtained through government funding, and (2) the immigrant women were not interested in doing this type of "pioneer" work. They understood that their difficulties in the labour force were serious enough without having to try to break gender barriers as well.

As might be imagined, over the years the training program has expanded both with regard to the number of people involved and the type of training received. In the first year two separate groups, each with nine women, were trained: now about 200 women go through the centre each year. And, while job training was originally confined to bulk mailing, it now encompasses a variety of different programs, including those that require relatively little time and are devoted to everything from job preparation to full-time comprehensive six- to eight-month programs associated with general clerical and bookkeeping training programs. These are conducted through computer software classes that deal with the whole range of preparation for this work. Introductory courses that offer extensive training in accounting software are available to people with no previous background.

All trainees are given Canadian work experience through the in-house business. The businesses conducted through the WSC include bookkeeping business service and direct mail. Trainees in the bookkeeping program apply their skills through direct work. Clerical trainees receive a range of practical experience in both businesses through database management, maintaining administration systems, and the production of flyers and spreadsheets. Those enrolled in the direct mail program gain work experience in bulk mail sorting as well as in processing other types of mail; the operation of various types of mailing equipment; and activities related to tracking documentation, shipping documents, and completing mailing statements. Trainees are also given on-the-job experience in businesses and organizations that are willing to hire them for a short period. This is a crucial part of the job-readiness aspect of the skills training because it gives the trainees a useful reference when they begin their permanent job search, although occasionally the firms who provide this experience hire from the WSC.

Because the government has funded the businesses of WSC and the workers have received government wage subsidies, the private sector has been vocal in ensuring that the businesses do not compete in its markets. As a result, the work performed is targeted for the non-profit, charitable, and community-based sector. As it became clear that the goals of the WSC's businesses were related to meeting social rather than commercial objectives, the for-profit business sector has been supportive in accepting two- or four-week training placements and in hiring the workers when their training is complete.

The language training the women received was specifically created by WSC to meet their needs. It focused on an intensive initial six-week period during which English for Special Purposes was taught in a classroom setting in the mornings, followed by classroom-type work in office-type situations where language training was combined with such skills-training as that related to keyboard work.[16]

Crucial Changes

The changes that occurred at the WSC were often the result of responding to the different needs of new groups of immigrants. However, too often the changes to the program involved desperate measures to cope with declining government funding and changes in government criteria for training programs.

Over time the origins of the new immigrants in Toronto changed, so, during the 1980s, WSC shifted its exclusive focus on Latin American and Portuguese immigrant women in order to become more eclectic in its selection of people for the program. Meeting the needs of immigrants from different countries sometimes necessitated a shift in program emphases. Occasionally, special groups of immigrants, such as refugees from Vietnam, Laos, and Cambodia, needed special treatment and required their own programs. To this end, WSC was instrumental in establishing organizations such as Skills for Change, and Davenport Immigrant Women's Services: two programs that focused on the needs of Vietnamese women. While, originally, WSC staff used to start up the programs, the goal was to have the Vietnamese women run them themselves. This was the model that worked for WSC, and it was successfully replicated in these new programs.[17] However, even with a new mix of trainees, which included women from a variety of backgrounds, the WSC was able to continue to meet its original goals.

This began to alter, however, with the changes in the way that the federal government dealt with immigrants and training. The dismantling of the National Training Act in 1996 was particularly threatening to programs like the WSC. As one former director noted, "It was a real tragedy for the immigrant community. It created an insurmountable obstacle to training and marked the beginning of the total abandonment of commitment to training by the federal government."[18] The most significant changes related to the wages that the women were paid. As noted above, this was considered to be an essential and integral feature of the training program not only because it allowed the trainers to insist on treating the program as a worksite but also because it provided an essential income to women who otherwise would not be able to afford training. By 1992 federal government grants would not provide funds for trainee wages. Because the WSC had been successful in the businesses it ran, it was able to continue to pay wages to trainees for another two years, although ultimately this had to be abandoned. Nonetheless, the WSC was one of the last training programs in the country to pay wages to trainees.

The significance of this change cannot be overstated. Once the shift from wages to training allowances occurs (i.e., funds that come from either unemployment insurance or social assistance go to individuals rather than to the program itself), "then you are providing income support and the trainees are not earning their wages – they are provided charity rather than work."[19] But, most significantly, it meant that the women who were most in need of training often could no longer receive any income assistance because they did not qualify for allowances that were established with unemployment insurance or social assistance criteria in mind.

Throughout the existence of the WSC federal government programs have changed in substantial ways; ultimately, what resulted was that the two main aspects of training for immigrants were separated into different ministries. In 1991 the Liberal government separated settlement and training programs by creating two new ministries – the Ministry of Citizenship and Immigration and the Ministry of Human Resources Development Canada. This separated language training for immigrants into two different ministries, one dealing with language as a settlement issue (Language

Instruction for Newcomers to Canada) and the other dealing with language as an employment issue (HRDC). This seriously complicated funding responsibilities for a program that combined language training for both employment and "settlement."[20]

With the devolution of training to the provinces in 1996, WSC lost its core funding and had to shift the nature of its training in order to deal with this. Ontario did not sign a training agreement with the federal government, so the levels of responsibility became opaque and resulted in the virtual elimination of federal funding transfers to the province for training. In an attempt to deal with this crucial funding issue, the WSC has downsized its programs, has shifted to a fee-for-training basis, and has pursued a wide variety of funding sources. This process is not simple and involves considerable staff resources – resources that used to be focused more on training. The WSC can no longer continue with an integrated training program as its core work. To generate income, the program has had to shift to a fee-for-service model that focuses on discrete modules or schools that can be sold to students as training units. All training is now "purchased" by students. The days of being able to target those immigrant women most in need of training are over: those who train now are those who either qualify through Employment Insurance or some other type of assistance, or those who can afford to pay for the programs on their own. The revenue from the business provides some funding so that bursaries can be made available to women who have no other source of income, and United Way funds twenty-two seats so that women living in shelters can enrol in the Freight Fowarding and Logistics Training Program.[21]

WSC continues to struggle with maintaining programming, particularly as the retrenchment in government funding continues. The situation is exacerbated by provincial cutbacks to community-based employability and language training programs. HRDC will fund assessment and placement programs, but the WSC has to find alternative ways to fund training. This takes the form of entering into a partnership with the Toronto Catholic School Board for ESL trainers, applying for funding through United Way, making applications to private foundations, entering into a barter-type arrangement with other community groups, and doing more in-house businesses.[22] Although the in-house businesses have been self-sufficient, and have generated sufficient revenue to pay for the salaries of three staff members (all of whom are graduates of WSC), generating a profit is more difficult. WSC is now considering moving into establishing a call centre business that would offer telemarketing to firms that need women with foreign language skills to reach immigrant communities. It also hopes to increase its mailing business by using the foreign language skills of the trainees by targeting freight from their countries of origin.

Community MicroSkills Development Centre

The early successes of the WSC provided a model for the development of another training centre for immigrant women in the Toronto area. A multicultural women's centre, Rexdale Women's Centre, initiated the project, and in 1984 Rexdale MicroSkills (later Microskills Development Centre) opened its doors for training immigrant women from a variety of countries in language, skills, and life skills training.[23] As with the WSC, the federal government provided start-up funding and wages for trainees, but the initial funding for skills training was fairly meagre, so finding an appropriate skill component was a challenge. The former executive director of WSC and the economist who had done the feasibility study for the WSC were once again asked to set up the program and to decide, given government parameters, what type of business and training would be possible.[24] Ultimately, it was decided that the preparation of microfiche for libraries and businesses would be appropriate and would not interfere with the business of established firms in the area.

Obviously the rapidly changing nature of information technology would give this type of training a fairly short shelf life, but, during the initial period, it served to meet the requirements of government funding, to provide women an entry to the labour market, and to generate a reasonable income for the whole program. Establishing a micrographics business provided an on-site business where women could learn business skills, practise precise record keeping, and have a way to receive Canadian employment credentials. When MicroSkills (MS) first trained women with microfilm it made strong connections with the microfilm industry and actually pioneered in bringing a level of professionalism to the industry. MS became certified to test anyone in the industry, and MS trainers were called upon to train outside the organization.[25]

In the early years of the program women were selected for this integrated training program on the basis of who could benefit most from the type of language and skills training that was provided.[26] This was possible because government funding allocated a training wage for the immigrant women who were selected. But the program also appealed to many candidates who needed training and Canadian work experience and who also faced additional and specific problems: some experienced violence in the home and some were political refugees who had been tortured in their home countries. The political refugees were often highly educated, skilled people who had had their lives turned upside down. They often had all the skills to succeed but, due to their devastating experiences, did not have control over their lives. The "holistic" program that MS offered was effective with regard to providing needed support, and, while these women often did not end up working in jobs requiring the skills training that MS provided, they were nonetheless integrated into the Canadian workforce through the initiatives of the MS programs.

Over the years the composition of the immigrant women's community changed, depending on the waves of immigration and refugee population, along with the wars, economics, and political climates in their home countries. The women experienced different barriers, which could vary from a lack of very specific skill sets and English language skills to inhibiting experiences with racism in Canada. Leaving dead-end, low-paying, and otherwise unsatisfactory employment required a great deal of resources and support in addition to the skills that are provided in more usual types of skills training programs. This was what made both WSC and MS unique: they were able to integrate responses to the multitude of barriers that immigrant women experienced.

During the 1990s MS went through a major reorganization not only in order to cope with the obvious changes that needed to be made in the skills training component of the program but also in order to deal with the radical changes in government funding. From the 1980s to the 1990s the work environment became driven by computer applications, and MS adapted to this change by introducing them to its programs. Programs were initiated to teach computer skills training in Word, Excel, Lotus, Access, and Power Point 2000. Courses in accounting software included those that focused on Simply Accounting and ACC PaC, PC repairs and technical help desk support, A+ Service Technician, Network+, and iNet+ entry-level skills training. Business English language training was also provided to accompany the computer programming training.

While the program changes in the 1990s were significant, several major changes occurred that transformed the character and direction of MS, most of which were related to coping with changes in government funding. These included instituting a fee-for-services basis for training; delinking the language and skills training programs; and, in many programs, shifting the focus for training to both men and women in the immigrant community.

These changes resulted in the retention of a substantial focus on immigrant women through programs designed to provide technical skills development, job-specific skills, language training, and job search, but they shifted substantially towards more discrete, fee-for-service programs offered to a wider public. This involved expanding certain training initiatives (like language training and computer skills training) so that people who were not part of the original target group could take them for a fee. Language training is delivered through two programs, Language Instruction for Newcomers to Canada (LINC), which provides ESL training to about 250 participants a year, and the Language Employment Related

Needs (LERN) program, a pilot program that targets information technology professionals for English language training. Thirty-four people received training under this fee-for-service program in 1999-2000.[27] MS also manages the HRDC Employment Resource Centre, a walk-in service that is open to the public but housed within the MS facility, and a women's enterprise and resource centre that offers support services to women pursuing self-employment. In addition, it has become a designated certified solutions provider for Microsoft programs. The wide variety of programs vary in intensity, with some requiring a year of training (the Women's Technology Institute pilot project) and others involving relatively brief consultations. Altogether MS services a huge number of people requiring some type of assistance: in 1999-2000 it served 12,527 clients.[28]

As with its original model, MS continues to operate a business in conjunction with its training program. MS Technical Solutions is a company that provides computer support services and computerized accounting. This involves providing technical services ranging from system set-up and installation, to hardware and software upgrades, to network solutions, to database development and management, to Web development, to troubleshooting and maintenance. The business is an integrated part of the training program, providing both funding for the program and a valuable way for trainees to gain work experience.[29]

One of the successful survival tactics that MS has used has involved developing diversified funding sources that are linked to its widely diversified programming. In large part this was a result of radical federal government changes in 1995 and the lack of provisions to accommodate funding cuts experienced by community-based training programs. The scramble to find funding meant that relatively few of all the trainees who go through MS each year are funded, and most now pay for training. However, with a variety of funding sources MS does not have to depend on a single funder for any particular program, and the organization is less vulnerable than others to changes in funders' priorities.[30] MicroSkills funding includes money from the federal, provincial, and municipal governments; the United Way; private foundations; corporate donors; individual donors; the Rexdale MicroSkills Alumni Association; and MS business services. But chasing funding is an ongoing challenge, and it takes considerable staff time that could otherwise be focused on the training initiatives themselves.

MS has made the changes that were necessary to its survival, but it is very clear that the government needs to re-invest in training if immigrant women are going to be able to find long-term meaningful work in Canada. The integrated nature of the goals of MS were well thought out, and they have worked; but they cannot reach the people who need training most without adequate funding for training, training allowances for immigrant women, and funding for support services that will enable women to take the training.[31]

Radical Changes
The changes in the nature of government funding through the shift of training responsibilities to the provinces, the shift from Unemployment Insurance to Employment Insurance, and the change in focus and expectations for training outcomes has greatly affected community-based programs like Working Skills Centre and Rexdale MicroSkills. As a review of Metro Toronto Immigrant Employment Services notes, the community-based, non-profit sector that has been developed with the active participation of users of services "has been at the forefront of program development for immigrants and refugees."[32]

The immigrants who participated in these programs consistently rated them very highly, much more highly then they did the traditional community college certificate and diploma programs, standard school board adult education programs, and private sector trainers. On three occasions the HRDC Employment Development Branch singled out WSC, from among all the non-profit community programs, as an exemplary model for training programs.[33] The federal governments have been so pleased with the efficiency and success rates at WSC and MS that both were frequently on the tour route of foreign government officials so that they could learn about their innovative model for incorporating language training into employment, counselling, and placement.

Yet, despite the obvious successes of community-based and comprehensive training for immigrants, the ability to target programs to reach those truly in need becomes increasingly difficult, if not impossible, as government criteria changes. Both organizations operate on an eclectic funding basis, always chasing small grants put together to fund permanent positions. Usually the grants are on a year-to-year basis and necessitate constant scrambling to keep together funding from a variety of sources. Funding is always tenuous.

The primary objective of government now appears to be saving money rather than training immigrants to improve market-ready skills. The community-based programs are so hampered by the shift to a market-based delivery system that they cannot target those truly in need; rather, they increasingly provide programs only to those who can afford them. As the above report noted, "it is becoming just as difficult for the sector to respond to the needs of unskilled recent immigrants as it is to meet the needs of the new class of professionals."[34] The women that WSC and Rexdale MicroSkills were designed to serve – that is, sponsored immigrants, those who lacked Canadian experience, those who were returning to the labour market after intense child responsibilities, and those who experienced labour market discrimination – are those who are most at risk for being excluded from training programs. This is because these are not only the women who are least likely to fit new criteria for training but also the women who do not have the resources to pay for the new training programs.

The emphasis now is on "self-reliance," pre-employment counselling, and market-based training services: all approaches that reduce government costs but that also considerably reduce the outstanding outcomes that were associated with community-based training and that allowed people with meagre resources to receive an income while working to improve their employability.

These community-based programs have succeeded so spectacularly because they have responded to what immigrant women said they wanted and what the women who worked with immigrant women said was essential to achieving these goals.[35] Equally significant has been the careful attention paid to the changes in the labour market: since these are employability training programs rather than formal education or career-oriented programs, their designers knew they had to be conscious of the changes in the labour markets. However, probably the most significant factor contributing to their success is that these programs are situated within, and run by, the community they serve. This means that they are more than simply training centres; rather, they are created and run by people who have a strong stake in meeting immigrant women's needs. Their role is one of advocacy and, as such, they are not removed from government policies but, rather, are important players when it comes to seeing what should be done and feeling the impact of what ultimately happens.

Notes

1 See, for example, Monica Boyd, "Migration Policy, Female Dependency, and Family Membership: Canada and Germany," in *Women and the Canadian Welfare State*, ed. Patricia M. Evans and Gerda R. Wekerle (Toronto: University of Toronto Press, 1997), 142-69; Tania Das Gupta, *Racism and Paid Work* (Toronto: Garamond, 1996); Andrea Brouwer, *Immigrants Need Not Apply* (Ottawa: Caledon Institute, 1999); Abigail B. Bakan and Daiva K. Stasiulis, "Foreign Domestic Worker Policy in Canada," *Science and Society* 58 (Spring 1994): 7-33; Sedef Arat-Koc, "Immigration Policies, Migrant Domestic Workers, and the Definition of Citizenship in Canada," in *Deconstructing a Nation: Immigration, Multiculturalism and Racism in '90s Canada*, ed. Vic Satzewich (Halifax: Fernwood, 1992), 229-42; Roxana Ng, "Racism, Sexism and Immigrant Women," in *Changing Patterns: Women in Canada*, ed. Sandra Burt, Lorraine Code, and Lindsay Dorney, 2nd ed. (Toronto: McClelland and Stewart, 1993), 279-301.
2 One of the early reports on the conditions of immigrant women was written by Sheila McLeod Arnopoulos, *Problems of Immigrant Women in the Canadian Labour Force* (Ottawa: Advisory Council on the Status of Women, January 1979).

3 This was originally known as "life skills" but has since changed because HRDC prefers the term "employment preparation."

4 Ravi Pendakur, *Immigrants and the Labour* Force (Montreal and Kingston: McGill-Queen's University Press, 2000), 13.

5 *Steps to Change Language Training: A Lobbying Kit for Immigrant, Refugee and Visible Minority Women's Groups* (1986-87) is available from ACTEW Reference Library, 401 Richmond St. West, Ste. 355, Toronto, ON, M5V 3A8.

6 Marjorie Cohen, *Evaluation of the Working Skills Centre* (Toronto: Working Skills Centre, 1979).

7 "Manpower" was the name of the federal government office that dealt with employment issues at that time.

8 Citizenship and Immigration Canada, *Milestones of the 20th Century: Citizenship and Immigration Canada,* (Ottawa: Minister of Public Works and Government Services Canada, July 2000), cat. no. Ci51-92/2000; Citizenship and Immigration Canada, *Forging Our Legacy, Canadian Citizenship and Immigration, 1900-1997* (Ottawa: Public Works and Government Services Canada, 2000), cat. no. Ci51-93/2000E), chap. 6.

9 Interview with Michael Barkley, June 2001. Barkley was the federal government representative from the Employment Development Branch at Canadian Immigration responsible for overseeing the WSC in the early years.

10 Ibid.

11 This was funded through the Local Employment Assistance Projects (LEAP).

12 Interview with Annamaria Menozzi, executive director of WSC from 1981 to 1991, June 2001.

13 The program was initially funded through LEAP, then LIP (Local Incentives Program).

14 The success rate, defined as three months of employment in the six months immediately following the completion of the program, ranged from 75 percent to 90 percent and was highly correlated to the health of the economy. Interview with Annamaria Menozzi, June 2001.

15 Interview with Eugenia Valenzuela, WSC's first executive director, May 2001. The stresses of immigration mean that immigrant women are unusually susceptible to violence. One of the senior trainees at WSC, who had been trained as a bookkeeper and was placed with the Bank of Montreal, was murdered by her ex-husband in 1990. A former executive director of WSC estimates that between 30 percent and 60 percent of the women in the training program were victims of violence in their homes.

16 English for Special Purposes involved tailoring the language lessons specifically to the actual situations these women were experiencing or were likely to experience. WSC created its own training manual, and this was used in the classroom. See, WSC, *Working Skills for Immigrant Women,* 2nd ed. (Toronto: Working Skills Centre of Ontario, 1996).

17 Interview with Annamaria Menozzi, June 2001.

18 Ibid.

19 Ibid.

20 Nakanyike B. Musisi and Jane Turritin, *African Women and the Metropolitan Toronto Labour Market in the 1990s* (Toronto: The African Training and Education Centre, June 1995).

21 Interview with Minerva Hui, June 2001.

22 This barter system is formally known as the LETS system. It is a computerized community-based trading system that allows members of the non-profit sector to accumulate and draw down credits by exchanging goods and services with other community members.

23 When Rexdale MicroSkills shifted its training and business away from preparing micro-fiche it changed its name to Community MicroSkills Development Centre, or MS.

24 These women were Eugenia Valenzuela and Marjorie Griffin Cohen (one of the authors of this study).

25 Interview with Hazel Webb, June 2001.

26 Interview with Shelly Gordon, first coordinator, June 2001.

27 MicroSkills Annual Report, 31 March 2001.

28 Ibid.
29 *MicroSkills Informs*, 2 (October to December 2000): 1. Rexdale: Community MicroSkills Development Centre.
30 Interview with Kay Blair, MS executive director, and Hazel Webb, MS director of communications and resource development, June 2001.
31 Ibid.
32 Annamarie Menozzi and Associates, and Quail Community Consulting Ltd., *Metro Toronto Immigrant Employment Services Review* (Ottawa: HRDC, January 1997).
33 Interview with Annamaria Menozzi, June 2001.
34 Ibid.
35 Interview with Jane Wilson, director of training and career development, June 2001.

9
Life Skills Training: "Open for Discussion"
Shauna Butterwick

Since the 1970s life skills classes have been commonplace in government-funded training programs designed to serve "the excluded" – the long-term unemployed, social assistance recipients, youth at risk, inmates in prisons, individuals with mental health and addictions problems, and survivors of violence and abuse. Life skills is a catch-all notion that often includes communication and problem-solving skills, assertiveness training, parenting skills, stress and time management, and other topics that come under the rubric of "personal development." Conger defines it as "the utilization of appropriate and responsible problem-solving behaviours in the management of personal affairs."[1]

Given its ubiquitous character and its multiple meanings and practices, this chapter begins with the assumption that life skills has become a keyword of postindustrial social welfare and labour market policies.[2] Examining keywords can help to illuminate the political struggles over definitions of social reality: "Keywords typically carry unspoken assumptions and connotations that can powerfully influence the discourses they permeate – in part by constituting a body of *doxa*, or taken-for-granted common-sense belief that escapes critical scrutiny."[3] The purpose of this chapter is to raise the notion of life skills, an idea now commonplace to many social welfare and employment-related programs for the "excluded," to critical consciousness, to open it for discussion. My particular intent is to explore the benefits as well as the problematic aspects of life skills curricula.

Although there are different approaches to life skills, those who are longtime practitioners in this field of adult education acknowledge the foundational work of the Saskatchewan NewStart project and the life skills curriculum developed during the duration of that program.[4] Saskatchewan NewStart began in 1968 and continued for five years, with funding from Canada NewStart, a federal government initiative concerned with exploring community-based approaches to addressing poverty and social exclusion. The Saskatchewan NewStart curriculum was created as an alternative approach to adult basic education pre-employment training for those participants facing significant barriers to finding paid work. Curriculum developers had noted that the structure and pedagogical approach of mainstream pre-employment training programs were not serving participants; they noted that these programs were similar in form and process to the schooling system in which many participants had experienced failure. Their task was to develop and test a training model that, instead of reinforcing inequalities, would be a space within which those living in cycles of poverty would be supported and would experience success.

A key element of this model was the experiential approach in which the classroom became a kind of living laboratory; that is, the lived reality of participants was a key part of the curriculum, making it relevant and meaningful to learners. Another important element was skills practising inside and outside the classroom with peers and with family. Furthermore, the philosophy of this model was oriented towards capacity building rather than a needs or deficits. These core characteristics continue to be found in some life skills programs and are central to the effectiveness of these programs and their ability to make a difference to participants who face significant barriers to employment. A further benefit of life skills programs is that the communication and problem-solving skills learned are often immediately applicable and transportable across participants' personal, community, and paid work contexts.

The benefit of life skills programs depends a great deal on the quality of instruction, whether sufficient time and resources are provided for this part of the curriculum, and whether programs are designed based on knowledge, respect, and appreciation of the lived reality of participants. Problems arise in these kinds of programs due to lack of funding and because funders and some providers have a limited understanding of the philosophy and proven benefits of the experiential pedagogical approach and the need for knowledgeable and skilled instructors. There has also been a tendency in the provision of employment-related training for "the excluded" to assume that "one size fits all" and that all participants in government-funded job training programs have the same needs and social biographies. Another problem related to life skills programs is that life skills have been positioned within a skills hierarchy. Individuals with limited resources, who already face significant barriers, can only gain access to life skills classes; they cannot gain access to other kinds of industry-specific training for jobs that pay a living wage.

In addition to these problems of administration and policy, it is important to direct attention to other concerns with life skills programs. Some life skills classes can reflect an extreme form of individualism – one that blames individuals for their impoverishment and unemployment, ignoring the structural and systemic forces that create barriers to paid work.

Those participants who do not find work often face a deeper despair than they did when they started life skills training as their initial sense of hope and possibility evaporates.

Another potential danger in life skills programs relates to the "generic" character of the problem-solving and communication skills. These skills and the individualistic orientation, however, are not neutral: they reflect a middle-class and Western orientation. The different gender, race, class, and cultural backgrounds of participants can be ignored in these skill-building lessons and, at times, may even be regarded as problematic. Furthermore, the experiential approach in which the lived reality of participants is explored can also become a context within which the private lives of those already vulnerable and excluded are "open for discussion."

The intent of this chapter is to explicate further the benefits and the problems of life skills classes. The research informing this discussion includes case studies of employment-related and coach training programs; analysis of policy and curriculum documents; and interviews with participants of life skills classes and instructors (coaches), program administrators, and curriculum developers.[5] A diversity of perspectives regarding life skills has been purposefully sought in order to illustrate the fluidity of life skills and the different ways this notion has been interpreted and practised.

Feminist and other critically oriented scholarship that challenges the taken-for-granted assumptions informing labour market policies and programs have informed this research. The following section of the chapter reviews some key authors and concerns found in this larger discussion and also examines other research into life skills programs. The remainder of the chapter illustrates in more detail some of the benefits and problems outlined in the introduction and the issues that surfaced in an analysis of conversations with providers, participants, and instructors of life skills programs.

The Bigger Picture

Nancy Fraser's[6] description of the dilemma faced by those who advocate for the maintenance of some form of welfare state as a component of a democratic government concerned with social inequalities clarifies the challenges I have faced in conducting this research. For Fraser, the struggle faced by activist scholars is that they must argue for both the maintenance of state intervention and, at the same time, critique the form that intervention takes. As outlined in the introduction, some aspects of life skills classes are beneficial while others are problematic. For those who are engaged in fighting *for and against* state intervention, as well as for welfare reform that would serve the excluded, Fraser calls for an approach based on critical discourse – an approach that examines the taken-for-granted notions (such as life skills) that are prevalent in policy discourse. Fraser also draws attention to the politicized and contested character of policy debates and the unequal access to these debates based on gender, race, and class inequalities.

Fraser calls this contested space "the social" – a space where "runaway needs" that are outside of the familiar institutionalized spaces of family and official economy are debated. The social is not exactly equivalent to the traditional public sphere, nor is it an extension of the state; rather "[it] is a site of discourse about problematic needs, needs that have come to exceed the apparently (but not really) self-regulating domestic and official economic institutions of male-oriented, capitalist societies."[7] In many respects, life skills have become a signifier for a complex grouping of runaway needs – needs that were not being effectively addressed within either the domestic or the public realm.

Investigating the taken-for-granted notions within policy reform was also central to Scheurich's[8] examination of educational policy as it relates to failing school children. He employed Foucault's notion of policy archeology in his study, which is an alternative to mainstream policy analysis – one that explores how some problems "enter the gaze of the state and policy researchers."[9] Policy archeology "critically probes why and how these strands and traces congeal (become visible) into what are thereafter labeled as a particular social problem."[10] A key element of policy archeology is the explication of social regularities: "the network of social regularities [which] constitutes what is socially legitimized (constructed) as a social problem and what is socially legitimized as the proper range of policy solutions."[11]

Human capital theory has become the dominant ideological orientation, largely uncontested, that informs how social problems and their policy solutions are constructed. In this orientation, the knowledge, attitudes, and skills of individuals are valued only in relation to their economic potential. Baptiste[12] explores the implications of this approach within adult education, arguing that human capital theory is socially bankrupt because "it treats humans as lone wolves: radically isolated hedonists, creatures of habit (not intentions) who temper their avarice with economic rationality."[13] He challenges adult educators who are concerned with social inequalities to be alert to the problems with programs constituted within a human capital orientation.

Central to the discourse of labour market and social welfare policies informed by human capital theory is the notion of "skill" and the assumption that skills (the lack of and the need for them) are both the problem and the solution to unemployment and economic restructuring. Braverman[14] was an early critic of this "skills" discourse, challenging notions of skilled and unskilled work and outlining the ideological assumptions, particularly of technology, informing how skill is understood. The patriarchal relations of capitalism that have contributed to the devaluing of women's work, and the argument that women's work is less skilled than men's, have been the focus of much feminist scholarship.[15] Jackson explores how "skill" has become the "lynch-pin" for a wide variety of initiatives and a "metaphor for the total output of all our institutions of learning, and a standard by which they should be judged."[16] Like other critics,[17] Jackson has challenged the educational rhetoric that positions skill as a neutral notion, one that hides "a long history of struggle between employers and workers for control over the organization of work processes."[18]

Disrupting the taken-for-granted approach to skill development as the key to economic prosperity in the United States, Noble[19] adds yet another critical voice to the discussion. He confronts this assumption and argues that the shortage problem is not in relation to skills; rather, there is a shortage of good jobs, and he suggests that the current "skills" ideology is a reflection of a state of denial. He further suggests that the flurry of activities related to identifying new skills requirements for the new economy are "pinning the rap for a bum economy on education and workers."[20] He calls for attention to be given to the restructuring of work in the name of globalization and increased productivity. "The insistent focus on human resources, education, and skills is thereby a convenient distraction from economic disasters caused by myopic managers with their relentless downsizing in the name of productivity."[21] In a similar vein, Livingstone[22] calls attention to the "talent-use gap," questioning the dominant argument put forward by labour market policy makers: that there exists a "skills-job gap." In a twelve-year study of the Ontario labour force, he found extensive underemployment or talent wastage among both overqualified and underqualified workers.

Taylor[23] examined how "employability skills," as articulated in 1991 by the Conference Board of Canada, were incorporated into Alberta school curricula. Her work, like other critical analyses of skills discourse, helps to illuminate the impact of focusing on employability rather than on employment. She argues that such a shift in focus "directs attention from workplace and labour market trends" and, as a result, further blames the victim and reinforces a process whereby "existing workplace inequities become 'naturalized.'"[24]

Life Skills Research

There have been few critical studies into life skills curricula and classes, which perhaps reflects how this notion has become so commonplace and naturalized that it tends to escape the radar of critical inquiry. However, some investigations have been undertaken within Canada and Britain.

Ainley and Corbett[25] examined a life skills curriculum, one that was central to the Enterprise in Higher Education Initiative (EHEI), a British program that introduced social and life skills for young people with learning difficulties. Their examination was built on work done by Cohen,[26] who challenged the assumptions informing social and life skills programs for the "academically less able," in particular, how, in these programs, contradictions were suppressed and displaced by "a magical resolution: the salvage of individual victories out of collective defeats."[27] Ainley and Corbett argued that most programs adopting the social and life skills curricula were based on "an absurd dislocation of behaviours from any kind of purposeful context ... and personal deficits were blamed for the influence of external factors."[28] They explored how the deficit model ignored circumstances of poverty, homelessness, violence, and high unemployment. Ainley and Corbett suggested that the "coping" skills of disadvantaged participants were measured against a White, masculine, and middle-class norm: "to present attitudes and habits dignified as skills as technical abilities that can be acquired piecemeal by practice and study not only divorces them from their real cultural context but represents them as equally accessible to all students whatever their class, culture, background, gender or race."[29]

The class, race, and gender bias inherent in life skills curriculum, these authors argued, was self-defeating and resulted only in making students "self-conscious of their failure to attain an impossible performance."[30] The "skills" emphasis, they proposed, was ambiguous and contradictory, representing opportunities for some to reskill and for others to experience a kind of deskilling and process of disempowerment. They also concluded that to label social and life skills as "personal and transferable" was misleading. These were not personal skills; rather, they were the universal and generic skills that related to "employers' demands for a multi-skilled workforce, as new technology renders formerly specialized expertise increasingly transparent and accessible to all."[31]

Ainley and Corbett's analysis is a powerful critique of the problems with life skills classes when they become disciplining tools that reinforce a "blame-the-victim" approach. It appears they found little of value in life skills classes. Griffith[32] articulated similar concerns in her investigation of the Ontario Ministry of Education's development of a life skills curriculum. She argues that the focus on skills has not arisen out of the concerns of people looking for paid work; rather, it is "the grammar of administration, a grammar obscured in the language of abstraction or generality."[33] Griffith examined the documents produced prior to the establishment of the Ontario Life Skills Curriculum and found that the problem was viewed as that of schools (and teachers) inadequately preparing students for the labour force.

She noted with interest, however, that the response was not to shift school curriculum towards more vocational or technical training but, rather, to focus on life skills. In addition to the supposed neutrality that others had noted with regard to the concept of skill, Griffith outlines the "positive moral connotations"[34] of life skills curricula and the difficulties of challenging the notion of life skills: it seems like such a good idea. She also noted the role that life skills curricula play in constructing issues like unemployment as a matter of individual responsibility: "life skills curricula enter students' lives and concerns into the curriculum while, at the same time, providing the basis on which those concerns can be rationalized and fitted to the cultural understandings generated in the capitalist mode of production – life as a series of skills."[35]

For Griffith, there are some constructive elements in this move to include life skills curricula in schools because such a curriculum recognizes, indeed mandates, that schools acknowledge students' everyday concerns. At the same time, however, this acknowledgment comes with a caveat that students' common sense understandings are incomplete and that it is teachers (and Ministries of Education) who know what students "need to know." Griffith concluded that class relations (and, I would argue, gender and race) are obscured in the neutrality of life skills language; however, by opening the door to discussing students' everyday lived experiences, life skills curricula contain emancipatory and political potential. As with Griffith's investigation, this study of life skills programs illustrates both the benefits of such training and the limitations.

Life Skills: Exploring the Terrain of "the Social"

Fraser's notion of "social spaces" in which runaway needs (needs that the domestic and public spheres are unable to satisfy) are discussed is an apt description of life skills classes in employment programs. In a study of three federally funded women's re-entry programs, particularly their life skills component, it became evident that the discourse about what women needed in order to find work was neither simple nor coherent.[36] In one of the programs that trained women for clerical work, some time had been spent on helping the participants review the skills and knowledge they had acquired through caring for their children, families, and communities, and how this was significant and useful to the world of work. These lists of strengths and "know-how" were then translated into a language for resumes – a language that would appeal to potential employers. This class illustrated the capacity for life skills to include contradictory elements.

The process began by valuing and naming the women's existing knowledge and skills, and there were positive shifts evident in the self-identity of many of the participants. In this respect the class reflected some of the principles of learner-centred adult education, where individuals are recognized as knowledgeable agents rather than as needing to be fixed. In that same "clerical" re-entry program another class focused on "dressing for success." The participants were given many strategies for finding ways, within a limited budget, to create an image of a professional business-woman. When the instructor emphasized that participants should avoid dressing as "housewives," a lively debate took shape. Several women commented on the contradiction between employers wanting their reception-ists to dress well in order to "represent" the employer and the company, and the low wages these same employers would be paying. Although the gendered inequalities of the labour market were not a formal part of the curriculum, as Griffith found in her study of life skills in schools, the issue of proper attire for work and the expectations of employers opened a space for participants to discuss and challenge unfair employment practices.

In another program, which offered bookkeeping training for immigrant women, students were receiving instruction on assertiveness training. In introducing the lesson, the instructor encouraged the women to know their rights and to demand respect from others. Within this same lesson, however, the same instructor made critical comments with regard to how some cultural behaviours (such as avoiding eye contact) were problematic. Another area of tension was noted in this program. While there was a strong message regarding women using their new assertiveness skills, at the same time these women were warned that, in order to succeed, they had to assimilate into Canadian business culture. The participants in these life skills classes were admonished to *lower* their expectations in order to gain entry to the Canadian labour market.

This program also displayed little acknowledgment of the diversity of cultures and experiences in the group: the women had become a mono-culture of immigrants. There was some space for the sharing of cultural differences, but they were limited to bringing "traditional" foods to pot-luck meals. It was ironic that one of the participants in this course was able to secure one of the better-paying jobs with an employer who did a lot of business with Latin American companies. A key aspect of getting the job was her ability to speak another language and that fact that she knew the values and practices of another culture.

The third program studied was for Aboriginal women and it was run by an Aboriginal organization. Within this context life skills classes had been designed using the notion of a medicine wheel that included the spiritual, cognitive, physical, and emotional dimensions. There was a significant focus on helping the participants come to understand their different Abo-riginal ancestries, the strengths of their cultures, and the impact of colo-nization on their families and communities. For many of the women, who did not have strong links with their tribal origins, this was the beginning of a long-term educational and cultural reorientation process – an element of the curriculum that was resisted by some of the participants. This program also made a great effort to establish a link with the women's families and communities. Weekly potluck meals and other activities were held, and friends and family members of the participants were encouraged to attend. Success in this program was not measured simply by whether the participants found paid work following its completion (although this was one of the central criteria imposed by the funders). For many women, given their everyday struggles with poverty and violence, maintaining regular attendance and imagining a better future was considered a major achievement. In comparison with the program for immigrant women, in which they were admonished to lower their goals in order to avoid disappointment, in the Aboriginal-run program the trainers pushed the women to dream of more for themselves, to imagine a career rather than just a low-waged entry-level job.

Examples of the contradictory character of life skills training continue to emerge in more recent research. Some of it describes life skills training as a positive element of programs for disadvantaged individuals and groups, and some of it considers it to be the failing of such programs. Often the same key elements of life skills classes (such as communication and expressing emotions) are described as both beneficial and problematic.

Opening the Door

Of the over thirty participants interviewed for this study,[37] many had very positive things to say about life skills and the difference it had made to their lives and to the lives of others. One interviewee described herself as "in recovery" from addictions and a life that had been constrained by poverty and violence. She found the lessons on problem solving and communication, particularly self-expression, very useful: "It's opened the door for me, where I can participate a little bit more in life ... I started feeling good last week and I was surprised with it. I never felt this good before." Students and coaches spoke about life skills classes working when they were relevant and when students were ready to undertake the process.

Another participant described a program developed specifically for women who had histories of trauma and abuse, and that had life skills classes at the core of its curriculum, as very useful: "I spent six months attending a weekly group for women in abusive relationships and it was great ... I went to the group when I was ready to go to it ... I learned a great deal and it gave me great strength." Required to attend life skills while on welfare, another individual described being initially resistant, particularly to being pushed into such classes. Although initially insulted, this person was surprised by how useful it was and how that first experience reoriented his career plans towards working in the life skills industry and running a coach-training program in a private postsecondary institute: "I thought life skills was for losers ... I thought it was making change for the bus ... I got into the class and thought ... I will take what I can. After about a week and a half I thought ... this is good stuff ... it really sparked me. I could see my own self-esteem and confidence going up, my communication skills were better, I was listening more actively."

Life Skills as Consciousness-Raising

In the earlier research on women's re-entry programs, as well as in a case study of a coach training program, shifts in consciousness and in skills that were occurring in the lives of learners were notable. The authority and power of life skills coaches was an issue for one coach with whom we spoke. She felt that this was both beneficial and dangerous: "What a life skills coach is doing is changing people. What I found significant was the power of it to do that, because you're in a position of authority, you sit in a position of social respect ... I think it actually scared me in some ways – the impact it could have on people." At the same time, this instructor was supportive of life skills classes because she believed that they provided resources for those with limited access. "I think one good thing about life skills is that I always perceived counselling and therapy as a privilege of economics; if you can't afford it you have to see a state conditioned psychiatrist or psychologist. So it gives people support when there is nothing else out there."

The experiential and practical aspects of life skills classes, where students who had not done well in traditional, more cognitively oriented, learning environments could succeed, was another source of value. As one longtime coach described it, life skills can be liberating because it changes participants' consciousness:

I think one of the ways that life skills elevates people's consciousness or pushes [them] into greater consciousness is that in that lab with those other people they are brushing up against other human beings all the time. And they are learning that this person does it this way, this person likes me. This person doesn't. How do I fit in here? And so they have to become more and more conscious of what is going on around them, how they fit into that ... it is harder for them to ever look at things quite the same again.

Dangerous Disclosures

Among those interviewed were several who commented on the asymmetrical power relations between life skills coaches and participants. Several spoke about the dangers of the kind of emotional disclosures demanded of the process – disclosures facilitated by those with limited training. As one life skills coach noted: "A lot of life skills is based on feelings, expressing feelings ... disclosing feelings ... folks have been forced to disclose, by the state and by institutions, their privacy."

One life skills coach with many years of experience, who had been trained in the NewStart model, felt that many of the problems were due to time constraints and not following the sequence that the NewStart model had developed: "Part of my role as a trainer is being able to give people honest and straightforward feedback, balanced with what a person can hear. So you can't just be there three days and just dump all this stuff on [students] ... People have to be able to grow and behave in a certain way."

Several participants noted the potential for life skills classes to shift towards a deficit model rather than acknowledging participants' experiences and existing capacities. One coach spoke clearly about the deficit approach and how it contradicted the intent of such programs to raise self-esteem: "It's believed that by learning these skills not only does society benefit but you'll benefit. Which, you know, says ... 'what you have isn't good enough.' It's interesting that a significant factor of life skills coaching [concerns] self-esteem. 'I will also give you self-esteem, I mean you have nothing. I have to teach you self-esteem because you don't have it.' Which is just an impossible situation for a student to be in."

One Size Fits All

Rather than receiving training in job-specific skills in occupations that would pay a living wage, those on the lower end of the training hierarchy find that life skills is the common denominator in their programs. As one student who was receiving income assistance commented: "The assumption is, yes, well you're on welfare, obviously you've screwed up your life." She went on to suggest that life skills might be useful but that it was taught in a demeaning way. "They've got the right idea in that people, as adults, maybe need to learn the stuff that they didn't learn as children, but ... it's not being approached in the right way. There's got to be some way of doing it that doesn't rob the participants of their dignity." She was also critical of the lack of transparency and the way life skills were inserted into the program: "I don't really think it has any place in a course like this at all. This course was not sold to me as get-your-life-together course."

Another criticism was that funders often require life skills to be part of the curriculum of job-specific training programs for those on Employment Insurance (EI) and those receiving Income Assistance. One student attending a trades exploration program while on EI expressed great frustration with two weeks of the program, which focused on life skills: "I was ready to quit the program because I just couldn't stand it any longer. I actually had a life that was happening [and] I didn't need to sit and discuss how to do my life ... I'm not having problems with my life, I'm having a problem with my career."

We spoke with one instructor who worked in a program serving immigrant women. She had not taken any coach training but ended up teaching this as part of the program because that was what the funders had required. She expressed concern that the coaches whom she had observed lacked any analysis of power with regard to their work. In order to address this issue, within the space of her life skills classes she presented a critical analysis of the economy and labour market structures and practices: "Most of the people teaching life skills [in this agency] don't have any analysis of oppression. So if you don't, then you're already starting from an unequal place or you're already starting from a model that will oppress. But in our program ... we look at employment standards, your rights [as workers], we do a lot of work around situations of racism, discrimination in the workplace, at home, within society and what you do with these situations."

Life Skills for Aboriginal Communities

Life skills classes have been a key element of training programs developed specifically for Aboriginal communities. There were different, at times competing, evaluations of life skills classes articulated by those First Nations participants to whom we spoke for this study. One of the interviewees had operated many government-funded employment training programs for First Nations communities and, for a few years, this agency offered programs that included life skills because it was one of the components required by funders. His initial perspective on life skills was that it appeared to offer some potential for Aboriginal communities. Efforts were made to hire Aboriginal instructors and to include visits by elders as well as lessons on the history of Aboriginal cultures and the impact of residential schools.

One of the concerns raised by this provider involved the difficulty of finding qualified Aboriginal instructors, those with sound training both within the academic sphere and also with regard to cultural beliefs and practices: "The scope of the qualified professionals that we had to choose from by and large don't have academic foundation. In any work we do ... we need to have solid references not only academically but culturally." One of the main concerns this provider expressed was the tension between the individualistic focus and traditional Aboriginal worldview, which values community and family. This individualistic orientation, he argued, helped to create divisions within Aboriginal communities. "[This approach] works against pursuing harmony and balance within the family ... you have those who are and those who aren't trained." Another criticism this provider made of these programs, particularly those of a short-term nature, had to do with the strong and outwardly shared emotions expressed by participants: "As somebody who grew up with our teachings ... that is not in keeping with our teachings about maintaining. No matter how high or low, you maintain. That might seem strange in a modern context for someone not to celebrate so widely. This [Aboriginal] society has a system of outlets for both the negative and the positive, it has the structures for grieving and the managing of big celebrations. They're built within the feasting system, they're built within the ceremony, they're built within the teachings."

This provider no longer offers such programs because he is concerned about the damage they may potentially cause to First Nations communities. He described attempts to raise critical questions with other coaches and with life skills organizations, but his concerns were not taken up. The focus of debate among life skills coaches at that time was whether the industry should be regulated and coaches licensed.

Another participant in our study was a First Nations woman who had been a life skills student and who had gone on to become a coordinator and life skills instructor in a high school. Her initial experience of a life skills program based on the NewStart model was very positive. She has subsequently adapted and added other elements to her approach to life skills in order to meet the needs of her Aboriginal students. Recognizing the dangers of not including family and community in the training process, this instructor spoke strongly about the importance of being open and inclusive: "What we do is invite students, potential students, their parents, administration and anyone else from the First Nations community that want to know about it. We hold a round of introductions. Coaches will talk about their experience with it, how valuable they think it might be for the community and then we do a little mini-lesson."

Another approach she brought to her work with life skills involved interviewing every student before accepting them into a class in order to get a sense of their history and current issues, as well as to let them ask questions about life skills. She also described conducting a capacity inventory rather than a needs inventory, which, in her view, implies that there is something wrong with a community: "[A capacity inventory] focuses on the strengths of the community, bringing those together ... imagine a spider web: bring those people and organizations and companies or whatever together."

We spoke with a First Nations student who was taking a life skills coach-training program (eight hours per day for twelve weeks). She had heard about it from another First Nations friend whom she had observed had made great strides after participating in a life skills class. "He seemed so self-assured and self-confident and he seemed to feel comfortable with himself and felt good about his life and the direction it was going in." She found the program very useful and described changing her communication style with her children, with positive results. She was planning to use these skills to work in a group home with youth at risk. She did find the class environment very challenging and different from anything she had experienced before: "I have to put myself out on a limb ... verbalize my opinions and my thoughts and that's a chore for me." She felt that the classes taught some values that were similar to those of her Aboriginal culture: "I think it teaches you respect, you know, people's feelings, emotions, thoughts, and acceptance of people as human beings. It's along the same wavelength [as my cultural teachings]." But she also noted that there were differences: "If it was an elder that I was speaking to, I wouldn't be staring in their eyes, out of respect, I wouldn't be staring at them ... I was at a ceremony this weekend ... I didn't ask a lot of questions ... you learn by experience and you gain wisdom and knowledge by watching and listening ... and I find myself quieter today than I did on Friday after being at the ceremony for the weekend. So there's a difference."

Open for Discussion
The purpose of this chapter was to bring into critical consciousness, to open for discussion, the concept of life skills as a keyword of social welfare and labour market programs serving the excluded. This exploration is situated within a larger debate about the ideological assumptions informing neoliberal policies and programs, which emphasize the need for skills training and individual responsibility for unemployment and poverty. Human capital theory, which values individuals and their skills only if they are considered to be economically productive, has become the dominant ideological orientation within which labour market and social welfare programs for the excluded have been developed. It is important to situate the discussion of life skills within this ideological framework.

Both the benefits and the problems of life skills are reflected in the perspectives of those students, instructors, and coaches with whom we spoke. Life skills offered a life-affirming experience for many. New ways of participating and considering problems created new possibilities for greater participation. It was a space of support and validation. It was an adaptable curriculum, one that was augmented so that it suited the issues facing Aboriginal high school students as well as their families. The therapeutic character of life skills classes was discussed as positive and as a way for individuals who would not otherwise have access to counselling to get support.

However, it seems that the benefits of life skills classes and the problems are closely tied together. Given the experiential model and the focus on participants' personal lives, life skills classes can be viewed as an example of governmentality – a process whereby individuals who are already vulnerable have their lives open for further surveillance. Governmentality refers to "a kind of governance that ... brings everything under its gaze."[38] Given the prevalence of life skills classes in programs for the most disadvantaged, life skills has, within some contexts, become a tool for a form of mandatory disclosure of one's personal and private struggles. Such demands are not made in other labour market programs that are open to those with greater socio-economic resources. The therapeutic quality of life skills classes has value, but, given the power that instructors (some of whom are not properly trained) have over participants who are engaging in psychological explorations, it is also dangerous.

Life skills is a curious concept, a keyword of late modernity, a concept that has become a signifier for a group of runaway needs – needs that were being addressed neither within family and community nor within the traditional adult basic education classroom. Its appeal to those running programs for the excluded is that it does provide some important tools for problem solving and communication – tools that have relevance to participants and that can be used by individuals to create change in their lives and to provide them with a sense of possibility and security. At the same time, these tools can become part of a curriculum that trains a generic worker who is flexible and adaptable to many work situations and who accepts the insecurity that characterizes postindustrial forms of capitalism.

Another way to look at the persistence of life skills programs is in relation to how they help individuals live in what German sociologist Ulrich Beck[39] has called a "risk society" – a term that designates the precariousness of social and personal life. According to Beck, within contemporary society, communities no longer supply the norms that shape the identity of individuals; individuals now face a diversity of options by which to map their identities and life course. There are dangers, however, in this kind of individual freedom. Building on Beck's work, Jansen and Wildemeersch[40] call for forms of adult education that counter the dominant orientation to individualization and economic rationality found in most employment-related programs, particularly for marginalized groups. Instead of programs that encourage a form of "entrepreneurship of the self," they call for programs that support a cultural approach to identity, whereby participants are supported as competent actors who can and do make a difference in their communities.

This analysis of life skills programs illustrates the ways in which these programs, with their emphasis on experiential learning and the acquisition of specific skills, can both promote self-sufficient individuals who are able to compete as economic entrepreneurs and support individuals in re-engaging with community, resisting hyper-individualistic economic rationality, and promoting the value of social dependency and engagement.

Notes

1 Stuart Conger and D. Mullen, "Life Skills," *International Journal of Advising Counseling* 4 (1981): 305.
2 Raymond Williams argued that keywords such as culture, society, and class were part of "an active vocabulary – a way of recording, investigating and presenting problems of meaning" and worthy of investigation not in order to resolve disputes about meaning but, rather, to bring such words and concepts into critical consciousness. See Raymond Williams, *Keywords: A Vocabulary of Culture and Society* (New York: Oxford University Press, 1974), 13.
3 Nancy Fraser and Linda Gordon, "A Genealogy of 'Dependency': Tracing a Keyword of the U.S. Welfare State," in Nancy Fraser, *Justice Interruptus: Critical Reflections on the "Post-socialist Condition"* (New York: Routledge, 1997), 121.
4 For a more detailed outline of the NewStart model, see Stuart Conger, "Life Skills Training: A Social Invention," in *Readings in Life Skills*, ed. Training Research and Development Station (Prince Albert, SK: Department of Manpower and Immigration, 1973), 1-5; and S. Conger and D. Mullen, "Life Skills," 305-19.
5 This research has been funded by the Social Sciences and Humanities Research Council (SSHRC) through the Western Research Network on Education and Training (WRNET), which is located in the Faculty of Education, University of British Columbia (Jane Gaskell, principal investigator).
6 Nancy Fraser, *Unruly Practice: Power Discourse and Gender in Contemporary Social Theory* (Minneapolis, MN: University of Minnesota Press, 1989).
7 Ibid., 156.
8 James Joseph Scheurich, "Policy Archeology: A New Policy Studies Methodology," *Journal of Education Policy* 9, 4 (1994): 297-316.
9 Ibid., 300.
10 Ibid.
11 Ibid., 301.
12 Ian Baptiste, "Educating Lone Wolves: Pedagogical Implications of Human Capital Theory," *Adult Education Quarterly* 51, 3 (2001): 184-201.
13 Ibid., 197.
14 Harold Braverman, *Labour and Monopoly Capital: The Degradation of Work in the Twentieth Century* (London: Monthly Review Press, 1974).
15 See Michele Barrett, *Women's Oppression Today: Problems in Marxist Feminist Analysis* (London: Verso, 1980); A. Phillips and B. Taylor, "Sex and Skill: Notes Towards a Feminist Economics," *Feminist Review* 30 (1980): 79-88; Cynthia Cockburn, *Brothers: Male Dominance and Technological Change* (London: Pluto Press, 1983); Nancy Jackson, "Skill Training in Transition: Implications for Women," in *Women and Education*, 2nd ed., ed. J. Gaskell and A. McLaren (Calgary, AB: Detselig Enterprises, 1991): 351-70; Jane Gaskell, *Gender Matters from School to Work* (Toronto, ON: OISE Press, 1992).
16 Jackson, "Skill Training," 353.
17 For example G. Lenhardt, "School and Wage Labour," *Economics and Industrial Democracy* 2 (1981): 191-222.
18 Jackson, "Skill Training," 354.
19 David Noble, "Let Them Eat Skills," in *Education and Cultural Studies: Toward a Performative Practice*, ed. Henry Giroux (New York: Routledge, 1997), 198-212.
20 Ibid., 206.
21 Ibid., 207.
22 David Livingstone, "Wasted Education and Withered Work: Reversing the 'Post-Industrial' Education: Jobs Optic," paper prepared for the International Workshop Conference, Human Resources Development in a Changing Economy, University of British Columbia, 19-21 August 1996.
23 Allison Taylor, "Employability Skills: From Corporate 'Wish List' to Government Policy," *Journal of Curriculum Studies* 30, 2 (1998): 143-64.
24 Ibid., 155.

25 P. Ainley and J. Corbett, "From Vocationalism to Enterprise: Social and Life Skills Become Personable and Transferable," *British Journal of Sociology of Education* 15, 3 (1994): 365-74.

26 P. Cohen, "Against the New Vocationalism," in *Schooling for the Dole: The New Vocationalism,* ed. I. Bates, J. Clarke, P. Cohen, D. Finn, R. Moore, and P. Willis (Basingstoke, UK: Macmillan, 1984).

27 Ainley and Corbett, "Vocationalism to Enterprise," 131.

28 Ibid., 367.

29 Ibid., 371-72.

30 Ibid., 372.

31 Ibid.

32 Allison Griffith, "Skilling for Life/Living for Skill: The Social Construction of Life Skills in Ontario Schools," *Journal of Educational Thought* 22, 2A (1988): 198-208.

33 Ibid., 200.

34 Ibid., 204.

35 Ibid., 205.

36 See S. Butterwick, "The Politics of Needs Interpretation: A Study of Three CJS-Funded Job-Entry Programs for Women" (PhD diss., University of British Columbia, 1993).

37 I am grateful for the research assistance of Lu Ripley, worked with me on parts of this study, conducted many of the interviews, and collaborated with me on the case study of the coach-training program.

38 Scheurich, "Policy Archeology," 306.

39 Ulrich Beck, *Risk Society: Towards a New Modernity* (London: Sage, 1992).

40 Theo Jansen and Danny Wildemeersch, "Beyond the Myth of Self-Actualization: Reinventing the Community Perspective of Adult Education," *Adult Education Quarterly* 48, 4 (1998): 216-26.

10
Pathways to Employment for Women: Apprenticeship or College Training?
Robert Sweet

There is a growing recognition that postsecondary credentials are essential to securing stable employment in Canada's emerging "knowledge economy." As a consequence, participation rates in universities, colleges, and apprenticeships have been rising for over a decade. These programs are not, however, equally valued. There is much greater public interest in the university as a means of acquiring essential knowledge and skill. Surveys of adolescents and their parents clearly indicate that most aspire to a university education.[1] These views are reinforced by empirical assessments of the relative value of postsecondary degrees, diplomas, and certificates. Allen,[2] Finnie,[3] and others have contrasted labour market outcomes for university and college graduates with results that consistently favour the university credential. These broad comparisons fail to recognize the economic importance of the skills taught in colleges and through apprenticeships. They also ignore the variety of school-work pathways that exist within the vocational stream and the training opportunities these represent for large numbers of young people, particularly women.

Women represent a potentially important source of skilled labour, and many have displayed an interest in vocational work. For at least two decades, more women than men have enrolled in college training programs.[4] In addition to the vocational pathways available through the college system, women have the option of registering in an apprenticeship.[5] This form of training requires the individual to alternate between the classroom and the workplace in order to obtain the necessary theoretical and practical knowledge of a particular trade or technology. As a complement to knowledge acquired in the classroom, exposure to the situated problems, processes, and rituals of the worksite develops in the apprentice a sense of personal competence as well as an understanding of working culture. Apprenticeships are considered by many as the preferred means of acquiring relevant work skills.[5]

Despite their evident interest in vocational employment, attempts by governments, employers, and unions to encourage women to consider careers in the apprenticed trades have failed. Throughout the decade of the 1990s the proportion of female apprentices never rose above 4 percent of total registrants. And among those who did register as apprentices, most chose a traditional women's trade – typically hairdressing, esthetics, or one of the baking or cooking trades.[6] Apprenticeships in nontraditional trades such as construction, manufacturing, or automotive repair nevertheless hold considerable promise for women. Sweet and Gallagher,[7] for example, found the transition experiences of women who completed their apprenticeship training in a nontraditional trade to be consistently successful. Nearly all were rewarded with stable employment and relatively high wages.

Women are obviously disadvantaged in the transition process when, despite possessing the same qualifications as men, they earn less. Gender differences in earnings exist in nearly all sectors of the economy but are most noticeable in the vocational trades and service industries.[8] It is important to know the extent to which choosing a particular form of training offsets the effects of a gendered workplace. At the present time, women appear to prefer the college system as a means of preparing for employment. Given the ability of apprenticeships to develop relevant skills and offer attractive initial wages, they may represent a more attractive option. Or it may be that only nontraditional trades training can offset the effects of sex-segregation in the workplace.

Making a successful transition from training to employment is essential to establishing and sustaining a career. While school-work transitions are complex and have been variously defined and measured, employment income (e.g., wages, earnings) remains a generally accepted indicator of overall transition success.[9] In this chapter, women and men's earnings are compared using data obtained two years after they had obtained either a college certificate or journeyperson's papers. A two-year transition period offered ample time within which to establish themselves in the workforce and, to the extent they were able, to experience transition success. In addition to analyzing gender differences in earnings based on choice of a school or workplace training format, I make a more focused comparison of earnings between women registered in either a traditional or nontraditional apprenticed trade.

An analysis of monetary outcomes associated with choosing a particular pathway to employment has obvious career planning implications for women. The emphasis on individual choice also reflects recent theoretical interest in the role of personal agency as a determinant of transition success.[10] Agency in this context refers to the individual's choice of a training format; and earnings differences are assumed to be a consequence of those choices. In exploring the dimension of agency in relation to women's vocational training opportunities and outcomes, this analysis extends previous research on the balance between social structural features of gender, age, ethnicity, or region and personal initiatives – such as selecting a field of study or training format – that represent attempts to cope with the uncertainties surrounding the movement from school to work.[11]

Background

Skills Priorities

In the early 1990s Canadian labour markets were characterized by high youth unemployment and the rhetoric of, inter alia, "downsizing," "flexible work organization," "technological revolution," and the "knowledge-based economy." Whether as a consequence of these pressures or other factors, young people were participating less in the labour market and more in post-secondary education.[12] Registrations in universities, colleges, and apprenticeships grew throughout the decade. However, participation was uneven, with the majority of young people preferring the university pathway. In 1994-95, at the mid-point of the decade, full-time, undergraduate enrolments in Canadian universities totalled 612,628 (including college university transfer students). College Career-Tech programs enrolled 272,003 students, and college and institute pre-employment trades programs enrolled 78,782.[13] Registered apprenticeships totaled 191,200 for the same period.[14]

National policy documents[15] advocate expanding basic technology and trades training. Underlying this concern for the vocational training sector is the growing shortfall in the national stock of skilled tradespersons, technologists, and service sector employees.[16] Profiles of rising skill requirements and projections of worker shortages are leading to calls for a major reconsideration of existing training facilities and programs with a view to attracting more young people to a vocational career.[17] Critiques of attempts to increase the stock of intermediate skills are not confined to Canada; other advanced economies are undergoing similar scrutiny.[18]

The vocational skills required are termed "intermediate skills" in Europe[19] or "mid-range skills" in the United States[20] and reflect the general trend towards up-skilling. More specifically, they describe job-related skills of an increased cognitive complexity. Ashton, McGuire, and Sung[21] refer to capabilities whose application "relies on the internalization of a body of theoretical knowledge and its usage in variable contexts ... that are transferable across a range of jobs ... constantly evolving with developments in theoretical understanding and in techniques utilized in the practice of such skills."

Mason[22] points out that employers are typically more interested in the nature of intermediate skill qualifications than in the level of attainment involved. Hiring tends to favour those graduates with relevant workplace experience. In response, colleges (and universities) have turned to applied curricula and co-op education programs to provide their students with the experiential prerequisites for successful entry to the workplace. And there is growing interest in the potential of the apprenticeship to serve as a model that achieves an appropriate balance between formal and applied learning.[23]

Preparing for Work

There have been numerous calls for reform of the Canadian approach to training. These range from curricular innovations in the community college[24] to more specific – and critical – analyses of the viability of the apprenticeship system.[25] In one form or another, all express concern for the relevance of the skills acquired through formal training and the disorderly school-work transitions experienced by many youth.

In response to these criticisms, the postsecondary education system has made significant changes to access policies, increased program diversity, and introduced greater flexibility in the use of program delivery technologies.[26] Universities and colleges have, however, retained their traditional approach to instruction. Most education and training institutions continue to emphasize conceptual learning and to employ direct instruction methods in classroom settings. This exclusive emphasis on discipline-based instruction may not be the most appropriate preparation for work in a rapidly changing society and a knowledge-based economy. An emerging view suggests that "alternation" methods – those combining experiential and cognitive learning – represent an effective instructional alternative for acquiring essential knowledge and relevant skills as well as for developing successful pathways from school to work.[27]

Teichler[28] frames the issue of relevance in terms of knowledge acquisition, the limits on its application, and the need for learners to possess an orientation towards practice. General knowledge is frequently differentiated from specific knowledge. The former is found in lists of "employability skills" presumed to incorporate general social and communicative competencies, intellectual flexibility, and personal initiative. Yet the need for task-specific knowledge is widely acknowledged in, for example, specialized trades training or professional education programs; and job-relevant skills are consistently rewarded by prospective employers.[29] Knowledge, whether general or specific, must be applied in the identification and solution of problems. It is therefore necessary to possess the capabilities of transferring knowledge or skill to the workplace. And finally, theoretical knowledge needs to be oriented to practice in the sense that it needs to inform activities in the workplace that are only partly expressible in words or symbols (or that may to some extent be automated or made routine). The task of education then is to ensure "systematic confrontation" between ways of thinking and problem solving within academic or disciplinary theories and the modes of craft or professional thinking and problem solving found in the workplace.[30]

Uncertain Transitions

As a consequence of the changing relationship between education and work, negotiating a successful transition between the two domains has increasingly become an individual responsibility. This emphasis on individualism is seen in the work of Beck[31] and Giddens,[32] who view social structures such as socio-economic status, gender, region, and ethnicity as exerting less influence over adult status attainment while the decisions and choices of individuals are crucial in determining their life chances. Recent research on the nature of school-work transitions suggests that, in emerging knowledge economies, transition processes are no longer linear and predictable; rather, they are more prolonged and the decisions involved in their successful passage more uncertain. Research on school-work transitions in Western European countries describes the trend to individualism in social policy. Heinz,[33] for example, describes the developmental task of youth as one of writing their own educational and work "biographies." Others take a more balanced view of the relative effects of structure and individual agency on transition success. Furlong and Cartmel,[34] and Rudd,[35] for example, suggest that expressions of personal agency, such as choosing a field of study (or trade), are substantially qualified by the individual's personal and social situation. All, however, acknowledge the greater risks associated with transition processes in postmodern economies.

Attempts to integrate notions of individualism, social structure, and social risk may be found in recent reviews of the transitions literature in Canada.[36] These analyses reflect an ongoing debate as to the applicability of the "individualism" thesis within the Canadian context. Lowe and Krahn,[37] for example, question whether aspirations may be met solely through personal decisions and actions. In their view, educational and occupational attainments remain very much determined by structural features of class, ethnicity, region, and gender. Other transition studies that address the relationship between personal agency and the effects of structure generally find significant social structural effects – principally, socio-economic status, gender, and rural-urban differences – although individual differences remained an important element in program choice and eventual transition success.[38] On balance, it would appear that individuals do exercise a measure of personal autonomy and control as they attempt to navigate the passage from school to work.

Women's Participation in Training

Women's participation in postsecondary education has grown steadily since the early 1970s, based on the belief that investment in education will produce tangible returns in the form of better pay and greater job stability. Studies of educational aspirations have shown that, over the previous two decades, women's aspiration levels have consistently exceeded those of men.[39] Gender differences in this regard have become so marked that educational analysts have expressed concern with the possible causes of adolescent males' relatively low levels of educational attainment and aspirations.[40]

Women have been actively pursuing both academic and vocational pathways to employment. Within the vocational training areas, however, their participation is selective. For the first half of the 1990s, women's participation rate (as a percentage of total enrolment) exceeded that of men in college trades and career-tech options. It is evident that women have invested heavily in school-based training. However, their participation in apprenticeships remains remarkably low. Skof's[41] analysis of women's participation in the largest trades categories (those with more than 3,000 registrants) revealed that fewer than 4 percent of apprentices in the nontraditional trades were women, while the proportions in cooking and baking trades, and in hairdressing and related areas of esthetics, were 25 percent and 75 percent, respectively. More recent analyses reveal essentially the same proportions.[42]

A similar pattern emerges among college students. Women tend to enrol in college programs that are linked to the business or service sectors. These include leisure and recreation, early childhood education, business, and, increasingly, specialized areas involving computer applications. Less interest is shown in areas of work traditionally occupied by men, such as manufacturing, construction, and automobile repair.[43]

Various attempts have been made to encourage women to enter the skilled trades. These include special training incentives and bridging programs designed to familiarize women with the nontraditional workplace. Although few in number and of limited duration, the record of these programs has been generally positive.[44] One of the reasons for the success of bridging programs is their recognition and acceptance of a range of interests and abilities.

The motivations for choosing a career and undertaking the necessary training are complex. They involve socialized preferences for particular types of work as well as an assessment of the return on investment in training. Other considerations are involved: balancing the demands of work and family limits many women's attempts to craft an autonomous career trajectory.[45] After weighing the alternatives, the majority of women have opted to train within the college system. While evidence of an adequate monetary return on an individual's choice of a particular form of training – college or apprenticeship – meets only one of many decision criteria, earnings are nevertheless an important consideration in the process of choosing how to train. Comparative information of this sort is not only of theoretical and policy interest but also of value to individuals contemplating or planning a vocational career.

System Comparisons

Attempts to empirically plot postsecondary participation and successful school-work transitions have used a variety of data sources. Skof[46] and Sharpe[47] used the Registered Apprentice Information System (RAIS) to compare recent college and apprenticeship enrolment and completion rates. Guppy and Davies[48] and others have used census data to track the initial labour market experiences of vocational graduates. While providing useful profiles of the state of vocational education in Canada, these studies have necessarily been limited by the broad demographic comparisons that the RAIS and census were designed to probe.

More detailed analyses of postsecondary school-work transitions have been undertaken using surveys specifically designed to assess graduates' success in the labour market, typically interviewing them at two- and five-year intervals following program completion. Finnie[49] used the National Graduates Survey (NGS) to examine the labour market outcomes of graduates from university and college graduates. And Boothby[50] used the same survey to examine graduate employment outcomes for trades graduates. The National Apprenticed Trades Survey (NATS) is similar in design to the NGS but was administered to a sample comprising completers and non-completers of apprenticeships. Analyses of the NATS data produced profiles of various groups (including women) as they attempted to establish themselves in the trades. For the most part, these were concerned with the effect of the credential (journeyperson's papers) on employment stability, continuity, and income.[51] Sweet and Gallagher[52] compared the transition success of women apprentices who had attained journeyperson status with those who had discontinued their training. While this analysis demonstrated the positive effects of program completion, it did not include a comparison of male and female labour market outcomes. Gender comparisons are important in examining transition success, given the evidence that initial labour market experiences of women – their earnings, employment status, and job satisfaction – are markedly different from those of men.[53] And to the extent that individual choice of a training program is reflected in the transition success of students, it is important to consider both college and apprenticeship graduate data in the analysis.

Comparing Graduate Surveys

Data from two surveys are used in the study – the 1990 *National Graduate Survey*[54] and the 1992 *National Apprenticed Trades Survey: HRDC*.[55] The NATS complements the NGS series and contains many of the same variables, although these are not always identical either in item wording or in the scales employed. The three programs of interest in the analysis were apprenticeships and the college trades training and career-tech streams. Apprenticeships typically last from three to four years, during which time apprentices are indentured to an employer who is responsible for their on-the-job training. This period of employment is interspersed with classroom instruction (typically at a college), where the theoretical and conceptual basis for the individual's trade is learned. There were approximately 170 apprenticeable trades available in Canada during the period of the study. Approximately 75 percent of all apprentices were registered in fifteen trades. The largest of these included the construction trades, automobile mechanics, and various manufacturing and mechanical trades.

College trades training comprises various pre-employment programs of relatively short duration – from three to twelve months. Typical fields of study included basic resource or primary industries skills (e.g., transportation), merchandising and sales, mechanical and small engine repair, journalism, secretarial services, and computer technologies and repair. The duration of career-tech programs was between thirteen months and three years. Most were eighteen-month or two-year programs leading to a diploma or certificate in a wide variety of fields. These included business services, computer technologies, various engineering technologies, health sciences, and management sciences.

The NGS and NATS data were not combined in this analysis. Separate samples were established that reflected the particular training program focus of these surveys. In the case of the NGS, respondents were selected from those classified as having graduated from (college) trades training and career-technology programs. These comprised 43,719 and 57,685 weighted cases, respectively. Only those respondents who had obtained their journeyperson papers were selected from the NATS data set. This resulted in a weighted sample of 21,080. Table 10.1 displays the working samples in relation to gender and school-work pathways.

Table 10.1

NGS and NATS working samples

	Program		
Gender	Trades (NGS-90)	Career-Tech (NGS-90)	Apprenticeships (NATS)
Male	20,955	23,669	19,895
Female	22,765	34,016	1,185
Total	43,720	57,685	21,080

Source: National Graduate Survey, Statistics Canada (1992) and National Apprenticed Trades Survey (1994).

Transition Indicators

Table 10.2 lists the annual earnings of college graduates and journey-persons. The most obvious pattern within programs is the uniform disadvantage of women. Regardless of the training program taken, their incomes were less than those of male workers. And in all cases the number of women in the lowest earnings categories exceeded that of men.

Comparing earnings across programs, it is clear that graduates from the Career-Tech stream fared much better than did any of the others. Higher proportions of both men (31 percent) and women (23 percent) from this program earned between $30,000 and $39,999. Their earnings, assessed two years after graduation, suggest they had made a successful transition to the labour market.

Gender differences can be seen in the lowest and highest earnings categories across programs reported in Table 10.2. Among Career-Tech program graduates, a greater proportion of women (31 percent) than men (20 percent) earned less than $20,000. Women were among the lowest earners in college trades programs and in apprenticeships. In both cases over 50 percent of respondents earned less than $20,000 per year. College trades programs are of short duration and, for that reason, may not be expected to

Table 10.2

Annual earnings: College graduates and journeypersons

| | Program | | |
Gender	Trades (%)	Career-Tech (%)	Apprenticeships (%)
Male ($)			
0-19,999	31	20	10
20,000-29,999	36	37	26
30,000-39,999	20	31	26
40,000-49,999	09	09	21
50,000-59,999	05	03	17
Valid responses (weighted)	13,316	18,893	17,064
Female ($)			
0-19,999	51	31	51
20,000-29,999	37	41	34
30,000-39,999	09	23	09
40,000-49,999	01	03	04
50,000-59,999	01	01	02
Valid responses (weighted)	14,031	25,911	994

Source: National Graduate Survey, Statistics Canada (1992) and National Apprenticed Trades Survey (1994).

have a strong impact on earnings. However, the longer training period required for apprenticeship completion would be expected to produce a correspondingly higher income. At the highest earnings levels, there are marked gender differences among those with apprenticeship training: 38 percent of males earned $40,000 or more while only 6 percent of women earned at those levels.

The results in Table 10.2 are discouraging to the notion that access to apprenticeships offers women an avenue to well remunerated vocational employment. However, differentiating traditional and nontraditional apprenticed trades in calculating women's earnings produces quite a different picture. Table 10.3 compares annual earned income for qualified women journeypersons two years after completing the apprenticeship requirements. Some 60 percent of women journeypersons in traditional trades – the majority of whom were registered in hairdressing and esthetics trades – earned less than $20,000 annually, while only 18 percent in the nontraditional training were in this category. In the middle and higher earnings categories – those earning $30,000 or more – the nontraditional group was clearly present in greater numbers. In fact, the earnings of women in nontraditional apprenticed trades compare favourably with the earnings reported in Table 10.2 for male career-tech and apprenticeship completers; and they exceed those of men in the college trades.

Earnings differences between the "traditional" and "nontraditional" categorization reflects the general devaluing of traditional women's work.[56] The distinction does, however, represent more than a difference in the male-female ratio of workers and an underlying gender bias. Nontraditional trades generally have higher rates of unionization. The positive effect of high unionization rates on earnings is substantial, especially in the construction

Table 10.3

Annual earnings: Women journeypersons

| | Trade category | |
| | Traditional | Nontraditional |
Annual earnings ($)	(%)	(%)
0-19,999	60	18
20,000-29,999	35	29
30,000-39,999	05	26
40,000-49,999	–	17
50,000-59,999	–	09
Valid responses (weighted)	797	226

Source: National Apprenticed Trades Survey (1994).

and manufacturing sectors. Unionization is also associated with successful attempts to narrow the wage gap between men and women.[57]

To the extent that annual earnings adequately represent the range of returns on investment in training, these results indicate substantial differences in relation to program choice. This pattern of earnings is even more sharply delineated by gender and, in the case of apprenticed trades, by the distinction between traditional and nontraditional trades.

Conclusion

This study contrasted annual earnings for graduates of two school-based training schemes – the trades and career-tech programs found in the college system – with those of recently certified journeypersons from the apprenticeship system. The analysis was conducted within a transitions framework that specifically examined gender differences in the ability of individuals with these credentials to establish themselves in the labour market. It appeared – from the number of enrolments – that women found the career-tech programs more attractive than either of the trades training or apprenticeship alternatives. Graduates also reported that career-tech training was able to provide a better return on their investment of time and money. The one exception was found among women who had completed a nontraditional (for women) apprenticeship.

From a theoretical perspective, establishing a link between earnings and the decisions individuals make with regard to training suggests that personal agency plays an important role in the school-work transition process. In this study, personal agency – expressed through selection of an apprenticeship or college training program – significantly affected transition success. However, the obviously gendered nature of earnings also demonstrated the continued presence and constraining influence of social structure. Men earned more than women irrespective of their training. And female apprentices gained a measure of parity only if they registered in one of the nontraditional trades.

Alternation models that combine classroom instruction with workplace experience can add to the effectiveness of training systems. The expansion of co-op education and work-experience programs in the colleges and universities attests to their general value. However, the potential of alternation approaches to contribute not only to skill development but also to educational and workplace equity is not being realized in the apprenticeship format. In the time period examined in this study (the early 1990s) few women were attracted to apprenticeship training; and, with the exception of the nontraditional trades, those who had apprenticed did not receive an adequate return on their investment in training. There is little evidence that conditions had altered by the end of the decade.[58] Despite these failings, apprenticeships are undergoing a process of modernization that, together with changes in the college approach to training, should result in greater diversity of choice for prospective trainees.[59]

Apprenticeships are being established in new sectors of the economy. The movie (film and video) industry, for example, is working with provincial apprenticeship boards to establish new and more flexible training programs. The existence of a wider range of apprenticeable trades will not guarantee improvement in the training and employment opportunities for women, but they are less likely to be burdened with the sexist attitudes of the more established trades.[60] The avenues young people can take to employment are also increasing. High school apprenticeships, while few in number and limited in scope, are nevertheless gaining support from provincial ministries of education and employers.

A potentially significant change is occurring in the relationship between colleges and apprenticeships with regard to the development of programs that involve both systems in skills training. The college-based entry-level trades training programs in British Columbia provide an opportunity to gain training credits that may be applied to an apprenticeship. Further evidence of greater flexibility in the college system is seen in the various industry-based training programs being applied to the rapidly expanding information and communications technology areas. In this sector of the economy knowledge and skill are often created and acquired on the job. The development of formal curricula and experiential programs cannot keep pace. New relationships between colleges and employers have been forged, and these involve students in workplace experiential learning that reflects many of the features of the apprenticeship approach to applied learning.[61]

The goal of increasing the pool of skilled workers in Canada would be more easily achieved by increasing the number of women enrolled in trades training. Doing so, however, requires greater flexibility in the provision of training. Women have family and work commitments that cannot accommodate rigid training schedules. And greater support in the form of work-related daycare is also an essential feature of any plan to increase the involvement of women. While institutional and programmatic changes are required in order to better accommodate women's priorities and schedules, even more fundamental social change is needed. Jenson[62] and others point to the necessity of reflecting upon the basic assumptions underlying relationships among families, work, and government. Certainly many of the existing norms surrounding employment and childcare make it difficult for women to undertake extensive periods of training.

Continued innovation in both apprenticeship and college programs will contribute to a more diverse training system. Greater diversity should enable women to choose from among a wider range of more appealing and rewarding training programs, including those that combine the resources and efforts of apprenticeship and college systems. In Canada the decade of the 1990s saw a need for substantial reform of vocational training. It is hoped that the next decade will see many of these needed changes implemented.

Notes

1 Ontario Premier's Council, *People and Skills in the New Global Economy* (Toronto: Queen's Printer, 1990); R. Sweet, P. Anisef, and Z. Lin, *Exploring Family Antecedents of Participation in Post-Secondary Education* (Ottawa ON: Learning and Literacy Directorate, Human Resources Development Canada, 2000).

2 R. Allen, *The Economic Benefits of Post-Secondary Training and Education in B.C.: An Outcomes Assessment* (Vancouver: Department of Economics, University of British Columbia, 1996).

3 R. Finnie, "Holding Their Own: Employment and Earnings of Post-Secondary Graduates," *Education Quarterly Review* 7 (2001): 21-37.

4 Statistics Canada, *Education in Canada* (Ottawa: Statistics Canada, 1996).

5 H. Schuetze, and R. Sweet, eds. *Integrating School and Workplace Learning in Canada: Principles and Practices of Alternation Education and Training* (Montreal: McGill-Queen's University Press), in press.

6 K. Skof, "Women in Registered Apprenticeship Training Programs," *Education Quarterly Review* 1 (1994): 26-35; A. Sharpe, *Apprenticeship in Canada: A Training System under Siege?* (Ottawa: National Apprenticeship Committee, Canadian Labour Force Development Board, 1999).

7 R. Sweet and P. Gallagher, *Women and Apprenticeships: An Analysis of the 1994 National Apprenticed Trades Survey* (Ottawa: Standards, Planning and Analysis Division, Human Resources Development Canada, 1997).

8 M. Charles, M. Buchmann, S. Halebsky, J. Powers, and M. Smith, "The Context of Women's Market Careers: A Cross-National Study," *Work and Occupations* 28 (2001): 371-96.

9 Finnie, "Holding Their Own."

10 W. Heinz, *Theoretical Advances in Life Course Research* (Weinheim: Deutscher Studien Verlag, 1991); P. Anisef, P. Axelrod, E. Baichman-Anisef, C. James, and A. Turrittin, *Opportunity and Uncertainty: Life Course Experiences of the Class of '73* (Toronto: University of Toronto Press, 2001).

11 Z. Lin, R. Sweet, P. Anisef, and H. Schuetze, "Consequences and Policy Implications for University Students Who Have Chosen Liberal or Vocational Education: Labour Market Outcomes and Employability Skills," *Applied Research Branch: Research Paper R-00-2-3E* (Ottawa: Human Resources Development Canada. 2000); R. Sweet, "Women and Apprenticeships: The Role of Personal Agency in Transition Success," working paper, Centre for Research on Work and Society, York University, Toronto, 2000.

12 G. Picot, A. Heisz, and A. Nakamura, "Were 1990s Labour Markets Really Different?" *Policy Options* (July/August 2000): 15-26.

13 Statistics Canada, Registered Apprenticeship Training Survey, *The Daily*, 4 August 1999.

14 Statistics Canada, *Education in Canada*.

15 Such as the Economic Council of Canada, *A Lot to Learn* (Ottawa: Economic Council of Canada, 1992); and similar provincial documents, including the Ontario Premier's Council, *People and Skills*, and the BC Labour Force Development Board, *Training for What?* (Victoria: Ministry of Skills Training and Labour, 1995).

16 Industry Training and Apprenticeship Commission (ITAC), *Ensuring a Skilled Workforce for British Columbia* (Victoria: Industry Training and Apprenticeship Commission, 2001); Centre for the Study of Living Standards (CSLS), *Report on Creating a More Efficient Labour Market*, <http://www.csls.ca/rt2/report-e.pdf> (April 2002).

17 S. Schetagne, *Building Bridges across Generations in the Workplace: A Response to Aging of the Workforce* (Ottawa: Canadian Council on Social Development, 2001).

18 G. Mason and D. Finegold, "Productivity, Machinery and Skills in the United States and Western Europe," *National Institute Economic Review* 162 (1997): 85-98.

19 P. Ryan, ed., *International Comparisons of Vocational Education and Training for Intermediate Skills* (New York: Falmer, 1991).

20 N. Grubb, *Working in the Middle: Strengthening Education and Training for the Mid-Skilled Labor Force* (San Francisco: Jossey-Bass, 1996).

21 D. Ashton, M. Maguire, and J. Sung, "Institutional Structures and Provision of Intermediate Skills: Lessons from Canada and Hong Kong," *International Comparisons of Vocational Education and Training for Intermediate Skills,* ed. P. Ryan (New York: Falmer, 1991), 234.

22 G. Mason, "The Mix of Graduate and Intermediate-Level Skills in Britain: What Should the Balance Be?" *Journal of Education and Work* 14 (2001): 5-27.

23 H. Schuetze and K. Rubenson, *Learning in the Classroom and at the Workplace: Elements of a Framework for the Analysis of Apprenticeship Training and Other Forms of "Alternation" Education and Training in Canada* (Vancouver: UBC Centre for Policy Studies in Education, 1996).

24 P. Gallagher, *Changing Course: An Agenda for Real Reform of Canadian Education* (Toronto: OISE Press, 1995).

25 Schuetze and Rubenson, *Learning in the Classroom;* Sharpe, *Apprenticeship in Canada.*

26 Council of Ministers of Education Canada (CMEC), *Transition from Initial Education to Working Life: A Canadian Report for an OECD Thematic Review* (Toronto: Council of Ministers of Education Canada, 1998); A. Gregor and G. Jasmin, *Higher Education in Canada* (Ottawa: Secretary of State, 1992).

27 Schuetze and Sweet, *Preparing for Work.*

28 U. Teichler, *Thematic Debate: The Requirements of the World of Work,* Paper ED-98/CONF.202/18 (Geneva: International Labour Organization, 2000).

29 Lin, Sweet, Anisef, and Schuetze, "Consequences and Policy Implications."

30 U. Teichler, *Thematic Debate,* 22-23.

31 U. Beck, *Risk Society: Towards a New Modernity* (London: Sage Publications, 1992).

32 A. Giddens, "Living in a Post-Traditional Society," *Reflexive Modernization: Politics, Tradition and Aesthetics in the Modern Social Order,* ed. U. Beck, A. Giddens, and S. Lash (Stanford, CA: Stanford University Press, 1994), 56-109.

33 Heinz, *Theoretical Advances.*

34 A. Furlong and F. Cartmel, *Young People and Social Change: Individualization and Risk in Late Modernity* (Buckingham, UK: Open University Press, 1997).

35 P. Rudd, "From Socialization to Post-Modernity: A Review of Theoretical Perspectives on the School-to-Work Transition," *Journal of Education and Work* 10 (1997): 257-78.

36 R. Marquardt, *Enter at Your Own Risk: Canadian Youth and the Labour Market* (Toronto: Between the Lines, 1998); H. Krahn, *School-Work Transitions: Changing Patterns and Research Needs* (Ottawa: Applied Research Branch, Human Resources Development Canada, 1996); CMEC, *Initial Education to Working Life.*

37 G. Lowe and H. Krahn, "Work Aspirations and Attitudes in an Era of Labour Market Restructuring: A Comparison of Two Canadian Cohorts," *Work, Employment and Society* 14 (2000): 1-22.

38 D. Looker, "In Search of Credentials: Factors Affecting Young Adults' Participation in Postsecondary Education," *Canadian Journal of Education* 27 (1997): 1-36; L. Andres and D. Looker, "Rurality and Capital: Educational Expectations and Attainments of Rural, Urban-Rural and Metropolitan Youth," *Canadian Journal of Higher Education* (in press); L. Andres, P. Anisef, H. Krahn, D. Looker, and V. Thiessen, "The Persistence of Social Structure: Class and Gender Effects on the Occupational Aspirations of Canadian Youth, *Journal of Youth Studies* 2 (1999): 261282; P. Anisef, R. Sweet, G. Plickert, and D. Tom-Kun, *The Effects of Region and Gender on Educational Planning in Canadian Families* (Toronto: Laidlaw Foundation, 2001); Sweet, Anisef and Lin, *Exploring Family Antecedents,* 2000.

39 Andres et al. "Persistence of Social Structure."

40 Elwood Epstein, J. Elwood, V. Hey, and J. Maw, *Failing Boys: Issues in Gender and Achievement* (Buckingham: Open University Press, 1998).

41 Skof, "Women."

42 Sharpe, *Apprenticeship in Canada.*

43 K. Hughes, "Women in Non-traditional Occupations," *Perspectives* 7 (1995): 14-19; K.

Hughes, *Gender and Self Employment in Canada: Assessing Trends and Policy Implications*, <http://www.cprn.ca/back_press/bgse_e.htm> (April 2001); Statistics Canada, *Education in Canada*.

44 M. Schneider, "Women in Non-Traditional Occupations: Educational Strategies that Work," *Education and Work*, vol. 2, *Proceedings of the International Conference Linking Research and Practice*, ed. D. Corson and S. Lawton (Toronto: OISE, 1990), 40-48; S. Wismer, *Women's Education and Training in Canada: A Policy Analysis* (Guelph: Canadian Congress for Learning Opportunities for Women, 1988).

45 S. Raudenbush and R. Kasim, "Cognitive Skill and Economic Inequality: Findings from the National Adult Literacy Survey," *Harvard Education Review* 68 (1998): 33-79; D. Looker and V. Thiessen, "Images of Work: Women's Work, Men's Work, Housework," *Canadian Journal of Sociology* 24, 2 (1999): 225-54; V. Thiessen and C. Nickerson, *Canadian Gender Trends in Education and Work* (Ottawa: Applied Research Branch, Human Resources Development Canada, 1999).

46 Skof, "Women."

47 Sharpe, *Apprenticeship in Canada*.

48 N. Guppy and S. Davies, *Education in Canada: Recent Trends and Future Challenge* (Ottawa: Statistics Canada, 1998).

49 Finnie, "Holding Their Own."

50 D. Boothby, *The Trade-Vocational Educational Pathway in Canada: 190 Trade-Vocational Graduates in the 1992 National Graduates and 1995 Follow-up Surveys* (Ottawa: Centre for Educational Statistics, Statistics Canada, 2000).

51 Schuetze and Rubenson, *Learning in the Classroom*; S. O'Hara and F. Evers, *Opportunity in Apprenticeship: An Analysis of the 1994/95 National Apprenticed Trades Survey* (Ottawa: Standards, Planning and Analysis Division, Human Resources Development Canada, 1996).

52 Sweet and Gallagher, *Women and Apprenticeships*.

53 I. Bakker, ed., "Introduction: The Gendered Foundations of Restructuring in Canada," *Rethinking Restructuring: Gender and Change in Canada* (Toronto: University of Toronto Press, 1996).

54 Statistics Canada, *Education in Canada*.

55 Human Resources Development Canada, *National Apprenticed Trades Survey* (Ottawa: Standards, Planning and Analysis Division, Human Resources Development Canada, 1994).

56 J. Gaskell, *Gender Matters from School to Work* (Philadelphia: Open University Press, 1992).

57 R. Sweet and Z. Lin, *Union Membership and Apprenticeship Completion*, working paper, Centre for Research on Work and Society, York University, Toronto, 1999; K. Hadley, "And We Still Ain't Satisfied": Gender Inequality in Canada – A Status Report for 2001 (Toronto: National Action Committee of the Status of Women and the Centre for Social Justice Foundation, 2001).

58 Sharpe, *Apprenticeship in Canada*.

59 Schuetze and Sweet, *Integrating School and Workplace Learning*.

60 K. Braid, "Neither Friendly nor Familiar: Language Styles, Stress and Macho," in *Surviving and Thriving: Women in Trades and Technology and Employment Equity, Proceedings of the Naramata Conference* (Winlaw, BC: Kootenay WITT, 1988), 61-68.

61 Business Council of British Columbia (BCBC), *The Third Option: Rewarding Careers via Non-University Pathways* (Vancouver: Business Council of British Columbia, 2001).

62 J. Jenson, *Shifting the Paradigm: Knowledge and Learning for Canada's Future* (Ottawa: Canadian Policy research Networks, 2001) (CPRN discussion paper no. F18).

11
Public Policy and Women's Access to Training in New Brunswick
Joan McFarland

From the Second World War until recently, the Canadian government saw providing training – including the sponsorship of training – to the labour force as one of its roles.[1] Since 1996, in the current neoliberal environment, all that has changed. It is now basically up to the individual to find and pay for her/his own training.[2]

Even during the period in which the government provided training, women's access to it was not equal to that of men. For example, in the early period much of the training was to prepare soldiers returning from the Second World War for re-entry into the labour force. However, from the 1960s to the 1990s, equity did become an issue in labour force training, and some programs that targeted women and other equity groups were offered. Although equality was not achieved, some progress was made. Beginning in the 1980s another group, this one comprised of social assistance recipients (SARs), was targeted for sponsorship in training programs. In fact, this was an overlapping group since most of the SARs were women. Then, in the late 1980s, women-only programs were dropped in favour of a gender-neutral approach – much to the dismay of women's organizations and programs.

By 1996, with the changes in the Employment Insurance (EI) program, all equity initiatives seem to have disappeared. In the new programs, such as Skills, Loans and Grants, participants have to meet Employment Insurance eligibility criteria even in order to receive loans. Women are given no special consideration and, in fact, at least in New Brunswick, are under-represented and, in some cases, grossly under-represented among the participants.[3]

Training has always been an area of federal jurisdiction. However, in 1996 a process of devolution began; that is, the delivery of training was transferred from the federal government to the provincial governments. The timing of the changes brought about by devolution coincided quite closely with the changes in the Employment Insurance program, and hence the two sets of changes are very much inter-related. On 13 December 1996

New Brunswick became the second province to enter into a devolution agreement, called a labour market development agreement, with the federal government. Under this agreement, the New Brunswick Department of Training and Employment Development receives monies transferred from the federal government and is in charge of the delivery of training.[4] However, New Brunswick is subject to various federally imposed conditions with regard to these programs.

Another trend that has been prominent in training and has affected women's access to it has been the increasing trend to the privatization of training. For example, in the 1980s in New Brunswick only a handful of private trainers offering secretarial skills training were operating. The community colleges provided the vast majority of training programs – even hairdressing. In the 1990s this all changed. The number of private training programs, many of them offering information technology, increased almost 100 percent while enrolment at the community colleges declined. In the year 2000 there were 4,548 students enrolled in private training programs, while in 2000-1 enrolment in the community college system was 9,578.[5] This despite the fact that the fees at private training schools are double (and more) those at the community colleges.

In this chapter I attempt to document the pattern of women's access to training in New Brunswick. In order to do so I have collected data, interviewed administrators, and held focus groups with potential and actual women trainees. I have found that data are available, broken down for gender, from most of the publicly funded programs (e.g., the community college system, the student loan program, and the recent Skills, Loans and Grants Program). Conversely, there is a great paucity of data on private training.

I approach the topic historically, providing an overview of training programs in New Brunswick from the 1970s to the present. I believe that this approach is not only useful but also necessary since it is the only way to see how the system actually works. The system is complicated and has been poorly documented, making generalization difficult.

During the period under consideration, training has come under the aegis of various federal strategies. These include, chronologically: the Canada Manpower Training Program, the National Training Act, the Canadian Jobs Strategy, the Labour Force Development Strategy, and the more recent shift to devolution and the labour market development agreements between Canada and each province. In looking at each program, I consider its social, political, and policy context; its purpose and rationale; its eligibility requirements; and the numbers and percentages of women and men trained under it. Then, taking a related approach, I examine female enrolment patterns at the community colleges in terms of programs and age of students. Both of these patterns are significant.

Based on such an analysis, and focusing on how availability of sponsorship functions as a barrier to women, my conclusion is that training
programs for women in New Brunswick have been spotty at best. There
have been few women-only programs, and those available have involved
relatively small numbers of specific groups of women. In some programs
men have been greatly favoured over women. Now both sponsored and
women-only programs have vanished, and discrimination in favour of
males is still evident.

Barriers to Women's Training

However, before beginning a discussion of the programs, I will briefly
review the barriers to training faced by women. While men and women
may face a number of the same barriers, these may affect them differently.
In addition, women face barriers that are not faced to the same extent-
by men. The literature on women's training identifies many barriers that
prevent women from getting the training that they want and need. These
barriers include those that are personal, family, societal, and bureaucratic.

Such personal barriers as lack of self-confidence and knowledge of how
the system works have prevented women from participating in some programs that have been available. In order to address these problems
pre-training bridging programs (i.e., programs that provide positive, supportive, safe, and woman centred-programming) have been advocated.[6]
None of these has been offered in New Brunswick, although there have
been a few in other provinces (Saskatchewan, Newfoundland, and British
Columbia).

Lack of family support is also a barrier to training. Too often this lack of
support escalates into violence when a woman engages in further education and/or training.[7] Broader societal barriers include poverty, various
forms of discrimination, and sex-role stereotyping.[8] In a family desper-
ately struggling to put food on the table, it is often not possible for the
wife/mother to take training. Another barrier is that many programs are
neither designed nor presented with appropriate sensitivity to the racial
and other diversities among women. Even when such women do begin
training programs, they may drop out because of this type of problem.

The sex-role stereotyping in our society dissuades women from taking
courses in so-called nontraditional areas (e.g., the trades). In addition,
women are often subject to sexual harassment when they do attempt to
enter these areas. The women who choose them need preparation (such
as that provided by bridging programs and ongoing support) in order to
succeed.

Bureaucratic barriers include access to information about programs.
Women often aren't aware of the programs that are available to them,[9]
and, if they are, they often have to persuade an employment counsellor of

their appropriateness for them. This may require a "selling job" (i.e., the woman has to sell herself as a good investment for the economy). This may be something that the woman either does not feel very comfortable with or is not very adept at.[10] As well, the eligibility criteria differ with different training programs. For some programs the woman must be an unemployment insurance (UI) recipient, for others she must be a social assistance recipient, and so forth. There are few programs for which all women are eligible. In terms of training allowances and other payments, the amounts paid compared to those paid in other programs (such as social assistance), the payment schedule, and inclusiveness of expenses are all critical issues. If any of these disadvantage a woman as compared to her previous status, then this is almost certain to prevent her from taking the training.[11]

The barrier that I stress in this chapter is a policy one – the lack of government-sponsored training. By sponsored training I mean training that covers tuition, living expenses, transportation, and daycare expenses for the trainee. Without the availability of such sponsorship, the other barriers listed above have little chance to come into play. And although private sponsorship (e.g., by industry) could also play an important role, in practice it has not done so.

Sponsorship has played a major role in government policy in Canada since the Second World War, with the introduction of the apprenticeship program. In the 1970s sponsorship was introduced in a number of other areas. In the 1980s and early 1990s, a number of programs covered daycare expenses. However, with the Employment Insurance Act, 1996, the concept of public sponsorship of training has apparently come to an end and loan programs have taken over. Where does this leave women and training?

Policies and Programs for Women's Training, 1970s to the Present

Women's training has taken place within the context of various national training strategies. Apprenticeship has been around since the Second World War. In the 1970s a Canada Manpower Training Program was introduced to reinforce the connection between training and economic development in Canada. The program also had equity and economic stabilization goals. In 1982 the National Training Act was passed. This program emphasized economic development over the latter two goals of the previous program, which included equity.[12] In 1985 a new strategy, the Canadian Jobs Strategy (CJS), was introduced with the stated purpose of linking job creation, work experience, and training under one labour market initiative. This strategy was replaced by the Labour Force Development Strategy (LFDS) in 1989. The latter's avowed purpose was to develop a "training culture" in the Canadian labour market.[13] Since 1996 changes in the Employment

Insurance Act and the policy of devolution of training to the provinces under labour market development agreements (LMDAs) have accelerated the adoption of a market-driven approach to training.

Along with each of these changes, proportionately fewer public funds have been spent on training. Since 1989, with the LFDS, no more funds from the federal government's consolidated revenues are being used for training. All training funds are taken from employee/employer contributions to UI funds.

Within the broad strategies outlined above, the design of particular programs has affected women's opportunities to gain access to training in New Brunswick. Figure 11.1 shows the various programs (indicated by downward pointing arrows) within the context of the broader strategies indicated on the right side of the chart. The length of the arrows indicates the starting and ending dates of the program, and the width of the arrows is an estimate of the numbers of women involved in the program on a yearly basis. As is clear from an initial inspection of Figure 11.1, some programs have lasted much longer than others. Similarly, some have offered training opportunities for large numbers of women while others have done so for only small numbers of women. Table 11.1 shows women's percentage representation in each of the programs. A brief description of each of the programs in terms of their special features in relation to access to women is given below.

CEIC Seat Purchase

CEIC (Canadian Employment and Immigration Commission) seat purchase consisted of the government purchasing seats in training institutions for unemployed and other prospective members of the labour force. This seat purchase began under the Canada Manpower Training Program in the 1970s and continued under various configurations until 1996. A participant, recommended for such training by an employment counsellor with CEIC, would be provided with a training allowance and transportation costs (where required).

In the early 1980s a certain percentage of training seats in nontraditional areas were reserved for women. However, it proved difficult to fill those seats on a regular basis, and by the time of the CJS in 1985 such reservation of seats had been dropped.[14]

In general, there has been very little gender-specific data available on the CEIC seat purchase program. When I requested some in the early 1990s it took almost a year for it to arrive, and it was both hand delivered and partly handwritten. It was for the fiscal year 1992-93.

The data were for training both inside and outside of the province. In that year – 1992-93 – 6,159, or 48.4 percent of the 12,721 who received private training through seat purchase, were females. Adding those who received training through the NB Community College system, 6,782, or 43 percent of 15,753, were females.

Apprenticeship

Apprenticeship is the oldest of the training programs, and New Brunswick began its program in 1944. One becomes an apprentice by either finding a tradesperson willing to take on an apprentice or by being placed with a tradesperson after a pre-employment course at a community college. Up until recently, a Grade 12 education was not required. Before the 1996 Employment Insurance Act changes, the courses (as well as transportation to them and a living allowance) were provided by CEIC.

Women have never played more than a very minor role in the apprenticeship program, probably because most of the trades are nontraditional for women. Most of the female apprentices are cooks. Formerly, hairdressing came under the program, but it does so no longer. However, barbers are still included, and some women choose this trade.

As shown in Table 11.2, in the period between 1986 and 2001 the average

Figure 11.1

Three decades of training programs for females in New Brunswick

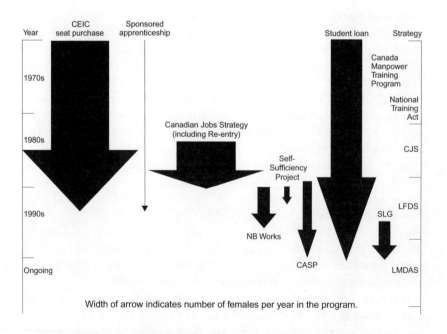

Width of arrow indicates number of females per year in the program.

annual number of female apprentices taking courses in the community college system was fifty-two out of an average of 2,115 apprentices in any given year. This means that, on average, female apprentices were 2.1 percent of all apprentices at the community colleges during this period. These numbers are down even from the 1986 to 1997 period, when there was an average fifty-two female apprentices annually and they formed 2.3 percent of the total (which is also in decline). Attempts have been made over the years to increase the number of female apprentices, and there has been some variation (as is shown in Table 11.2), but the numbers are still extremely low.

Table 11.1

Female participation in various programs in New Brunswick

Program	Females yearly # (est.)	Females as % of total participants
Seat purchase CEIC (1970s-1996)	6,782	43.0
Apprenticeship (1944-present)	48	2.3
Canadian Jobs Strategy (CJS) (1985-89)	9,758	38.9
Re-entry (Sept. 85-Sept. 89)	341	99.7
NB Works (1992-98)	811	84.0
Self-Sufficiency Project (1992-94)	293	95.4
Community Academic Services (CASP) (1991-present)	985	57.0
Student loans (net of university) (1997-98)	5,087	56.6
Skills, Loans and Grants (SLG) (Oct. 1997-present)	1,628	35.8

Sources: Seat purchase: data provided by Human Resources Canada regional office; Apprenticeship: data provided by NB Department of Training and Employment Development; CJS: Background paper, "Women's Training Needs in New Brunswick," doc. 2 (prepared for the New Brunswick Advisory Council on the Status of Women, March 1993), 20; Re-entry: *Evaluation of the Job Entry Program, Final Report* (Ottawa: EIC Strategic Policy and Planning, July 1989), 12-15; NB Works: Joan McFarland and Bob Mullaly, "NB Works: Myth vs. Reality," in *Remaking Canadian Social Policy: Social Security in the 1990s*, ed. Jane Pulkingham and Gordon Ternowetsky (Halifax: Fernwood, 1996), Tables 1 and 2, pp. 17-18; Self-Sufficiency: *When Financial Incentives Encourage Work: Complete 18-Month Findings from the Self-Sufficiency Project* (Vancouver: SRDC, September 1998), 16, 17, 76; CASP: *Final Report, CASP Program Evaluation* (prepared for Literacy NB Inc., 31 December 1997), 14; Student loans: calculated from *New Brunswick Student Aid, Statistical Profile, 1997-98*, 3, and data provided by NB Student Aid; SLG: data provided by NB Department of Training and Employment Development.

The Re-Entry Program under CJS

The CJS, which was initiated in 1985, was made up of five programs. One of these was Job Entry. Within Job Entry was Re-entry, which was a program to aid housewives returning to the labour force after at least a three-year absence. Re-entry could be coordinated by a public institution, a private trainer/consultant, or a voluntary organization. The programs included life skills, job search, as well as on-the-job training and were of relatively short duration – four months to one year. Sponsored by CEIC, all costs for participants were covered, including living expenses, transportation, and childcare.

In New Brunswick, from September 1985 to September 1987, there were sixteen privately sponsored Re-entry programs and seven publicly sponsored ones.[15] The Re-entry program overlapped for several years with the LFDS. As is shown in Figure 11.1 and Table 11.1, there were on average 341 participants annually in Re-entry programs in New Brunswick between September 1985 and September 1987, a relatively small number in terms of the overall CJS picture (e.g., 25,085 participants in New Brunswick in

Table 11.2

Females in apprenticeship, New Brunswick, 1986-2001[a]

Year	Female apprentices at community colleges[b]	Total apprentices at community college[b]	Females as % of total apprentices at community colleges	Active apprentices[c] in NB
1986-87	34	1837	1.9	3328
1987-88	42	1905	2.2	3546
1988-89	58	2017	2.9	4003
1989-90	71	2651	2.7	4200
1990-91	86	3061	2.8	4712
1991-92	69	2895	2.4	4666
1992-93	56	2447	2.3	4362
1993-94	61	2396	2.5	4145
1994-95	53	2067	2.6	4082
1995-96	27	1879	1.4	3526
1996-97	19	1596	1.2	3205
1997-98	25	1483	1.7	3070
1998-99	21	1620	1.3	2957
1999-2000	31	1787	1.7	3376
2000-1	35	2079	1.7	–

[a]   Apprentices at community colleges: data supplied by NB Department of Education; Active apprentices: data from *Annual Report, Department of Training and Employment Development*, various years.
[b]   Taking courses that year at the community college.
[c]   Registered as apprentices that year, male and female.

1989-90). Women constituted 99.7 percent of the participants in the Re-entry program.

NB Works

NB Works was Premier Frank McKenna's showpiece, and it was touted as "a wonderful opportunity for the women of New Brunswick."[16] Launched in 1992, the three-year program targeted "employable" social assistance recipients with a less than Grade 12 education. There were places for three cohorts of 1,000 participants each. The program involved an initial community workplace placement followed by academic upgrading and training of the participant's choice. Participants were supported with living expenses, transportation, and childcare. Over the 1992-98 period of the program, there was an average of 811 participants in each cohort (taking account of drop-outs). Eighty-four percent of these were female.

Self-Sufficiency Project (SSP)

The SSP was an experiment with earnings supplements, and it was conducted through CEIC by the Social Research and Demonstration Corporation (SRDC) between 1992 and 1995.[17] It was carried out in both British Columbia and New Brunswick. In New Brunswick it ran concurrently with the early part of NB Works. The targeted participants were single parents who had been on social assistance for at least one year. The basic idea of the SSP was to give participants a chance to prepare for and find employment, then to supplement their earnings from that employment up to some minimum level (e.g., $30,000) for a certain period. The outcomes were then compared with those in a control group of social assistance recipients not in the SSP. Employment was the main goal. Training was sponsored, but voluntary, under the SSP and, if taken, had to be completed during the preparation for employment phase.

In New Brunswick an average of 293 female participants received an earnings supplement under the SSP each year. The overwhelming majority of participants (95.5 percent) were female.[18]

Community Academic Services Program (CASP)

CASP is a literacy program that was developed in 1991 and that provides literacy training free of charge in communities throughout the province.[19] Considered by some as a cost-cutting initiative, it replaces literacy training previously given in the community colleges.[20] The communities involved are expected to make a contribution to the program in terms of fundraising and the provision of space and so on. CASP is a program within which the majority of students are female. Data show that, for the 1991-97 period, 5,417, or 57 percent, of the total 9,504 participants in CASP were female.[21] Sponsorship in the program is sparse. From 1991 to 1994, under a Canada-New Brunswick LFDA, allowances were provided for UI recipients attending CASP, but that has ceased. Now only income assistance recipients receive support while in the program.[22]

Canada Student Loans (CSL) Program

Obviously, the CSL program is not a sponsorship program since the loans have to be paid back with full interest.[23] However, they do play a role in women's access to training.

The CSL program has been around since 1964. Originally, New Brunswick only supplemented CSL with bursaries. However, in recent years provincial loans have been given, with reduced monies for bursaries. Support is provided for attendance at all forms of secondary education, including university, community college, and registered private trainers.

The CSL program is very large and covers many students. For example, in 1997-98, 8,985 students received student loans to study in New Brunswick. Women were the majority of these students – 56.6 percent – as they have been for the past number of years.[24]

Some of the reasons put forward for this is that, due to their disadvantaged position in the labour market and the fact that there has been a higher level of sponsorship for men under such programs as apprenticeship and seat purchase, women are unable to earn as much as men in summer jobs.[25] It should be noted that these figures are for the number of students not the amount spent. Thus, the fact that women's courses may be shorter and/or cost less than men's courses is not taken into account.

Skills, Loans and Grants (SLG) Program

The SLG program came out of the Employment Insurance Act, 1996.[26] It replaces all seat purchase with provisions for present employment insurance (EI)[27] recipients or for those who have been recipients within the past three years (five years if maternity leave was taken during the period) with a combination loan/grant to be used for training purposes. The loan/grant is intended to cover tuition and living expenses, and a case manager for the program assesses the individual.

In New Brunswick this assessment is based on the perceived return on investment to the province. The loan/grant division initially adopted by the province was $3,500 in a loan, with the rest made up in a grant.[28] However, because New Brunswick has not been able to find a financial institution to underwrite the loan portion of the program, to date all of the monies have been in the form of grants. Thus, the SLG program has been a bonanza for those who have received support under it.

Data supplied by the SLG program for two periods – 1997-99 and 1999-2001 – show that participants in the bonanza were 64 percent males during the former and 61.1 percent males during the latter (see Table 11.3).

Gender disparity is also reflected in the amounts of funds granted – over $18 million in total to male participants in the first period and $38 million in the second period, whereas the corresponding amounts for females were $13 million and under $31 million. As had been the case in the CEIC seat purchase program, the discretionary aspect of the case manager's role may play a considerable part in the lower support rate for women.

One example of this lower rate is the support for students at the Information Technology Institute (ITI) in Moncton, New Brunswick. ITI is a private trainer that claims to have a high job placement rate for its graduates; however, it also has a high tuition (e.g., $23,000 for a ten-month program). Females made up only 25 percent of the students sponsored in 1997-99, and this dropped to 22 percent in the 1999-2001 period. See Table 11.4.

Women's Participation in the Community Colleges
Over the years, aspects of women's access to training may be seen from a different perspective by looking at women's participation in the community colleges. The main determining factor for such access would again seem to be government policy – specifically, the availability of training sponsorship. However, perhaps the trend to information technology training has been another factor that has led to some shifts in enrolment patterns, with young people from universities not only attending private training institutions but also community colleges.

Enrolment
Data supplied by New Brunswick community colleges show that female enrolment reached a peak in 1995-96, at 7,109, and that it has since

Table 11.3

Male/female grants under the Skills, Loans and Grants (SLG) program in New Brunswick

	Number	% of total	Average size of grant	$ spent	% of $ spent
1 October 1997-1 May 1999					
Males	4965	64.2%	$3658.20	$18,162,967	58.7%
Females	2767	35.8%	$4610.60	$12,757,524	41.3%
Total	7732	100%	$3999.03	$30,920,491	100%
1 May 1999-30 May 2001					
Males	7419	61.1%	$5103.10	$37,859,900	56.3%
Females	4934	39.9%	$6209.54	$30,637,852	44.7%
Total	12353	100%	$5545.03	$68,497,752	100%

Source: Calculated from data provided by NB Department of Training and Employment Development.

declined to 4,182 in 2000-1. Much of this very significant decline reflects an overall decline in enrolment at the community colleges. As a percentage of total enrolment, females reached a peak of 45.9 percent in 1988-89, a low of 34.9 percent in 1991-92, and were back up to 43.7 percent in 2000-1.[29]

Programs Women Are Taking

Data show that although, in some cases, it appears that there are "male" and "female" programs, over the years there have been considerable shifts in the programs women are taking.[30] As examples of the first pattern, apprenticeship is clearly a male program, while second language is a female program. And job readiness, a small program in terms of total enrolment and that has not been offered in New Brunswick since 1994, had been a female-dominated program. In a greater number of cases, however, there have been dramatic switches in gender domination in various programs. These switches suggest that gender dominance depends on which sponsored programs are being offered and on who is eligible for them. In the programs relating to academic upgrading and pre-employment, male-dominated enrolment has switched to female-dominated enrolment. The former switch may be explained by the NB Works program, which had almost solely female participants. In the special program category there had been a dramatic shift from female- to male-dominated enrolment. This suggests something about the difference between the CJS and the LFDS, with the latter paying far less attention to equity.

Changing Age Groups in Training

The community colleges enrolment data also show a considerable change in the dominance of certain age groups in training over the period 1985-

Table 11.4

Male/female grants to Information Technology Institute students under the Skills, Loans and Grants (SLG) program in New Brunswick

	Number	% of total	Average size of grant	$ spent	% of $ spent
1 October 1997-1 May 1999					
Males	73	75.3%	$10,664.42	$708,475	73.5%
Females	24	24.7%	$ 9,705.14	$255,946	26.5%
Total	97	100%	$ 9,942.48	$964,421	100%
1 May 1999-30 May 2001					
Males	69	75.8%	$ 8,825.03	$608,927	75.7%
Females	22	24.2%	$ 8,870.50	$195,151	24.3%
Total	91	100%	$ 8,836.02	$804,078	100%

Source: Calculated from data provided by NB Department of Training and Employment Development.

2001. This offers further evidence of the sensitivity of enrolment to the sponsorship of training and the eligibility for such sponsorship, but it also suggests that, in this neoliberal era, some young people are choosing skills training over university education.

The data for both males and females show that, whereas in the earlier period, 1985-86 to 1992-93, the 30- to 34-years age group was in the majority; since 1993-94, the 20- to 24-years age group has taken over that position. Looking at female enrolments alone, again the younger age groups dominate in the latter period. Table 11.5 gives some of the details of this information by comparing the dominant age groups for each of the programs for the years 1987-88, 1997-98, and 2000-1. The main pattern that emerges shows the switch from dominance from the 30- to 34-years age group to the 20- to 24-years age group. This is the case in academic upgrading, pre-employment, and technical programs. In technology, the switch downward is from the 25- to 29-years age group to the 20- to 24-years age group. In upgrading, the shift is from the 45+ years age group to the 25- to 29-years age group in 1997-98, and it is shared between the 25- to 29-years and 20- to 24-years age groups in 2000-1. In second language, it is from 45+ years age group to the 20- to 24-years age group: an even more dramatic shift. In two programs the direction of the switches varies during the 1997-98 and 2000-1. In job readiness, the younger age group in 1997-98 is 25-29 years old rather than 20-24 years old. However, in 2000-1 the dominant age group has shot up to 45+ years. In apprenticeship, the two moves are in the reverse direction: the dominant age group moves up from 30-34 years to 35-39 years in 1997-98, whereas in 2000-1 it moves down to 20-24 years. In only one instance does dominant female enrolment move to a higher age group: in the category "special," the move is from 30-34 years to 45+ years in both 1987-88 and 2000-1.

What Are the Issues?

Under-Representation
Women's numerical and percentage representation in training programs in New Brunswick has been shown above.[31] Women have been under-represented in the sponsored training programs that have been available – drastically so in apprenticeships but also in CEIC's seat purchase scheme, the CJS, and the new SLG program. And this trend is increasing rather than decreasing in some aspects of the latter program. Women have only been well represented in the few programs that have been specifically targeted at them – Re-entry, NB Works, and the SSP. However, these programs were all short-lived and, relatively speaking, covered few women.

What is the appropriate representation of women in sponsored programs? There is little discussion of this question in any of the documents,

Table 11.5

Changes in dominant age groups in female enrolment at the community colleges, various programs, 1987-88, 1997-98, and 2000-1

Program	1987-88		1997-98			2000-1		
	Largest age group	% of total	Largest age group	% of total	Direction of change 87-88 to 97-98	Largest age group	% of total	Direction of change 97-98 to 2000-1
Academic upgrading	30-34	26.7	20-24	19.4	→	20-24	33.7	k*
Apprenticeship	30-34	31.0	35-39	32.0	←	20-24	40.0	
Job readiness training	30-34	50.0	25-29	18.2	→	45+	33.0	
Pre-employment	30-34	31.4	20-24	47.2	→	20-24	60.9	k
Second language	45+	43.5	20-24	29.7	→	20-24	26.7	k
Special	30-34	26.4	45+	25.5	←	45+	20.0	k
Technical	30-34	36.1	20-24	52.4	→	20-24	52.2	k
Technology	25-29	51.5	20-24	53.6	→	20-24	53.9	k
Upgrading	45+	44.4	25-29	24.9	→	25-29	28.0	k
Overall	30-34	27.9	20-24	34.9	→	20-24	39.7	k

*k = no change
Source: Data provided by the NB Department of Training and Employment Development.

although one source suggests that the CEIC's target in the early 1990s for the CJS was 40 percent, "the same as women's representation in the labour force."[32] I believe that this number should receive some discussion. In postsecondary education generally, female enrolments outnumber male enrolments. In New Brunswick this is reflected in university enrolments – women making up as much as two-thirds of the enrolment in liberal arts programs.[33] The fact that women outnumber men in New Brunswick's student loan program also suggests that they are seeking at least equal access to postsecondary education and training. The exception is the male/female enrolment ratio at the community colleges, which has remained pretty steady at 60/40 since the mid-1980s (now 57/43). However, this may well be a reflection of the sponsorship pattern and the apprenticeship situation.[34]

Sponsorship

If the availability of sponsorship has been a major factor in women's access to training, then what has happened with the virtual withdrawal of such sponsorship following the 1996 changes in the Employment Insurance Act? The impact of this withdrawal is quite clearly illustrated in Table 11.6, which compares sponsorship at the community colleges for both males and females in 1996-97, 1997-98, and 2000-1. The 1996-97 and 1997-98 figures show the situation before and directly after the Employment Insurance changes, while the 2000-1 figures show the current situation. A large percentage of the students are now non-sponsored. Specifically, non-sponsored students increased from 42.8 percent of total enrolments in 1996-97 to 62.3 percent in 1997-98 to 73.4 percent in 2000-1. CEIC sponsorship declined from 13.4 percent in 1996-97 to just 0.1 percent in 2000-1, while industry sponsorship declined from 10.2 percent to 0.9 percent over the same period. The decline in the "other" category has been less severe – from 33.6 percent in 1996-97 to 25.6 percent in 2000-1. This probably reflects NB Works sponsorship in 1996-97 and SLG program sponsorship in 2000-1, which is being recorded in the "other" category.

Table 11.6

Sponsorship by category at the community colleges: Males and females, 1996-97, 1997-98, and 2000-1 as a % of all enrolments

Source	1996-97	1997-98	2000-1
CEIC	13.4	2.8	.1
Industry	10.2	4.4	.9
Other	33.6	30.5	25.6
Non-sponsored	42.8	62.3	73.4

Source: Calculated from data provided by the NB Department of Training and Employment.

Looking at the situation for females only, Table 11.7 and Figure 11.2 show female sponsorship at the community colleges for the period from 1985-86 to 2000-1. The data make clear the increase in the numbers of females in the non-sponsored category and the virtual elimination of CEIC sponsorship, which had peaked in the late 1980s – the CJS era. The very small amount of industry sponsorship of females decreased even further during this period. The quite substantial sponsorship in the "other" category in the 1988-91 period in the CJS era and later in the mid-1990s in the NB Works era dropped sharply in 1998. In the 1999-2001 period, female sponsorship in the "other" category has returned to approximately 1,000, about one-quarter of the mid-1990s level. The current numbers in this category are probably a reflection of SLG program sponsorship.

In fact, in terms of data on females as a percentage of those sponsored, women are most highly represented in this "other" category. In industry sponsored training, women as a percentage of the total were higher in the late 1980s and early 1990s and have since become very low. Women as a percentage of the total in CEIC sponsored training show a steady decline to 1998-99 while the recent higher percentage numbers are not significant because the absolute numbers are so very low. The decline in CEIC sponsorship up until 1997 is also a reflection of the fact that with other programs being dropped, apprenticeship – with its chronic under-representation of women – had become one of the few remaining programs.

Figure 11.2

Sponsorship of females at the community colleges, 1985-2001

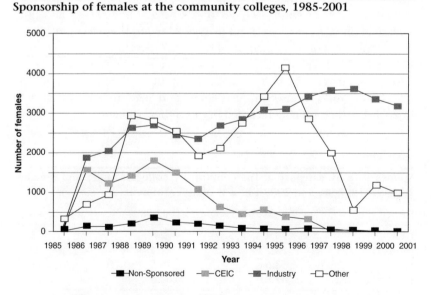

Table 11.7

Sponsorship of females at the community colleges, 1985-2001

Year	Non-sponsored		CEIC-sponsored		Industry-sponsored		Other sponsored		Total sponsored	
	Number females	Females as % of non-sponsored	Number females	Females as % of non-sponsored	Number females	Females as % of non-sponsored	Number females	Females as % of sponsored	Total females sponsored	Females as % of total sponsored
1985-86	128	44.6	131	36.9	24	70.6	335	34.4	490	35.9
1986-87	1886	45.1	1565	34.0	155	19.2	701	37.2	2421	33.2
1987-88	2044	46.5	1214	32.5	113	11.8	939	37.5	2266	31.5
1988-89	2618	48.2	1416	32.5	196	38.3	2946	55.0	4558	44.6
1989-90	2689	48.0	1787	31.2	353	35.4	2799	53.4	4939	41.3
1990-91	2454	47.5	1488	26.6	225	28.0	2542	45.7	4285	35.8
1991-92	2347	44.1	1066	21.7	189	31.8	1912	38.6	3167	30.2
1992-93	2672	44.0	623	17.0	150	24.2	2101	41.7	2874	30.9
1993-94	2825	42.4	433	13.6	70	10.5	2735	46.6	3238	33.3
1994-95	3073	45.1	557	17.6	67	7.8	3410	55.0	4034	39.5
1995-96	3093	45.4	377	14.2	42	5.3	4147	53.2	4566	40.5
1996-97	3404	45.6	313	13.4	96	5.4	2857	48.6	3266	32.7
1997-98	3567	39.4	17	4.2	71	11.1	1996	45.0	2084	38.1
1998-99	3602	43.4	30	2.9	27	16.2	524	44.7	587	24.8
1999-2000	3346	44.9	39	23.9	7	5.4	1175	45.3	1221	42.3
2000-1	3173	45.1	3	33.3	20	24.19	986	40.2	1009	39.6

Source: Data supplied by NB Department of Training and Employment Development.

Eligibility for Sponsorship

Only CEIC's seat purchase program was officially an open eligibility program. Both UI recipients and non-recipients were eligible for training sponsorship. However, it has been alleged that discretion on the part of the employment counsellor and persuasiveness on the part of the potential trainee played a major role in determining who did and who did not get sponsorship.[35]

Under the new SLG program, in order to receive training a person has to be on EI or to have been on it within the last three years (or five years if on maternity leave). This greatly narrows the number of those eligible for the program. With women being a smaller percentage of EI recipients, as mentioned above, they are in a disadvantaged position.

The targeted and/or women-only programs have all been for specific groups of women. Re-entry was for women who had been out of the labour force for at least three years; NB Works was for women on income assistance who had a less than Grade 12 education; the SSP was for single parents who had been on income assistance for at least one year. Obviously, these programs excluded many potential trainees.

Women-Only and/or Bridging Programs

There is the issue of women-only and/or bridging programs. In the late 1970s and early 1980s, places in the seat purchase program in nontraditional occupations were held for women.[36] However, as has been mentioned, when a number of these seats were left unfilled, this practice was dropped. Various women's groups suggested that, in order to deal with the situation, women needed more support when entering into training, particularly in nontraditional occupations. Bridging programs were proposed, and a few were offered in Saskatchewan, Newfoundland, and British Columbia.[37]

However, in 1989, with the introduction of the LFDS, not only bridging programs but also the concept of women-only programs lost support. Such programs were abandoned, with the explanation that "they were not needed."[38] Many women's groups disagreed with this.

In New Brunswick, up until the late 1980s, career orientation for women courses were offered in the community colleges. They fell by the wayside as Re-entry and other programs were dropped, and so far they have not reappeared.[39]

Training for SARs

Up until 1985 individuals receiving social assistance were not permitted to gain access to training programs. Social assistance was a so-called passive program. However, the thinking of policy makers was changing, and in the early 1980s active programs were being promoted for SARs. The 1985 employability enhancement agreements for SARs – financed fifty-fifty by the federal and provincial governments, respectively – embodied this new approach. Training for SARs was encouraged, and New Brunswick signed its first agreement with the federal government in 1987. The program in New Brunswick was called "Focus," and it attempted to get as many SARs as possible into the Re-entry programs under the CJS. It is estimated that SARs made up 27 percent of the Re-entry participants across Canada.[40]

In 1992 New Brunswick signed a second employability enhancement agreement. This led to the financing of the NB Works program, which was exclusively directed towards SARs. NB Works had an 84 percent female participation rate. The SSP, also financed by CEIC but under a different program, was also for SARs only. These two programs, both starting in 1992, were short-lived. NB Works ended in 1998, the SSP in 1995.

Now, at the beginning of the new millennium, there are few training options for SARs. They are still permitted to take training, but sponsored training, such as that under NB Works, is non-existent. The only options left for a social assistance recipient are either to take a CASP literacy program or to borrow funds for training under the student loan program. The only sponsored program would be SLG, but eligibility would be limited to those who have been recent EI recipients. Other than that, the only recent programs for SARs have been short-term job placement programs such as Jobs Plus and Rural Experience (and now the Workability Program).[41] None of these programs contains a training component.

One of the major criticisms of the training programs of the 1980s and early 1990s was that, in the high unemployment economy, they never seemed to lead to a job for participants. "I've been on programs and programs and never got a job," complained one female social assistance recipient.[42] However, instead of responding by enhancing the job placement phase of the programs, policy makers cut out their training aspect altogether. The result of this is that participants are placed in minimum skill jobs. The whole purpose of the training seems to have been abandoned.

The Present/Future

Women's access to training has experienced ups and downs from the 1970s to the present. In general, access has been variable, but there have been some programs that sponsored training for women. Most of these were short-lived and only covered particular groups of women; however, they did exist and some women did benefit from them. In the new market-driven economy, sponsorship has virtually disappeared. Women-only programs have disappeared. A woman wishing to undertake training has few choices if she or a family member does not have the funds to pay for it.

To persuade people to engage in employment training, promotion by trainers – mostly private but also community colleges – seems to have replaced sponsorship. Every day the newspapers are full of ads suggesting that the trainer in question offers the "ideal" training program leading to the "ideal" job. A member of the New Brunswick Status of Women Council suggested to me that this promotion seems to rest on "selling dreams" – quite a powerful message in a jobless economy.

Conclusion

If the premise of this chapter is true – that the absence of sponsorship is the most significant barrier to women's training – then with the virtual elimination of such sponsorship during the market-driven approach to training of the present era, we can expect a significant decline in women's training. Recent evidence in New Brunswick on enrolments, sponsorship, and programs for women seems to bear this out.

Notes

1 I would like to thank my research assistants, Maggie Gorman and Jennifer Flavin of St. Thomas University; the people in New Brunswick who either provided me with data, allowed me to interview them, answered my questionnaire, or participated in focus groups; and Mary Shortall, the CLC regional training advisor, for all of her help.
2 For more details, see Joan McFarland and Abdella Abdou, "What's Happening with Training in New Brunswick?" in *Training Matters: Working Paper Series, Labour Education and Training Research Network* (York University, Centre for Research on Work and Society, May 1998).
3 I do not consider the fact that women who have been on maternity leave are eligible for SLG if they have been on EI during the previous five years rather than the previous three to be significant enough to constitute "special consideration for women."
4 The current Department of Training and Employment Development has had different names and configurations during the period examined here. At the time of the signing of the devolution agreement it was the Department of Labour. Before that it was the Department of Advanced Education and Labour, and before that it was the Department of Advanced Education and Training. In an attempt to avoid confusion I refer to the department by its current name.
5 Data on enrolments provided by the Department of Training and Employment Development.
6 Aisla Thomson, "Editorial: Training for Whom?" *Women's Education des femmes,* Special Issue, *What's Happening with Women's Training in Canada?* 10, 3/4 (1993): 2. See also Sylvia Ash, Helen King, Dorothy Robbins, Gladys Watson, and WISE participants, "Women Interested in Successful Employment: Perspectives on a Bridging Program," *Women's Education des femmes* 7, 2 (1989): 30-34.
7 Kathleen Rockhill, "Literacy as Threat/Desire," *Women's Education des femmes* 5, 3 (1987): 9-12.
8 Ingrid Wellmeier, "Transitions Research by the Women's Reference Group," *Women's Education des femmes* 10, 3/4 (1993): 37.
9 This was emphasized by women in the focus groups I organized.
10 This came out in a number of my interviews with women.
11 This was another point that was emphasized in the focus groups, especially the one with SARs. Of particular concern was the possibility of keeping their health cards while they were in training.
12 Stephen McBride, "The Political Economy of Training in Canada," in *Training Matters: Working Paper Series*, Labour and Education and Training Research Network (Toronto: York University, Centre for Research and Society, May 1998), 4.

13 Elspeth Tulloch, "Background Paper: Women's Training Needs in New Brunswick," document 2 (prepared for the New Brunswick Advisory Council on the Status of Women, March 1993), 4.

14 Susan Wismer, "Women's Training and Education in Canada" (prepared for the Canadian Congress for Learning Opportunities for Women, 1988), 8.

15 CEIC, *Program Evaluation Report: Evaluation of Job Entry Program, Final Report* (Ottawa: CEIC, July 1989), 62.

16 Joan McFarland and Bob Mullaly, "NB Works: Image vs. Reality," in *Remaking Social Policy: Social Security in the Late 1990s*, ed. Jane Pulkingham and Gordon Ternowetsky (Halifax: Fernwood, 1996), 202-19.

17 Social Research and Demonstration Corporation for HRDC, *When Financial Incentives Encourage Work: Complete 18 Month Findings from the Self-sufficiency Project* (Vancouver: SRDC, September 1998).

18 Ibid., 16.

19 Baseline Market Research for Literacy NB, *Final Report: CASP Evaluation Program* (Fredericton: Baseline Market Research Ltd., 31 December 1997).

20 Dorothy MacKeracher, "CASP! Do You Really Want One in Your Neighbourhood?" *Women's Education des femmes* 11, 1 (Spring, 1994): 49-52.

21 Baseline Market Research for Literacy NB, *Final Report*, 14.

22 Information from CASP administrator, New Brunswick Department of Training and Employment Development, June 1999.

23 In New Brunswick the student loan program is variously referred to as NB Student Aid and NB Student Financial Assistance. It is under the Department of Education.

24 *New Brunswick Student Aid: Statistical Profile 1997-98* (Fredericton, NB: Department of Education), 2.

25 Information from NB student loan administrator, April 1999.

26 The SLG program is now called Training and Skills Development.

27 With the passing of the Employment Insurance Act in 1996, unemployment insurance (UI) is now referred to as employment insurance (EI).

28 Information from interview with SLG administrator, New Brunswick Department of Advanced Education and Labour, summer 1998.

29 From data supplied by the New Brunswick Department of Training and Employment Development.

30 Unfortunately, similar data from private trainers are not available.

31 See Table 11.1.

32 Tulloch, "Background Paper," 21.

33 For example, at my university, St. Thomas, which is a liberal arts college, women made up 71 percent of full-time enrolment in the academic year 1998-99. Information from registrar's office.

34 Joan McFarland, and Abdella Abdou, "What's Happening with Training," 36.

35 This information came from interviews with women. One woman had gone three times over a number of years before she was given a training seat. Her qualifications had not changed during this period.

36 Wismer, "Women's Training and Education."

37 See note 6.

38 Elspeth Tulloch, "Where Are the Women? Federal Training Policy and the Gender Factor," *Women's Education des femmes* 10, 3/4 (1993/94): 4-7.

39 Tulloch, "Background Paper," 22.

40 CEIC, *Program Evaluation*, 12ff.

41 Information from interview with administrators in Human Resources Development New Brunswick, fall 1998, and from the SAR focus group.

42 Joan McFarland, "Combining Economic and Social Policy through Work and Welfare: The Impact on Women," in *Papers on Economic Equality* (Ottawa: Status of Women Canada, 1994), 157.

12
Still Shopping for Training: Women, Training, and Livelihoods
Karen Lior and Susan Wismer

Shopping for Training

In 1996 the government of Canada decided that people should shop for their labour market training. As part of a general shift in policy towards privatization and "market-driven" solutions, changes to the federal Employment Insurance (EI) Act as legislated in 1996 shifted funding away from sponsored training programs and towards individual subsidies.[1] The result has been that, today, women's choices for training and employment services are, at the same time, more limited and greater than ever before. For the woman on social assistance, there are typically a very restricted number of programs offering minimal training opportunities. On the other hand, for the declining number of people who qualify for EI-related training, changes in federal policy have created a wide range of potential choice.

As every wise shopper knows, making a good purchase depends on availability, quality, and price. What range of choices is there? Do the available choices offer something suitable in the way of size, fit, and style? What about quality? Is the quality high enough to make for a durable, usable, and attractive purchase? And price? Is it affordable and good value? In situations where any of availability, quality, or price is a problem, the shopper is faced with a difficult dilemma: accept an unsuitable, inferior, and/or overly expensive product or go home empty-handed.

Information on the impacts of the new policy has only recently become available. As of Spring 2001 Labour Market Development Agreements (LMDAs), finalizing devolution to the provinces, had been signed in all provinces but Ontario. Most agreements, however, are still in the early stages of implementation. Ontario's agreement negotiation process as of fall 2000 was "on hold" and may stay on hold indefinitely. Training-related changes to the EI Act have been effectively implemented since 1997, with the first statistical information on impacts becoming available in late 1999. As a result of social welfare reform at the federal level in 1996 through the Canada Health and Social Transfer (CHST), changes to training available to social assistance recipients in various provinces have also come into effect from 1997 on. In Ontario, for example, "women seeking to re-enter the paid workforce may have little recourse to programmes other than work-for welfare."[2] There are very few options for women on social assistance to gain access to programs that will significantly change their lives, moving them to self-sufficiency and financial security. In this area too, systematic information about the impacts and effects of the changes that have taken place during the past five years is still largely unavailable.

Emerging evidence, from available reports and from a short study we carried out during the summer and fall of 2001, indicates that, increasingly, women are returning home from their training shopping trips empty-handed.[3] The power to purchase means little if there is nothing to buy. Shopping can be a frustrating and discouraging process when a much-needed item is unavailable, out-of-stock, or financially out of reach.

Women: In and Out of Fashion
One aspect of the problem is that women, never entirely *in* fashion with policy makers, have now clearly and definitely gone out of fashion. Although the particular training needs of women have been recognized in Canada and around the world for over twenty-five years, the direction of Canadian policy since 1989 has progressively moved away from specific mechanisms directed towards meeting women's needs and interests. At the same time, policies have moved towards increasingly privatized, market-driven arrangements that place responsibility for gaining access to and arranging training in the hands of those who qualify.[4]

The unique and important labour market training needs of women were first clearly articulated in 1970 in the Report of the Royal Commission on the Status of Women chaired by Florence Bird.[5] Recommendation Number 82 in that report called for

> the federal department of Manpower and Immigration, in co-operation with provinces and territories, [to] develop policies and practices that will result in an increase in the number of women undertaking educational upgrading programmes and training for more highly skilled occupations, and the enrolment of women in courses in line with their capacities without regard to sex-typing of occupations, an increase in the number of women training for managerial and technical positions, and the consideration by women of the whole spectrum of occupations before choosing training courses.

The next recommendation called for postsecondary educational institutions to develop programs to meet the special needs for continuing education of women with family responsibilities.[6] Neither of these recommendations was ever fully implemented. In the 1970s Canada's Manpower Training Program provided some limited support for women's training as part of its equity provisions. Later, a number of federally purchased seats in training courses were reserved for women, in conjunction with the National Training Act, 1982. Three years later, in recognition that this "quota" system was having limited success, "re-entry" programs specifically for women received funding as part of the Canadian Jobs Strategy (CJS) (1985). Also, as part of the CJS, Human Resources Development Canada (HRDC) established the Designated Group Policy (DGP), identifying women, Aboriginal peoples, people with disabilities and visible minorities as identifiable equity groups with specific training needs. Eventually, in 1986, more than fifteen years after the publication of the Bird report, in a major policy initiative, ministers responsible for the Status of Women endorsed a nineteen-point strategy aimed at enhancing women's education and training opportunities in all Canadian jurisdictions.

When the Canadian Labour Force Development Board (CLFDB) was established in 1991, as part of a national labour force development strategy, women continued to be identified as a designated "equity" group. Other parts of that strategy included provincial labour force adjustment and training boards, and a web of local boards in the province of Ontario. The CLFDB was devised as a national advisory group on labour market development policy, and it was modelled on similar structures in the United Kingdom and Europe. Each of the four "equity groups" (women, Aboriginal peoples, visible minorities, and people with disabilities) was allocated one director on the board. Concurrently, the National Women's Reference Group was created to advise and support the women's representative to the board. As part of its work, the Women's Reference Group produced a draft set of principles as guidelines for a national women's agenda on training.[7]

Despite the recognition in policy of women's unique training needs and concerns, and the articulation of a set of principles as guidelines for the implementation of policy through programs, allocation of resources to programs for women was never significant during this period. Recognizing that progress in implementation at the joint ministerial level had been slow, a federal-provincial-territorial working group, including officials responsible for labour market development and also officials responsible for the Status of Women, was formed in 1993. The Joint Working Group was mandated to identify a comprehensive strategy for women's training and, to that end, identified principles, models, and best practices for women's training across Canada. These principles were similar to those articulated earlier by the National Women's Reference Group.[8]

All of this represented slow and painstaking progress over a twenty-five-year period. Despite the recognition in policy of women's important labour market role and our unique constellation of training needs, resources and mechanisms for implementation were never adequate to meet the policy goals. Targeted training for women was only briefly available, disappearing when the Labour Market Development Strategy (LMDS) replaced the CJS in 1989, and it was hard to get even when it was available.[9] In her report to the Women's Reference Group in 1993, Marcy Cohen, the women's representative, writes:

> From 1984 until 1993, the overall federal government expenditures on labour market programming have declined by 45.5 percent in real terms. In addition ... in the first year of the CLFDB's operation, training expenditures for women declined by 108 million dollars, or 18 percent. Over a five year period, from 1987 to 1992, federal government expenditures on training for women declined by 30 percent ... even though women comprise 44 percent of the labour force and represent over 60 percent of new labour market entrants.[10]

The supportive policy framework did have impacts, however. It created a context that legitimated training for women and that allowed for community-level responses to the particular needs of women. During this period community-based organizations and agencies emerged that had a particular interest in women's training and that developed programs especially for those women who were multiply disadvantaged and/or who were not well served by the range of courses and programs available through schools, colleges, and universities.

One early response, for example, came in 1985 from the Committee for Alternative Training and Education for Women (CATEW). The committee's proposed programming grew out of a (then) growing concern that programs offered by traditional educational institutions "are not providing women with the essential core life and generic skills that will prepare them for long term financial independence." The proposal noted that "there is a broad consensus that the new technology is causing large dislocations in the labour force, particularly in traditionally female occupations and that every effort must be made to ensure that women in and entering the labour force will have equal access to available employment and that the trends which have led to job and economic segregation be reversed."[11] Women's training agencies started up in various parts of the country and included the Women's Training and Employment Coalition in British Columbia's Lower Mainland; YWCA training and employment programs in Ontario, Alberta, and British Columbia; and the HRDC Women's Employment Service. Until 1997 there were ten community-level programs for women in Ontario that were funded through the HRDC Outreach Program.[12]

In conjunction with the creation of the national labour force development strategy, after 1991 women across Canada also organized reference groups and elected women's representatives to provincial and local boards.

In principle, the Canadian government remains committed to equity for women. The decision to devolve responsibility for training delivery to provinces and territories, however, has effectively removed existing mechanisms for the implementation of that commitment with respect to women's training, partial as they may have been.

In 1996, in tandem with the EI Act, the federal government and various jurisdictions embarked on a series of negotiations leading to the signing of Labour Market Development Agreements (LMDAs) in all jurisdictions, with the exception of Ontario. These agreements have different frameworks in various parts of the country. Three types of models have emerged for the agreements: co-management, full transfer, and strategic partnership.

Under the co-management model, there is no transfer of resources to the provinces, although there is joint management of program design and implementation. Co-management agreements are in place in British Columbia, Prince Edward Island, Newfoundland and Labrador, and the Yukon.

Nova Scotia has negotiated a strategic partnership. The agreement calls for two levels of government to collaborate and coordinate efforts to improve their respective labour market programs and services. The key requirement is that a joint management committee examines areas of joint cooperation and collaboration.

The third LMDA model, full transfer or devolution, involves the provinces in assuming responsibility for labour market policy and program delivery within the framework of federal funding and client eligibility criteria (Part 2 of the EI Act). The federal government keeps the responsibility for delivering EI benefits and pan-Canadian initiatives such as the national labour market information and exchange. Provinces with full transfer agreements are New Brunswick, Quebec, Manitoba, Saskatchewan, the Northwest Territories, and Alberta.[13]

For all models, primary responsibility for implementation rests at the provincial/territorial level. None of the agreements contains any equity provisions or equity guidelines. Further, the 1997 cancellation of the federal DGP removed all requirements for equity-based criteria from the provision of employment training and services.[14]

In all jurisdictions, the federal transfer of labour market training has created a climate of considerable confusion for women. On the one hand, the transfer created the possibility for an integrated and seamless system for the delivery of labour market services, something that women's organizations had been advocating for years. Submissions made in the early 1990s to the federal government (prior to its Social Security Reform process) and various other briefs and position papers on training and adjustment services argue strongly for a seamless system of training and adjustment services (with numerous access points and with services not tied to any income support program) as the kind of system that will best meet women's diverse training and adjustment requirements.[15] On the other hand, the erosion of public entitlement-based income support and employment services has increased the potential for arbitrary and uneven standards for access; program content; and delivery in training, adjustment, and related employment services. In the midst of the confusion, however, it has become clear that women, as a group, are not a priority. In fact, across the country, women-only programs were one of the first casualties of the LMDAs.[16]

In Ontario, for example, twenty-five local labour training and adjustment boards were formed, starting in 1994. These boards were originally intended to be "a community-voice" on training and adjustment issues.[17] Their mandate was to develop, deliver, or purchase training for their geographical areas. The boards had elected representatives from business, labour, the education and training community, and four designated equity groups: women, people with disabilities, visible minorities, and Francophones. With the elimination of the federal DGP and with a provincial political climate of declining interest in equity issues, the boards are no longer required to have any equity representation; directors do not have to be elected by or accountable to reference groups; and the boards no longer have any identified policy function. The removal of the requirement for equity representation supported by reference groups is, in turn, affecting the composition of the boards in that they are no longer required to reflect diverse community voices and interests.

At the federal level, the Canadian Labour Force Development Board was dissolved in December 1999. The federal Women's Reference Group has incorporated, changing its status from a national reference group related to a government advisory body to a separate not-for-profit organization. The Women's Reference Group no longer has a mandated advocacy role in federal policy or program development, as it did in the days of the CLFDB. Further, with the recent cessation of most of the activities of the Canadian Congress for Learning Opportunities for Women (CCLOW), there is now no national organization that can provide coordinated visibility for women's training needs at the national, provincial, and territorial levels.[18]

All Dressed Up and Nowhere to Train
The changes to the EI Act, which took place in concert with the transfer of training responsibility from federal to provincial and territorial levels, are resulting in a situation that ignores women's concerns. Among the first casualties of the changes to the EI Act were women's training and employment services in Alberta, New Brunswick, and British Columbia. In New Brunswick Joan McFarland's research has found that, under the CJS

(1995-89), nearly 10,000 women annually received federally funded training in New Brunswick. Since 1997 that number has dropped to just over 1,600 annually.[19] A recent review of the organizations listed in ACTEW's Employers' *Guide to Community-Based Training* (1991) found that, of thirty-six Toronto-area organizations actively involved in women's training ten years ago, fifteen either no longer exist or have ceased to carry out core programming, effectively reducing community-based training opportunities for women by about 40 percent.[20] In jurisdictions across Canada the changes mean less training for fewer people.

Although access to training is limited for people who are officially unemployed, the unemployed do have the advantage of being identified as suitable for training. Social assistance recipients, however, find themselves in another, more restricted, category. In Ontario in 1999, less than 5 percent of federally transferred expenditures on training were allocated to SARs through the Ontario Works Program, which is predominantly a work-for-welfare program.[21] There is very little skills training available to people in this category. Programs are primarily limited to providing interventions geared to attaching people to employment, although there are some exceptions. In Quebec, for example, the Centre de documentation sur l'éducation des adultes et condition féminine provides computer-based and distance-learning support through collaborative development and dissemination of training kits on various employment-related issues.[22] In Ontario, Sistering, a multi-service agency working with women facing a variety of issues, including homelessness and mental health problems, offers a program called "On the Path," in which women choose various aspects of training based on their own sense of what the barriers are that keep them from employment. While the focus is on employment preparation, the definition of what that entails is highly flexible and is based on participants' self-defined needs. For example, one aspect of the program has been a chronic pain management workshop.[23]

The decline in funds available for labour market training and the increasingly restrictive means of access to the training that is available affect both men and women. A recent survey of 175 agencies and organizations offering training in British Columbia found that "an overwhelming number of agencies (83 percent) indicated that they are turning away large numbers of people who have been determined by the funders to be ineligible. They are however, in desperate need of training. Furthermore, 80 percent of respondents indicated clients have to go through so many hoops to qualify for government assistance, that many of them give up. This, combined with the elimination of federal government block funding has resulted in a profound lack of services for clients, particularly the most disadvantaged."[24]

Women are disproportionately affected by these changes. They are over-represented in the temporary and part-time jobs that do not lead to EI eligibility, resulting in a situation in which 31 percent of unemployed women, compared to 39 percent of unemployed men, are EI-eligible.[25] A recent study of contingent workers in the Toronto area also found that, relative to men, women are over-represented in part-time, temporary, and self-employed jobs. In the Toronto study, 85 percent of people responding to a widely distributed survey were women. Just under half of the respondents in the Toronto study were not EI-eligible, and fully two-thirds were not eligible for benefits in the event of accident or injury through the Workers Safety and Insurance Board. Over 70 percent of the respondents in the contingent workers study reported that financial barriers prevented them from gaining access to training and education.[26]

The barriers between women and the training they need have been repeatedly studied and documented, and the findings have been remarkably consistent.[27] Access to appropriate, high-quality training has been an identified problem for women for a long time.[28] Many of the issues identified by the Bird Commission Report on the Status of Women in 1970 have not disappeared. The wage gap between men and women persists and means that women have little in the way of disposable income to allocate to training. Women continue to be concentrated in low-paying, part-time, entry-level, and temporary jobs or self-employment – all of which are highly unlikely to include workplace-based training. The top ten occupations for women are: retail sales clerks, secretaries, cashiers, nurses, accounting clerks, elementary school teachers, waitresses, office clerks, daycare workers, and receptionists.[29] A 1999 Statistics Canada study found that 28 percent of working women, compared to 10 percent of working men, had part-time jobs. From 1976 to 1999 the self-employment rate of women jumped from 5.7 percent to 12.5 percent, an increase of 75 percent, while men's rate of self-employment increased by 46 percent.[30] The contingent workers study cited above states that "69.4 percent of contingent workers earn less than $1,500 a month, $18,000 a year. Women earn less than men do. Seventy-two percent of the 250 workers surveyed stated that they would prefer permanent, full-time jobs."[31] In 2000, Status of Women Canada examined the impact of restructuring on women's labour market participation and found that women make up 68.8 percent of the part-time labour force, occupying primarily temporary, minimum-wage jobs.[32] Researchers have found a negative correlation between wages and the percentage of female workers in an occupational category. In other words, the more women workers in a given career, the lower the average wage. Based on 1997 data from the Survey of Labour and Income Dynamics (SLID), in Toronto women's average hourly wage is about 84 percent to 89 percent of men's average wage.[33] Requirements under the new federal-provincial training agreements stipulate that participants may be expected to contribute up to 70 percent of course costs in order to qualify for assistance.[34]

For sole-support women living on limited incomes, such requirements are often prohibitive.[35]

Women bear a heavy domestic burden, despite their strong presence in the labour force, which means that access to childcare, training schedules that do not conflict with family responsibilities, and some flexibility in training programs and requirements are necessary if they are to gain access to training.[36] Further, at least one in ten women is affected by domestic violence, which not only makes it difficult to carry out regular activities outside the home but also has a major impact on their self-esteem.[37]

Training that does not acknowledge the full range and diversity of needs and requirements of participants is highly likely to leave out many people. Discussing women as a group, as we do in this chapter, tends to mask the reality of women's lives. Women come in all shapes and sizes, from all races and ethnic backgrounds. Some are young; some are old; some live with mental or physical disabilities or chronic illnesses. Some bear children; some do not. All live multifaceted lives, meaning that a "one-size-fits-all" approach to training results in something that is hardly ever a good fit.

These well documented barriers continue to be critical issues for community-based organizations and the women they serve. In 2000 a series of focus groups and a "think tank" coordinated by Advocates for Training and Employment for Women (ACTEW) found that changing federal and provincial policy regarding labour force development, employment insurance, and access to training services has resulted in programs that, for the most part, do not meet the needs of the women who rely on those services as an access point to the labour market. Focus group participants described in detail their frustration over the lack of relevance to women's lives of government employment policy and the importance of continuing to build capacity in the women's training community to "mobilise decision-makers to address their priority issues."[38] Participants in the focus groups and the think tank noted the lack of coordination among women's training providers, the need for networking at all levels, and the importance of continuing to develop ways to share information provincially and locally.[39] As one participant stated: "Policy initiatives are short-term and often unresponsive to the training needs and time commitments of our clients."[40]

Less Shopping, More Training, More Sustainable Livelihoods

Women seeking training are not doing so because they enjoy shopping. Women want training because they see it as a means of obtaining and retaining meaningful employment. Since the passing of the National Training Act, 1982, federal training policy, for the most part, has been developed and implemented in isolation from initiatives directed at job creation. Since 1996 one result has been a proliferation of bureaucratic mechanisms and requirements that focus on: information provision, screening, monitoring, and directing applicants for training based on various eligibility criteria; promoting competition among service providers; limiting skills development opportunities to areas of pre-identified economic need; and on asking women to go shopping for programs that, increasingly, have eligibility requirements that either screen them out or do not exist at all. For example, one of the most well identified and thoroughly proven models for successful training for women has been bridging programs. These programs have offered skills training that focus on overcoming or compensating for systemic and structural barriers to optimal labour market participation. Despite their importance, effectiveness, and efficiency as a training approach, in the post-1996 period bridging programs have all but disappeared. Those that continue do so by cobbling together their programs from funding sources designed for other purposes. They do so with considerable difficulty and under conditions of tenuous financial security.[41]

The changes to the EI Act in 1996 have not only altered availability of programs but have also changed the way training and employment services are delivered. One significant change is that federal funds no longer support training programs; instead, training funds are allocated to the individual deemed eligible for training. This has made "shopping for training" more complicated than ever. The new system demands that clients investigate a number of training options, develop a career path, do extensive research, and have their plans approved before they can begin any type of training program. This, in turn, has affected the availability of training. Women are now shopping with less money and greater restrictions.

Service providers as groups have also been affected. There are three main categories of service provider for employment-related training: community-based trainers, private vocational schools, and community colleges.[42] Private trainers offering competitive and effective services at market rates have, in general, been well served or unaffected by the changes. Community colleges have had varied experiences. In some jurisdictions, such as British Columbia, they have been able to advance their situation by negotiating as partners in developing LMDAs.[43] Community-based trainers have been most negatively affected, as a group, by the changes. From 1985 to 1989, under the CJS, community-based trainers were a key source of service provision. Their role shifted but remained relatively strong, particularly in equity-related areas, from 1990 to 1996, under the LFDA. Since 1996, and with the removal of the concern for equity provisions from federal training policy in 1997, community-based trainers have found it increasingly difficult to provide accessible, high quality services to the traditionally marginalized or underserved groups that are their traditional area of focus.

The purpose of employment-related training services and programs is not to send women on difficult, unrewarding shopping trips. Their lives are already far too busy to be taken up with such fruitless activity. Since the main purpose of training is to assist women to secure jobs and to create sustainable livelihoods, then the shrinkage of the community-based training sector is of particular concern. Community-based training organizations arose in order to provide an integrated, sustainable livelihoods approach to the provision of training for women. With their commitment to equity, their non-profit orientation, their demonstrated capacity to adapt to changing social and economic circumstances (as a matter of organizational survival), and their local networks and connections, community-based trainers have the range of experience necessary to act as a bridge between women and suitable employment – a bridge that takes into account the complexity of their multiple responsibilities in the workplace, at home, and in the community.[44] The shrinkage we identified for this study (i.e., 40 percent in the community-based training sector in Toronto) is not unique to that city. In our recent interviews of providers in British Columbia, Quebec, and Ontario, we heard repeatedly that the scramble for inadequate and/ or unsuitable funding is taking its toll, causing organizations to close their doors or to curtail their services. The results of our interviews are further supported by a recent HRDC-funded study of the community-based training sector in Canada, which notes: "The Community-Based Training (CBT) sector has faced significant change in Canada in recent years, and there are few signs that changes affecting the sector will subside ... These changes have placed significant pressure on CBT providers to continuously increase funding targets and rapidly develop and change curriculum."[45]

The information we have gathered suggests strongly that the market-driven focus of the post-1996 changes is benefiting a decreasing number of women. Moreover, they are missing the point. Effective labour market training assists people to get the jobs they need. The main issue here does not concern information or services or eligibility criteria, although all of these matter. The main issue involves developing and offering training that enhances the sustainability of women's livelihoods through structured learning experiences. Training and job creation have been considered separately, in policy and programming, since the passing of the National Training Act, 1982. Developing training policy and programs without considering how women can secure the jobs they need in order to generate income certainly creates problems for the seamless, integrated consideration of livelihood needs for which women and their advocacy organizations have argued long and hard.[46] Further, women's livelihoods are about much more than paid work and the training that should be attached to their pursuit of it. The sustainability of livelihoods is based on a broad and integrated consideration of the unpaid work in the home and the community, which is as necessary as is paid work with regard to creating individuals, families, and communities that can live well supported and rewarding lives.[47]

Training that Works for Women

The Federal-Provincial-Territorial Working Group, in its 1994 report, set out five principles for women's training. The National Women's Reference Group on Training produced a similar list of seven principles, endorsed by the CLFDB in 1996. These training standards were to be used in designing programs funded with federal monies, including those funded through federal-provincial training agreements. The cancellation of the federal DGP in 1997 effectively removed any requirement that these principles be honoured in developing and offering training supported through federal funding or federal transfers. The seven principles themselves, however, remain useful and offer a set of criteria for evaluating the suitability of training for women as well as for understanding why so many women, despite their need for training, are returning home with no training purchases:

Access: Training programs work best when they acknowledge that a variety of mechanisms are needed in order to ensure that those who need a program can participate in it fully. These include: information, support services, childcare, training allowances for those who need subsidies, broad eligibility criteria, counselling, accommodation measures, available means of transportation, bridging courses, and programs.

Equity: Equity means fair treatment for everyone. It means equal rights and benefits regardless of race, gender, country of origin, class, religion, sexual orientation, geographic location, income, age, and ability. No one should be excluded from or not fully included in training because of characteristics not relevant to the tasks or skills for which she/he is being trained.

Right to basic education: Integrated and flexible programs that provide adult basic education, literacy skills, life skills, administrative and technical skills, and language training are a necessary foundation for all advanced skills training. Advanced skills training programs may not offer basic skills directly, but they need to partner with or have strong working relationships with basic skills programs.

Recognition of skills: Recognition of acquired skills, education, and experience is important and can be addressed through prior learning assessment and recognition, flexible accreditation criteria, and other forms of formal and informal recognition.

Quality: Five competencies that all high-quality training programs should design for in curriculum development include the following: ability to decide on a career or occupation, acquisition of the skills necessary to be successful at the chosen job, experience in using those skills to search for a job, ability to maintain employment, and the ability to find and gain access to the resources to master all of the above.

Accountability: Programs need to arrange for regular evaluation. Participants should be able to ask for and receive information about the experiences of other participants. Evaluation procedures should include participants as a key source of information.

Integration of training, economic development, and livelihoods: Training programs must be linked to available jobs. Programs should address relevant community issues and should be linked to local/regional/ national economic development planning processes. Training must be part of an overall economic development framework designed to promote sustainable livelihoods.

The conditions and requirements for training adopted at the ministerial level in 1994 and endorsed by the CLFDB in 1996 are just as relevant now as they were in the mid-1990s. Women's need for high-quality training that leads to good jobs and the barriers that affect their access to that training have not changed. Nor have the characteristics of a good job. Women still need stable, secure jobs with satisfactory health and safety provisions that take into account the requirements of their unpaid work responsibilities and that provide meaningful work at a rate of pay sufficient to support themselves and their families.

The search for training that will lead to good jobs is neither frivolous nor greedy. Women in Canada and around the world play a critical economic and social role in ensuring the well-being of their families and communities. Their income-producing work is only one component of a dynamic and carefully crafted approach to livelihood. Sustainability of livelihoods in Canada and elsewhere for both women and men rests on three legs: income generation, subsistence and domestic work, and community support/voluntary work. All are essential to the longer-term economic, social, and ecological viability of families, communities, and countries. None can be ignored. Training may well focus on income generation and employability, but if it does not also take into account the other two dimensions of sustainable livelihood, then it will be ineffective with regard to contributing to the longer-term sustainability of livelihoods, communities, and nations. Policies and programs and their implementing organizations and institutions play a key role in ensuring that training enhances, rather than interferes with, the sustainability potential of individual livelihoods.[48]

All of this is well recognized in Canada and internationally as well as in developing countries.[49] Unfortunately, in the rush to offer shopping opportunities to people in need of training, and despite its commitment to sustainable development, Canada seems to have lost its perspective on the value and purpose of training. For women, who wish to use the seven principles as a "Shopper's Guide" to choosing well, chances of coming home empty-handed are greater than ever.

Still Shopping for Training

Although women and their training needs may be out of fashion with labour market policy makers, the importance of their contribution to the labour market has not diminished in any way. In an era in which there is increasing concern about skills shortages, women represent fully half the social capital available for labour market development in Canada. The concern for mobilizing women's current and potential contribution to Canadian economic well-being through the labour market, which motivated federal and provincial ministers in 1986 and 1993, is no less valid now than it was then. Equally valid are the needs and interests of women across the country who want to find meaningful, safe, and secure work in order to create sustainable livelihoods for themselves and their families.

Women's contribution to the Canadian economy has been calculated in a variety of contested ways. Whatever means are used, however, the conclusion is always that women's current contribution is typically underestimated and that their potential contribution continues to be hampered by structural barriers. Many of these barriers are the same as those that prevent women from gaining access to the training that they need and want.[50]

Training in isolation cannot solve structural economic problems and certainly cannot solve problems of unemployment. However, training as part of an integrated strategy for the creation of sustainable livelihoods can make an important contribution to dismantling the barriers that are currently keeping women away from the jobs that they need. The decision made to separate training from development considerations appears to have taken us down a road that, twenty years later, has led us to an overly bureaucratized, fragmentary, and ineffective labour market training system that focuses on shopping rather than livelihoods, and on information and services rather than on jobs. Until these things change, women's shopping trips for training are likely to continue to be difficult and discouraging. Far too often, despite their well identified needs and the genuine interest of service providers in meeting those needs, they will continue to return home empty-handed.

Notes

1 Susan Wismer and Karen Lior, "Shopping for Training," *Canadian Women's Studies* 17, 4 Winter (1998): 122-26.

2 Jennifer Stephen, *Access Diminished: A Report on Women's Training and Employment Services in Ontario* (Toronto: ACTEW, 2000), 3.

3 See, for example, ASPECT, *Analysing the Impact and Challenging the Assumptions* (Victoria: Association of Service Providers for Employability and Career Training, 1999); Clarence Lochhead and Katherine Scott, *The Dynamics of Women's Poverty in Canada* (Ottawa: Status of Women Canada, 2000); Joan McFarland, *Women's Access to Training in New Brunswick* (Toronto: Labour Education and Training Research Network, York University, 1999); Jennifer Stephen, 2000); Workfare Watch, *Broken Promises: Welfare Reform in Ontario* (Toronto: Welfare Watch, 1999). This study is being carried out on behalf of the Labour Education and Training Research Network, York University, Toronto (Fall 2001).

4 Organisation for Economic Cooperation and Development, *Education and Policy Analysis* (Paris: OECD, 2001).

5 Florence Bird, Chair, *Report of the Royal Commission on the Status of Women in Canada* (Ottawa: Supply and Services Canada, September 1970).

6 Ibid., 406.

7 Susan Wismer and Linda Szeto, *Towards a Women's Agenda on Training* (Toronto: National Women's Reference Group on Labour Market Issues/Canadian Congress for Learning Opportunities for Women, 1991).

8 Joint Federal Provincial Territorial Working Group, *Rethinking Training* (Ottawa: FTP Working Group/Status of Women Canada, 1994); Susan Wismer and Karen Lior, *Meeting Women's Training Needs: Case Studies in Women's Training, Phase 2 Report* (Ottawa: FTP Working Group/Status of Women Canada, 1994).

9 Elspeth Tulloch, "Where Are the Women? Federal Training Policy and the Gender Factor," in *Women's Education des femmes,* Special Issue: *What's Happening to Women's Training in Canada?* 10 (3/4) Winter (1993): 4-7.

10 Marcy Cohen, *Report to the Second Annual Consultation of the Women's Reference Group on Labour Market Issues* (Ottawa: National Women's Reference Group, 1993), 2-3.

11 Committee for Alternative Training and Education for Women (CATEW), Proposal to Secretary of State, unpublished, 1985, 2-4. CATEW was the original name of ACTEW, which now stands for Advocates for Community-Based Training and Education for Women.

12 Idalia Gonzalez (Counsellor, Times Change Women's Employment Service), personal communication, October 2001.

13 Thomas Klassen, "The Federal-Provincial Labour Market Development Agreements: Brave New Model of Cooperation," in *Federalism, Democracy and Labour Market Policy in Canada,* ed. Tom McIntosh (Kingston: McGill-Queen's University Press, 2001), 159-203.

14 The cancellation of the policy actually affects all transfers of federal funding authority to other levels of government, not just the LMDAs.

15 Windsor Women's Incentive Centre (WIC), *Submission to the Parliamentary Standing Committee on Human Resources Development* (Windsor: WIC, 1994); National Action Committee on the Status of Women, *Training and the Social Security Review,* Fact Sheet 2 (Toronto: NAC, 1994); Canadian Congress on Learning Opportunities for Women, *CCLOW and the Social Security Reforms* (Toronto: CCLOW, 1994).

16 Stephen, *Access Diminished,* 14.

17 Ontario Premier's Council, *People and Skills in the New Global Economy* (Toronto: Queen's Printer for Ontario, 1990).

18 The National Women's Reference Group on Labour Market Issues, *Voices from the Field: Impacts of the Changing Federal Funding Context on Women's Access to Training* (Ottawa: Canadian Labour Force Development Board, 1998).

19 Joan McFarland, *Women's Access to Training in New Brunswick* (Toronto: Labour Education and Training Research Network, York University, 1999). See Chapter 11, this volume.

20 Advocates for Community Based Training and Education for Women (ACTEW), *Employers' Guide to Community-based Training* (Toronto: ACTEW, 1991).

21 Stephen, *Access Diminished.*

22 Sharon Hackett (Executive Director, Centre de documentation sur l'éducation des adultes et la condition féminine), personal communication, October 2001.

23 Teresa Roberson (Coordinator, Sistering,) personal communication, October 2001.

24 The Association of Service Providers for Employability and Career Training, *Analysing the Impact and Challenging the Assumptions: A Report that Demonstrates the Impact of Government Policies on Unemployed Persons and on Community Service Deliverers* (Vancouver: ASPECT, 1999), 3.

25 Stephen, *Access Diminished.*

26 Alice de Wolff, *Breaking the Myth of Flexible Work: Contingent Work in Toronto* (Toronto: Contingent Workers Project, 2000).

27 See, for example, Susan Wismer, *Women's Education and Training: A Policy Analysis* (Toronto: Canadian Congress for Learning Opportunities for Women, 1988); Wismer and Lior, "Shopping for Training"; Ursule Critoph, *Background on the Training System in Canada* (Ottawa: Canadian Labour Congress, 1997); McFarland, *Women's Access.*

28 See, for example, Wismer, *Women's Education.*

29 Leela Viswanathan, Toronto Training Board, Environmental Scan Update, November 1999, 29.

30 Status of Women Canada, *Women's Economic Independence and Security: A Federal/Provincial/Territorial Strategic Framework* (Ottawa: Status of Women Canada, March 2001), 14.

31 Alice de Wolff for the Contingent Workers Project, *Breaking the Myth of Flexible Work: Contingent Work in Toronto* (Toronto: Contingent Workers Project, September 2000), i-ii.

32 Ibid., 15.

33 Leela Viswanathan, *Toronto Training Board 2000-2001 Environmental Scan: Training for Toronto's New Economy* (Toronto: Toronto Training Board, 2000).

34 Stephen, *Access Diminished,* 17.

35 Clarence Lochhead and Katherine Scott, *The Dynamics of Women's Poverty in Canada* (Ottawa: Status of Women Canada, March 2000).

36 Ann Zelechow and Anne Morais, *ACTEW Survey of Training and Employment Programs for Women in Metro Toronto* (Toronto: ACTEW, 1997), 8.

37 Jenny Horsman, *Too Scared to Learn: Women, Violence, and Education* (Toronto: McGilligan Books, 1999).

38 ACTEW, *Building the Capacity of the Women's Training and Education Community: A Plan for Sustainable Action* (Toronto: ACTEW 2001), 1.

39 ACTEW, Think Tank Highlights (unpublished, June 2001), 2.

40 Ibid., 3.

41 Eva Pakyam, *YWCA-LEAP,* personal communication, October 2001.

42 Wismer and Lior, "Shopping for Training," 122-26.

43 "The Provision of Training in Canada: Regional Comparisons, National Perspectives – Conference 2000 Report," *Training Matters/Recherche en Formation: Newsletter of the Labour Education and Training Research Network,* Spring 2001, no. 5, p. 1.

44 William Wolfson, *The Second Century: Community-Based Training in Canada,* National Human Resources Study (Toronto: Canadian Coalition of Community Based Training, 1997); Ursule Critoph, *Background on the Training System in Canada* (Ottawa: Canadian Labour Congress, 1997); Ontario Network of Skills Training Projects, *A History of Community Based Training in Canada* (Toronto: ONESTEP, 1998).

45 Canadian Coalition of Community-Based Training, *A Study to Investigate, Analyse and Organise Community-Based Training Roles in Canada* (Ottawa: CCCBT/HRDC, 2000).

46 Canadian Congress for Learning Opportunities for Women, Canadian Research Institute for the Advancement of Women, National Organisation of Immigrant and Visible Minority Women, Canadian Farm Women's Education Council, *A Collaborative Response to the Green Paper on Social Security Reform from Four National Women's Groups* (Toronto: CCLOW/CRIAW/NOIVMW/CFWEC, 1994).

47 Michael Redclift, ed., *Life Chances and Livelihoods* (London: Routledge, 2000); Beth Moore Milroy and Susan Wismer, "Communities, Work and Public/Private Sphere Models," *Gender, Place and Culture* 1, 1 (January 1994): 71-90.

48 Michael Redclift, *Life Chances;* Diana Carney, *Livelihoods Approaches Compared* (report prepared for the United Nations Development Program, Februrary 2000); Caroline Moser, *Gender Planning and Development: Theory, Practice and Training* (London: Routledge, 1993).

49 Morley Gunderson, *Women and the Canadian Labour Market* (Ottawa: Statistics Canada, 1998); Status of Women Canada, *Women's Economic Independence and Security: A Federal/Provincial/Territorial Strategic Framework* (Ottawa: Status of Women Canada, March 2001); Organisation for Economic Cooperation and Development, *Education and Policy Analysis* (Paris: OECD, 2001).

50 Louise Toupin, *Social and Community Indicators for Evaluating Women's Work in Communities* (Ottawa: Status of Women Canada, February 2001); Isabella Bakker, *Unpaid Work and Macroeconomics* (Ottawa: Status of Women Canada August, 1998); Susan Wismer, *Counting Ourselves In: Women's Contribution to the Canadian Economy* (unpublished, prepared for the Canadian Women's Foundation, Toronto, January 1997).

13
Youth Employment Programs in British Columbia: Taking the High Road or the Low Road?
Linda Wong and Stephen McBride

Contemporary labour markets are characterized by heightened insecurity and the distinction between good and bad jobs. As a result of this, the transition from youth to adulthood has grown more difficult. Labour market conditions for young people in Canada are poor on a variety of indicators. Rhetoric about lifelong learning and the extension of education hides the fact that many experience difficulties and delayed independence because of poor labour market conditions. Entry into the labour force is delayed, and this postpones the age of independent living. The fact that more young people are continuing their education represents a struggle for positional advantage within a difficult environment, and it is as much an indicator of lack of adequate jobs as it is of a desire to invest in their own human capital resources.

Human capital theory holds that the knowledge and skills possessed by individuals is a factor of production in the same way as is physical capital (buildings, raw materials, machinery, etc.). Higher levels of skill and knowledge, achieved through education and training, lead to higher productivity, which is expressed in higher earnings for those who possess them.[1] To the extent that labour market problems are accompanied by higher education enrolments, this theory enables policy makers to take a benign view of developments.

A high skill economy, the result of major investments in human capital, is often referred to as a high road strategy – one that should be followed in preference to a low road strategy, which is based on low wages and leads to a race to the bottom in terms of labour and social standards. The high road strategy is portrayed as resulting in a virtuous circle of high skills, high productivity, and high wages. In general, this chapter concludes that British Columbia has failed to develop a "high road strategy" – a training system geared to a high skill economy. This failure has led, in turn, to a pursuit of policies that re-enforce the inequities of a neoliberal labour market, such as high unemployment, underemployment, greater use of contingent labour, and so on, rather than striving to overcome them.

Labour Market Conditions for Canadian Youth

We start with an examination of labour market conditions for Canadian youth. While labour market conditions for adults remained poor during the 1990s, the situation for Canadian youth was worse. Unlike after the recession of the early 1980s, after the recession of the early 1990s the labour market for youth aged fifteen to twenty-four was very slow to improve. Teenagers were particularly affected. Through much of the 1990s the youth unemployment rate was about 1.8 times higher than was that of adults. During late 1996 and 1997 the adult unemployment rate dropped, while the youth rate continued to increase. As a result, the youth-to-adult unemployment rate ratio went above 2.00, and it remained around 2.2 in the late 1990s.[2] The same bleak picture holds for earnings. Between the early 1980s and the early 1990s, the average earnings of youths fell by about 20 percent.[3]

Young people make up a high proportion of those earning the minimum wage and a disproportionate share of the part-time workforce. In total, the youth population constituted 58 percent of those making minimum wage.[4] In 1970, 29 percent of young earners worked full year, full time; however, by 1995 this proportion had declined to only 16 percent.[5] Participation rates among youth also decreased substantially during the 1990s. The adult participation rate declined moderately from 85.1 percent in 1990 to a low of 83.7 percent in 2000, compared to the drastic drop from 73 percent for youth in 1990 to 61.6 percent in 2000.[6] While the adult unemployment rate was on a pattern of slow decline, youth unemployment increased until it hit a decade high of 17.3 percent in 1998. Since then there has been a modest decline, but it has yet to reach the 1990 level of 12.8 percent.[7]

While demographic factors may explain some of the decline in youth participation in British Columbia, there are indications that structural barriers and challenges in the labour market continue to challenge a young person's ability to find work. For example, the number of fifteen- to nineteen-year-olds not in school, not employed, and not actively looking for work increased from 12.6 percent in 1990 to 20.7 percent in 2000.[8] One explanation of this is that young people in the 1990s showed a greater preference for enrolment in education and training programs. It is reasonable to suppose, however, that this "preference" was driven by a deteriorating labour market.

Underemployment, in the sense of individuals working fewer hours than they would like, makes young people's situation even more difficult.[9] In the first quarter of 1997 the underemployment rate for youth was 4.7 percent, double that of adult women and nearly three times that for adult men.[10] In 1996 the involuntary part-time rate among youth aged fifteen to twenty-four was 10 percent, twice the rate of those over twenty-four.[11] Canadian youth see themselves as "occupationally challenged," and they believe that, at best, the labour market can give them short-term contracts, part-time work, and sales and telemarketing work on commission.[12]

The implication of these findings is that there are an insufficient number of jobs to absorb the potential workforce and that the jobs that are available provide insufficient hours to fully employ the existing workforce. Logically, the solution should lie in expanding the demand for labour, in creating more jobs, and in making policies to stimulate the development of a high skill economy. However, since the triumph of neoliberal ideas in the 1980s[13] the employment policy has relied upon the market to create jobs, thus reducing the barriers to the operation of markets (such as social programs that are deemed overly generous) while addressing the alleged deficiencies, in skill or attitude, of the existing workforce.

The Neoliberal Labour Market and Training

The Organisation for Economic Cooperation and Development (OECD) is a leading advocate of neoliberal labour market policies. Its recommendations, in its Jobs Study,[14] can serve as a model of the deregulatory neoliberal approach to labour market problems. It outlined a set of policies that it claimed would reduce unemployment, raise employment, and increase productivity. The OECD Jobs Study had two complementary components: one that focused on skills development and investment in human capital as a route to high wage, high value-added production, and one that was designed to encourage low-waged employment.[15] Far from being competing strategies, these were, in fact, complementary.[16] Policies associated with human capital development include educational reforms designed to make the system more responsive to the needs of a competitive economy; to provide greater access to education, including postsecondary education; to improve school-to-work transitions through co-op education, internships, and youth apprenticeships; to provide more effective counselling; and to provide information.

Encouragement of low-wage employment is achieved by policies that target "rigidities" like payroll taxes, minimum wage, unemployment insurance coverage and benefits. Reducing these, it is claimed, will increase incentives to find work. Other rigidities lie in the welfare system. The solution here is to create welfare-to-work schemes involving low-end training and work experience, to encourage self-employment and entrepreneurship among young people, and to provide work-experience programs for those not going on to postsecondary education.

Neoliberals hold that if rigidities are removed from the operation of the labour market, then jobs will be created by the private sector. In such a market workers are expected to demonstrate flexibility and adaptability. Viewed differently, insecurity can be said to be characteristic of labour markets in the "new," post-Fordist, and neoliberal era.[17] Moreover, the individual is increasingly held responsible for his or her success in navigating the labour market and the market economy. These markets are increasingly deregulated and operate either without or with much reduced safety nets for those who are displaced.

Restructuring of training and other employment programs plays a role in structuring such a labour market. Two basic approaches to training can be observed. The first approach involves education and training for high road occupations – highly skilled positions resulting from technological innovations and automation.[18] The second approach to training concentrates on low road occupations – those with low wages, low skills, low job security, and harsh workplace conditions.[19] Since the neoliberal job market is increasingly bifurcated into good and bad jobs, both approaches are consistent with it. To the extent that training programs channel young people into bifurcated occupations, with little laddering between the bad and the good jobs, they can be viewed as the guinea pigs for this type of social engineering.[20]

The development of national labour market strategies based on neoliberalism has been "conditioned"[21] by international organizations and agreements. The model of neoliberal labour market deregulation has been pursued by many governments and was vigorously proselytized by the OECD.[22] It reflects the two approaches to training and employment preparation noted above – each approach slotting individuals into different points within a hierarchy of occupations.[23] Measures taken to develop human capital have run afoul of other governmental imperatives; notably, federal expenditure reduction has adversely affected funding for postsecondary education, with the result that tuition fees, except in Quebec, have risen significantly while expenditure on vocational training has declined.[24] This, though, is consistent with the neoliberal view that individuals should bear more of – in extreme versions all of – the responsibility for investing in their own human capital and thus preparing themselves for the labour market.

The influence of international models reaches down to provinces. There has been an attempt to create an integrated strategy between labour market, education, and social welfare policy, generally in ways consistent with the prevalent neoliberal paradigm. For example, in many provinces there has been a change in education policy towards cultivating skill-sets that cater to making young people more "job ready." This approach stresses applied studies and training, scientific and technological fields, and, at the primary and secondary levels, core skills. Likewise, social welfare policy has shifted towards what is widely referred to as a "welfare-to-work" approach, in which those deemed unduly dependent on government transfers and social services must work for social benefits and in which participation is increasingly mandatory. The effect of this is to enlarge the pool of low-skilled labour – an effect that seems predicated upon an acceptance of growing inequality in Canadian society.[25]

The three main types of training and employment programs are wage subsidy programs, apprenticeships, and active social benefit policies.[26] We outline each type below and then apply the typology to youth employment programs in British Columbia.

A wage subsidy program consists of providing employers public money in order to provide work experience and training opportunities. Wage subsidies are often criticized for creating "dead weight" – that is, windfall payments to employers who would have hired without the subsidy – and "displacement," through which subsidy workers displace those who otherwise would have continued working. Evaluations of wage subsidies in Australia, Belgium, Ireland, and the Netherlands have suggested that the combined dead weight and substitution effects amount to around 90 percent. Others argue that the positions that are created are merely temporary and do not address the need for full-time work.[27]

Proponents argue that dead weight and displacement can be limited if the positions are newly created and the tasks involved do not overlap with existing jobs or positions.[28] Another defence of such programs is that they provide youth with experience and contact with the labour market, thus preventing loss of motivation and long-term unemployment. An equity justification is also commonly advanced: those who usually benefit from these programs are frequently disadvantaged members of society who would not otherwise have found work. In these cases, the end result is usually low-waged, low-skill employment. However, programs of this type may also be focused on high road occupations – as with the BC First Job in Science and Technology Program.

Apprenticeships involve an agreement between the individual, the government, and the employer with regard to training in a specific government-regulated trade. Apprentices receive training from the employer while on the job as well as formal educational training. Apprenticeship allows for more direct and more secure attachment to the labour force through the acquisition of certifiable, and usually portable, skills. Not all of these are necessarily at the high end of the skills spectrum, but the attention to skill, and its reinforcement through part-time education accompanying on-the-job skills training, leads us to classify it as a high road program. According to Bowers, Sonnet, and Bardone, countries with comprehensive apprenticeships do a good job of getting young people a firm foothold in the labour market.[29] Apprenticeship systems in these countries have a good track record with regard to keeping youth unemployment at low levels and quickly integrating a high proportion of those newly leaving school into jobs. They do this by raising the incentives and motivation of high school students; by providing clear pathways and transitions from school to careers through expanding contextualized learning, which goes beyond firm-specific training; by increasing the relevance of training; and by encouraging employers to upgrade the quality of jobs and to give young workers a chance.[30]

Training schemes within active social benefit programs assume that individuals who need social benefits must be deficient in life skills or attitudes, and it is this that the training is designed to address. These programs have gained popularity in the last decade. The assumption is that individuals in need of social assistance need to be redirected from state dependency towards active behaviours that will enable them to achieve independence. Entirely dismantling benefit entitlements has so far been viewed as politically impossible, so the preferred approach in the majority of OECD countries has been to make only marginal cuts in the generosity of benefit entitlements while tightening up eligibility conditions and developing "activation" strategies. The aim of the latter is to induce the unemployed to be more active in job search and to maintain a closer attachment to the labour market. Activation strategies include attempts to provide more effective job search assistance to the unemployed as well as attempts to oblige them to satisfy work tests or to participate in active programs (or in education and training) in order to continue to draw benefits.[31] The latter forms have been described as "workfare." Other activation strategies include a combination of training, job search, career counselling, remedial education, subsidized work experience, and job placement (or "job brokering"). Typically, these measures are combined with increased monitoring and enforcement,[32] and the programs are geared to low road occupations at low wages.

BC Training Programs

Our examination of BC youth training and employment programs argues that British Columbia followed the neoliberal pattern of focusing on removal of rigidities through implementation of work-to-welfare schemes and individualization of responsibility for acquisition of human capital. Given the social democratic composition of the BC government from 1991 to 2001, this might seem surprising. However, changes in federal policy beginning in 1996 conditioned provincial options. Critoph[33] shows how reduced federal funding and new rules governing the training and employment services transferred to the provinces led to the individualization of responsibility for labour market training. As well, there was a focus on short-term results, typically measured by removing individuals from social assistance rolls rather than adequately placing them in the labour market.

Of course, reviewing the broad picture, one can see that there is evidence that having a social democratic government did produce a different approach in a number of areas. First, tuition fees in postsecondary education were frozen and remain among the lowest in Canada. Second, within a context in which training was being privatized, steps were taken, through initiatives like the Training Accord, to maintain a significant public presence in the training area.[34] Third, young people in entry-level jobs benefited from successive increases in the minimum wage, which is the highest in Canada. Fourth, there was some initial interest, though this was not sustained, in buying into the rhetoric of a high skills, high wage economy.

Certainly official pronouncements reflected the high road strategy. For example, the 1995 Throne Speech outlined the following choices:

> There are two opposing visions of how a government should move forward in a modern economy. We can stop building infrastructure, cut public services, reduce wages and lower social standards in a race to the bottom; to compete with less developed economies in attracting new jobs. Or we can invest in our strengths, in up-to-date skills, increase our productivity, and add value to what we produce, in an effort to match the advanced economies of Japan and the European Community in attracting new jobs.

> Investing in people. To fill those jobs and ensure that prosperity, BC will need a highly skilled workforce. Investing in our people, equipping them with the knowledge and skills they need to meet the global challenge, is fundamental to keeping our economy strong.

> Fundamental to this government is that every young person in our province feels valued. New steps will be taken in the coming months to move young people off welfare into jobs and job training. BC's kids will get the helping hand they need to grow with our economy. Together we will build British Columbia one dream at a time.[35]

For a variety of reasons,[36] the attempt to forge a high skills training strategy was abandoned in 1996, though a less ambitious institutional initiative, centred on the Industrial Training and Apprenticeship Commission, was launched in 1997. The main reasons the high skills strategy was abandoned included conflicts between business and labour, and considerable variation among industrial sectors (in British Columbia and elsewhere) with respect to the demand for highly skilled workers.[37] Within that context, for many firms or sectors a low skill, low-wage strategy made more sense. In practice, British Columbia's social democratic government pursued policies that re-enforced the inequities of a neoliberal labour market rather than polices that strove to overcome them. This direction was partly conditioned by the changes in federal policy noted above. Despite the high road rhetoric, training policies reinforced polarization in the labour market rather than altering its structure. An analysis of training and employment programs geared to young people sustains this point.

Youth Training Programs in British Columbia[38]
Under Youth Options BC, which is the provincial government's comprehensive initiative to provide youth with labour market assistance, there are
fifteen youth programs, nine of which were chosen for closer examination
(see Figure 13.1). The programs we chose included examples of wage subsidy (targeted at high-, medium-, and low-wage levels), apprenticeship,
active social benefits, and information/career preparation programs. Addi-
tionally, programs were chosen in order to cover groups targeted according
to socio-economic and educational background.[39]

Youth training programs under "Youth Options" typically provide entry-
level work experience. As indicated in Figure 13.1 a number of programs
are targeted at those in or on their way into postsecondary education.
These participants may reasonably be supposed to be destined for high
road occupations. But Youth Works, the largest program both in terms of
budget and number of participants, typically provides entry-level work experience in low-wage sales and service occupations. Youth Works assumes
the participant will continue to work in the occupation for which they are
trained even if s/he does not stay with the employer beyond the subsidy.
The goal of Youth Works is not to concern itself with the professional
development of the participant but, rather, to reduce social assistance
caseloads.[40] The training provided is at a rudimentary level. Other programs aim at particular niches in the occupational hierarchy.

The generic term "training" implies that all training increases an individual's human capital and leads to a better situation in the labour market.
However, this obscures the fact that not all programs are equal, that not all
youths are treated equally, and that youth programs in British Columbia
are segmented along occupational and socio-economic lines as well as
between good jobs and bad jobs. Youth Works and Job Start tend to focus
on the low-wage service sector while the public sector program and the
First Job in Science and Technology (FJIST) tend to focus on high-wage
occupations. Interviews with program officials revealed that many of the
programs were not evaluated. When they were, evaluations mainly consisted of employer and employee surveys asking for opinions of the program and what the trainees thought they learned. From this information,
the program administrators would extrapolate and interpret the kinds of
skills the employee had gained from the program. But there was no attempt
to find out how effective the program was with regard to providing skills
or permanent labour market attachment. Such procedures are consistent
with low road concepts of training rather than with high road concepts.

Explaining the Paradox
Globalization and technological progress have created heightened competition and economic change that can cause instability and difficulties in

Figure 13.1

Nine youth programs chosen for analysis

Program	Type of program	Target group	Training goal	Participation numbers*	Budget*
First Job in Science and Technology	High-wage subsidy	Post-secondary diploma	Work experience	230 (1999)	2 million[b]
Public Sector Youth Employment	High-wage subsidy/ employment	Post-secondary students	Work experience	957 placements ministry-funded and 160 corporate-funded (1999-2000)	N/A**
Student Summer Works	Mid-wage subsidy	High school and post-secondary students	Work experience	5,445 (1998)	$8.9 million[a]
Youth Community Action	Tuition credit (mid-wage subsidy)	Geared towards post-secondary students	Work experience	1,731 (1998-99)	$2.4 million[a]
Job Start	Low-wage subsidy	Those not intending to further their education into post-secondary school	Work experience	1,229 (1998-99)	$2.2 million[a]

Program	Description	Target	Services	Participants	Cost
Youth Works	Active social benefits using low-wage subsidy and labour market information	On social assistance	Work experience, job readiness, and basic skills training	The average monthly Youth Works caseload in the 1999-2000 fiscal year was 19,615	$65.7 million and $3,500 per participant in WPBT[a]
YouBET!!	Labour market information	Seeking entrepreneurial opportunities	Planning a small business	1,800 participants, 1998-99 YEAR[f]	1.3 million[b]
Apprenticeship (secondary school apprenticeship)	Apprenticeship	High school students who want to enter a trade	Work experience	In 1997-98, there were 397 students enrolled in the SSA program in BC in 1999 there were over 400[d]	$.17 million[d] ($2,800 per SSA student, $85,000 for scholarships)[b]
Bladerunners	Low/mid-wage subsidy towards apprenticeship	At-risk youth with very little work experience	Work experience, job readiness, and basic skills training	120	1.2 million[e]

* Unless otherwise indicated the information came from interviews with participants working in the Youth Programs.
** The amount per student ranged between and within programs so calculation of the total amount was unavailable.
a BC Annual Reports.
b Inventory of Canada's Youth Employment Programs and Services.
c <http://www.elp.gov.bc.ca/main/newsrel/may/nr126.htm> (August 2001).
d <http://www.bced.gov.bc.ca/careers/ssa/intro.htm> (28 August 2001).
e <http://www.cdcv.gov.bc.ca/publicinfo/newsreleases/nr2000/114nr2000.htm> (September 2000).
f <http://www.sbtc.gov.bc.ca/news/2000march/youth_program_stats.htm> (September 2000).

maintaining the employability of large segments of a country's labour force. At the same time, these new economic forces provide new opportunities for economic growth and employment expansion. Yet these same global forces appear to be reducing opportunities and incentives for training for many workers by undermining long-term employment relationships and marginalizing low-skilled workers.[41]

The assumption "that appropriate and well targeted investment in training through a reduction in skill mismatch can result in a net creation of productive employment in a national economy"[42] is a dubious one, even where it is followed. Trends created by technological and organizational innovations have led to a polarized labour market. Without action on the demand side to create more employment, there is no reason to expect supply-side actions to solve the employment problems of young people.

Despite the high road rhetoric, policy responses create training policies that feed the polarized labour market rather than altering its structure. In British Columbia's *Training for What* report, one of the recommendations was to implement an industry-led workforce development strategy and another was to ensure the greater relevance of publicly funded education and training. The point of both was to ensure that training and learning is industry- and market-driven.[43] The 1998 BC report of the Premier's Business Advisory Committee on Youth Employment reconfirmed this goal.[44] In an interview, a Youth Options representative indicated that programs and initiatives relied upon *current* demand. Representatives from FJIST, Youth Works, the Secondary School Apprenticeship all indicated that their strategies and placements were primarily focused upon *market-driven* occupations and industries. Rather than constructing ways to move into the high road, the objective is to identify and to define the skill requirements of the *existing* labour market, to develop occupation-specific curricula, to award credentials to individuals, and to set outcomes for education and training.[45]

Training for occupations in the low road does not lead to higher levels of training; that is, what we see is a churning of the low-waged labour force rather than laddering, which would enable individuals to progress from lower to higher skill occupations. In many cases, training does not go beyond basic work experience. At most, trainees will be subjected to human resource strategies that make them feel responsible for what happens at work.[46] However, in the low-end service sector, while it may make the person feel like s/he received "training," it does not change the contingency and insecurity of the work or the level of pay. There is no vertical movement in the training process. There is no necessary integration of the separate task into a new whole that would constitute a higher-skilled performance. Nor is there a new level of knowledge open to accommodate the various bits of information needed to carry out the various subtasks or competencies of the new role.[47] Moreover, high road jobs are not being created fast enough to absorb displaced workers. While organizational and technological shifts have created a core of functionally flexible white-collar workers who have secure employment, many of them used to have secure jobs but were made redundant. The high road logic is based on economic sectors and firms that use capital-intensive technologies and relatively little labour.[48] Because such firms produce few jobs, the periphery, the underemployed, and the unemployed can only expand. Thus, the high road is a high unemployment strategy that reinforces the labour-market polarization between "haves" and "have nots."

There is a sizable literature suggesting that labour market training programs do little or nothing to improve the demand side of the unemployment problem.[49] Rather than training ameliorating the polarized labour market, it has reinforced the polarization between a "core" of Canadians with well-paid, permanent, full-time jobs and an emerging "periphery" with dead-end, low-paid, part-time, and temporary McJobs (or no jobs at all).[50]

This polarization can be explained by considering the labour market as a balkanized market, with different occupations inhabiting different territories guided by institutional rules.[51] These rules create certain barriers to entry that serve to stratify the labour market. Political forces create two essentially non-competitive sectors: (1) a core, primary workforce occupying relatively secure jobs with relatively good pay and conditions and (2) a peripheral secondary workforce with insecure jobs and relatively poor pay and conditions. There is no definitive line of demarcation between categories of people; rather, classes fade into each other through slight gradations. Ultimately, individuals find their power to compete limited to a certain range of occupations.

In the case of British Columbia, those on social assistance and with not much more than a high school education were being targeted for programs that would set them on the path to the low road. Those with postsecondary degrees were targeted with programs that not only provided higher wages but also better placement in the labour market with regard to employment security. Despite provisions made through the student loan system for some Youth Works participants to attend university, the reality is that the vast majority of clients are not initially presented with that option. Instead, they are either shunted into job clubs to look for the first available job they can get or into short workplace-based training programs.

Developments elsewhere are consistent with this interpretation of BC training programs. For example, Lee et al.'s study involving interviews with over 200 trainees and former trainees from Southwick, England, found that participants in the better schemes (and with favoured backgrounds or good school records) were now becoming established in well-paid work with good prospects, some buying homes and living with partners. In contrast, the life chances of most former trainees on inferior schemes were unaffected or made worse by the further disillusionment of Youth Training Schemes.[52] Once one is in a low road occupation it is difficult to get out.[53] These youth receive low training investments from their employers and may also acquire unstable work histories due to job turnover in secondary jobs. This creates barriers in their effort to find better employment. The screening mechanisms used by employers become a self-fulfilling prophecy as youth, women, and minorities fail to acquire the characteristics that employers desire. As a result, the social division of labour is maintained in industry and occupational labour markets, with youth, women, and minorities concentrated in secondary jobs and peripheral industries.[54]

The reality of BC youth employment programs does not challenge social divisions; instead, they complement them by slotting individuals into appropriate places in the jobs hierarchy and by increasing the numbers available for low-waged employment. Rather than seeking social and economic solutions to the policies that create the polarized and insecure labour market, existing training programs assume that individuals must adjust to economic conditions. But this only serves to perpetuate the structural inequalities of the neoliberal labour market.

Notes

1 See Gary Becker, *Human Capital: A Theoretical and Empirical Analysis, with Special Reference to Education,* 3rd ed. (Chicago: University of Chicago Press, 1993).

2 Statistics Canada, *Labour Force Update: Youth and the Labour Market, 1998-1999* Cat. No. 71-005-XPB (Autumn 1999), 8.

3 Ibid., *Labour Force Update: An Overview of Average Wages and Wage Distribution in the Late 1990s,* Cat. No. 71-005-XPB, 4, no. 2 (2000), 11.

4 Ibid., *Labour Force Update,* Cat. No. 71-005-XPB (Summer 1998), 27.

5 Ibid.

6 Cansim label D987879 and D987882.

7 Statistics Canada, Cansim label D987852 and D987856.

8 BC Stats, Ministry of Finance and Corporate Relations, April 2001.

9 David W. Livingstone, *The Educational Jobs Gap: Underemployment or Economic Democracy* (Toronto, ON: Garamond, 1998).

10 Statistics Canada, *The Daily,* 14 July 1997. <http://www.statcan.ca/Daily/English/970714/d970714.htm#ART1> (28 August 2001).

11 Statistics Canada and the Council of Ministers of Education, Canada (CMEC) *Education Indicators in Canada: Report of the Pan-Canadian Education Indicators Program, 1999,* Cat. No. 81-582 (Toronto: Statistics Canada, Council of Ministers of Education, Canada, 2001).

12 Canadian Youth Foundation, *Youth Unemployment: Canada's Rite of Passage* (Ottawa: Canadian Youth Foundation, 1995).

13 Stephen McBride and John Shields, *Dismantling a Nation: The Transition to Corporate Rule in Canada* (Halifax: Fernwood, 1997).

14 OECD, *The Jobs Study* (Paris: OECD, 1994).

15 As Richard Marquardt, *Enter at Your Own Risk: Canadian Youth and the Labour Market* (Toronto: Between the Lines, 1998), 133, observes, these designations are equivalent to the distinction between "progressive competitiveness" and "competitive austerity" drawn by Albo. See G. Albo, "'Competitive Austerity' and the Impasse of Capitalist Employment Policy," in *The Socialist Register 1994: Between Globalism and Nationalism,* ed. Ralph Miliband and Leo Panitch (London: Merlin Press, 1995), 144-70.

16 Marquardt, *Enter at Your Own Risk,* chap. 7.

17 George S. Callaghan, *Flexibility, Mobility and the Labour Market* (Brookfield: Ashgate, 1997).

18 Graham S. Lowe, "The Future of Work: Implications for Unions," *Industrial Relations* 53 (1998): 235-57; David Wells, "Speak Softly and Carry a Big Carrot: Why the High Road to Competitiveness Is the Wrong Road," *Canadian Dimension* 31 (1997): 23-25.

19 James Swift and David Peerla, "Attitude Adjustment: The Brave New World of Work and the Revolution of Falling Expectations," in *The Training Trap: Ideology, Training and the Labour Market,* ed. Thomas Dunk, Stephen McBride, and Randle W. Nelsen (Winnipeg/Halifax: Society for Socialist Studies/Fernwood, 1996), 29-51.

20 Robert Hollands, "Crap Jobs, 'Govy Schemes' and 'Trainspotting': Reassessing Youth, Employment and Idleness Debate," in *Work and Idleness: The Political Economy of Full Employment,* ed. Jane Wheelock and J. Vail (Boston: Kluwer Academic Publishers, 1988), 103.

21 Ricardo Grinspun, and Robert Kreklewich, "Consolidating Neoliberal Reforms: 'Free Trade' as a Conditioning Framework," *Studies in Political Economy* 43 (1994): 33-61.

22 For an outline and critique of the OECD jobs strategy, see Stephen McBride and Russell A. Williams, "Globalization, the Restructuring of Labour Markets and Policy Convergence: The OECD Jobs Strategy," *Global Social Policy* 1 (2001): 283-311.

23 Marquardt, *Enter at Your Own Risk,* chap. 7.

24 These developments carry the potential for access to postsecondary education to be narrowed sociologically. There are, in any case, grounds for believing that human capital theory, which underlies this approach, may prove an inadequate guide to policy. See Marquardt, *Enter at Your Own Risk,* 125-26; Greg Albo, "The Cult of Training: Unemployment and Capitalist Employment Policy," in *Work and Idleness: The Political Economy of Full Employment,* ed. J. Wedlock and J.J. Vail (Amsterdam: Kluwer, 1998); Stephen McBride, "Policy from What?" in *Critical Perspectives on Canadian Public Policy: Restructuring and Resistance,* ed. Mike Burke, Colin Mooers, and John Shields (Halifax: Fernwood, 2000).

25 Marquardt, *Enter at Your Own Risk,* 133-34; Arimine Yalnizyan, *The Growing Gap: A Report on Growing Inequality between the Rich and the Poor in Canada* (Toronto: Centre for Social Justice, 1998).

26 International Labour Office (ILO), *World Employment Report 1998-99: Employability in the Global Economy – How Training Matters* (Geneva: ILO, 1998).

27 John P. Martin, *What Works among Active Labour Market Policies: Evidence from OECD Countries' Experiences,* OECD Working Papers: Labour Market and Social Policy Occasional Papers 6 (35) (Paris: OECD, 1998), 21.

28 Ibid., 14; Robert G. Fay, *Enhancing the Effectiveness of Active Labour Market Policies: Evidence from Program Evaluations in OECD Countries,* Labour Market and Social Policy Occasional Papers 18 (Paris: OECD, 1996), 43.

29 Norman Bowers, A. Sonnet, and L. Bardone, "Background Report: Giving Young People a Good Start – The Experience of OECD Countries," in *Preparing Youth for the 21st Century: The Transition from Education to the Labour Market Proceedings of the Washington, D.C., Conference, 23-24 February 1999* (Paris: OECD, 1999), 18.

30 Ibid., 25.

31 Martin, *What Works,* 26.

32 W. Norton Grubb, "Lessons from Education and Training for Youth: Five Precepts," in *Preparing Youth for the 21st Century: The Transition from Education to the Labour Market Proceedings of the Washington D.C. Conference, 23-24 February 1999* (Paris: OECD, 1999); Bowers, Sonnet, and Bardone, "Background Report," 33; ILO, *World Employment Report 1998-99;* OECD, *Key Employment Policy Challenges Faced by OECD Countries,* OECD Working Papers, Labour Market and Social Policy Occasional Papers 6 (50) (Paris: OECD, 1998); Fay, *Enhancing the Effectiveness,* 1996; W. Norton Grubb, *Learning to Work: The Case for Reintegrating Job Training and Education* (New York: Russell Sage Foundation, 1996).

33 Ursule Critoph, "Who Wins, Who Loses: The Real Story of the Transfer of Training to the Provinces and the Impact on Women," in this volume.

34 John Calvert, "The British Columbia College, University College, Institutes and Agencies Accord on Government Contract Training," York University Centre for Research on Work and Society Working Paper No. 00-08, 2000.

35 Lieutenant-Governor D.C. Lam, "Speech from the Throne," *Hansard Legislative Debates*, 22 March 1995 <http://www.legis.gov.bc.ca/1995/hansard/h0322pm.htm> (15 August 2001).
36 See Rodney S. Haddow, "How Malleable Are Political-Economic Institutions? The Case of Labour Market Decision-Making in BC," *Canadian Public Administration* 43, 4 (2000): 387-441.
37 Ibid., 407.
38 For a history of federal training policy, see Stephen McBride's working paper, "The Political Economy of Training in Canada." For a history of the provincial training policy, see Lara Lackey's working paper, "We've Got to Have Skills: Exploring Meanings, Contradictions and Implications of British Columbia's Skills Now Policy," written for the Western Research Network for Education and Training, UBC, Department of Curriculum Studies, April 2000. This essay can be downloaded from the Web site at <http://www.educ.ubc.ca/wrnet/Working%20Papers/WPS00-05.PDF>.
39 For further analysis of youth training programs in British Columbia see Linda Wong, "The Foundations of British Columbia's Youth Employment Programs" (MA thesis, Department of Political Science, Simon Fraser University, 2002).
40 British Columbia, *Hansard Legislative Debates, 4th Session, 36th Parliament* (March 2000), 16281-2.
41 Ibid., 1-2.
42 Ibid., 136.
43 British Columbia, Labour Force Development Board, *Training for What* (Victoria: Queen's Printer, 1995).
44 British Columbia, Premier's Business Advisory Committee on Youth Employment, *Working Together, Working Now: Combating Youth Unemployment* (Victoria: Premier's Business Advisory Committee on Youth Employment, 1998).
45 Ibid., 38-39.
46 Marquardt, *Enter at Your Own Risk;* Catherine G. Johnston and Carolyn R. Farquhar, *Empowered People Satisfy Customers* (Ottawa: Conference Board of Canada, 1992); Jacques Ellul, *The Technological Society,* trans. John Wilkinson (New York: Knopf, 1964).
47 Patrick Ainley, *Learning Policy: Towards the Certified Society* (New York: St. Martin's Press,1999), 184.
48 David Wells, "Speak Softly"; John Shields, "Flexible Work, Labour Market Polarization, and the Politics of Skills, Training and Enhancement," *The Training Trap,* ed. Thomas W. Dunk, Stephen McBride, Randle W. Nelsen (Halifax: Fernwood, 1996), 53-72.
49 Greg Albo, "Competitive Austerity," 1995; Marquardt, *Enter at Your Own Risk,* 129-30; David W. Livingstone, "Wasted Education and Withered Work: Reversing the 'Postindustrial' Education-Jobs Optic," in Dunk et al., *The Training Trap.*
50 Isik U. Zeytinoglu and Jacinta K. Muteshi, "Gender, Race and Class Dimensions of Nonstandard Work," *Industrial Relations* 55 (2000): 133-67; Lowe, "Future of Work"; Wells, "Speak Softly."
51 Callaghan, *Flexibility.*
52 David Lee, D. Marsden, P. Rickman, and J. Duncombe, *Scheming for Youth: A Study of YTS in the Enterprise Culture* (Philadelphia: Open University Press, 1990), 137.
53 David Lee, "Poor Work and Poor Institutions: Training and the Youth Labour Market," in *Poor Work: Disadvantage and the Division of Labour,* ed. Phillip Brown and Richard Scase (Philadelphia: Open University Press, 1991), 137.
54 Robert G. Sheets, Stephen Nord, and John J. Phelps, "The Impact of Service Industries on Unemployment," in *Metropolitan Economies* (Toronto: DC Heath and Company, 1987), 40-41.

14
Training Youth at Risk:
A Model Program in Quebec
Sylvain Bourdon and Frédéric Deschenaux

Despite the relative improvement of the job market in the last few years, a significant portion of the population still appears to be headed for exclusion from work and full citizenship. The increased qualifications required for job entry, combined with the school system's inability to ensure that all young people obtain a diploma,[1] are leaving a disturbing number of youth at risk of exclusion, first in terms of work (because of their lack of access to jobs) and subsequently in terms of social status (because of their lack of resources and lack of access to the networks and status imparted by paid employment).[2]

To counter this situation, a number of initiatives have been developed to provide young people at risk of exclusion with opportunities to acquire the qualifications they need for job integration. Many of these initiatives form part of government programs, but some are issued from actors directly involved in community development. One such community initiative, which we consider particularly interesting by virtue of its dynamism and impact, is the CIFER[3] Angus project that recently transformed into Insertech Angus.[4]

We present here a case study of this project, a community initiative conducted by community partners with the point of offering training within the context of a real, paid work set-up. In the first part of this study, we describe the organization's current activity, how it functions, the young people it accepts, the admission process, and the personnel team. Next, we present the initiative's community origins, its partnership links, and its funding. In conclusion, we discuss the difficulties involved with this type of initiative within the context of current government training and employment policies.

On-the-Job Training

The CIFER (Centre intégré de formation et de recyclage) Angus, which has been operating since 1998, is a job-entry firm specializing in computer recycling. Its business is refurbishing computers, printers, and peripherals – equipment that is donated by the provincial and federal governments and some large corporations as it becomes outdated or is replaced – then reselling them at the added-value price (i.e., the cost of the refurbishing process). Eighty percent of the organization's customers are schools; the remaining production goes to community organizations and individuals.

Thus, the centre is a real production facility, subject to real market constraints. Evidence of this reality is its physical location in a renovated industrial complex at the site of the former Angus shops in the heart of Montreal's working district as well as the physical layout of its work space, which is organized into a receiving area, management offices, shop, warehouse, and shipping area. The architecture and atmosphere serve as constant reminders that this is a work, not a school, environment.

The centre's business orientation also colours its training practices. While initially much more formal, the instruction rapidly evolved to become largely informal as centre personnel became aware that knowledge could be passed on through practice, with minimal hours spent in the classroom. According to the project director, this change in approach has been positive for the centre's young clients, who have often had a strained, if not antagonistic, relationship with the usual school "format."[5]

To further underscore its identity as a workplace, the centre regards it as essential that the young people benefiting from its services be considered employees. This status enables them to experience work, in a setting very similar to the regular labour market, and fosters their social integration by letting them become wage earners. In fact, it is by offering jobs, rather than training, that the centre recruits its young participants.

Recruitment takes place by means of posters, which are put up in places where young people congregate (pool halls, arcades, parks) and, increasingly, by word-of-mouth. The typical recruits are aged eighteen to twenty-four and have limited education and almost no work experience. During the first year, approximately one-third were women and two-thirds were men, but an increase in the number of men brought the proportion of women down to 21 percent in 2000-01 (Table 14.1). Although the targeted candidates are high school dropouts, they are required to have some mastery of written French as the training involves a large reading and writing component and demands rapid learning and adaptability. Young people unable to handle written work easily are considered better served by other resources.

Of the young people recruited, about half are welfare recipients; the other half are categorized as "cheque-less," meaning they don't receive any salary or government allowance of any kind. They rarely come from Employment Insurance, because to be eligible for EI they would have to have worked (for some time), which goes against the centre's eligibility criteria. Many of these youths have numerous handicaps in relation to the current labour market: they have limited education and little or no work experience; those who have worked have often had difficulty keeping their job. Most admit to having problems dealing with authority, and centre personnel note their low self-confidence levels. According to the centre's director, many recruits also have major personal problems. Some of the young women were heads of single-parent families and some have been victims of violence.

Another notable feature of the centre's clientele is multi-ethnicity. In 2000-1 there were participants from Haiti, the Dominican Republic, the Congo, Somalia, Pakistan, El Salvador, Mexico, Rwanda, Burundi, and Laos. Almost half of the participants are recent immigrants whose mother tongue is something other than French. However, a minimal knowledge of French is required for admission because all training at the centre is provided in French.

Not for Everybody
The centre does not automatically accept candidates seeking a job. In fact, according to the director, only about one in ten is admitted and begins training. The first step of the admission process is a group meeting, during which interested youth are given information about the centre and have an opportunity to visit. After this meeting, those who are still interested are invited to submit a job application – not to register for training! Applicants are then called for an interview, which allows the personnel to assess their motivation; an applicant's failure to come to the interview is considered very revealing.

According to the centre's director, an essential condition for hiring is that the young person have, or be in the process of acquiring, his or her

Table 14.1

Descriptive profile of the CIFER Angus clientele

| Cohorts | Gender | | Average age | Average education |
	Men	Women		
1 (September 1999-March 2000)	6	4	23	Sec. III (Grade 9)
2 (November 1999-May 2000)	8	4	21	Sec. III (Grade 9)
3 (March 2000-August 2000)	10	3	21	Sec. III (Grade 9)
* July 2000-June 2001	45	12	22	Sec. IV (Grade 10)

* Aggregated data only since cohort is unavailable for this period.

own living arrangements. The purpose of this condition is to ensure some stability, without which, experience has shown, it is almost impossible for young people to adhere to an established work schedule. This condition excludes itinerant or homeless youth.

Another consideration influencing hiring is group heterogeneity. The director explains that her aim, for each cohort, is to have a mix of personal characteristics as work in the different functional units requires a broad range of skills and interests. We note that, here again, production requirements rather than training considerations determine eligibility, thus reaffirming the centre's business orientation.

Strange as it may seem, some applicants are rejected because they appear to have too few difficulties. Given the centre's mission, young people who do not really need its services are directed to other resources. Applicants who present excessive problems are also not accepted because the centre lacks the resources required to work with them.

Learning without the School Feeling

The centre's formal training program, which consists of about thirty hours, is organized into modules. These are spread out over the first few weeks in order to avoid saturating the participants. The program was developed internally, in relation to the operations required for the efficient functioning of the production facilities. To ensure that the training reflects the reality of the job market, centre staff frequently visit local businesses in order to observe what really happens there and to determine the skills that will enhance the participants' entry into employment.

According to the director, the centre's hands-on approach, while maintaining the young people's interest and facilitating their learning, has proven challenging for staff members, who often associate training with classroom instruction. However, an effort has been made to adapt the training practices because the centre is intent upon operating as a business rather than as a place of training or, even less, as a school.

The young people hired by the centre stay for a maximum of six months and are paid minimum wage for thirty-five hours a week. During the first few months, they undergo thirty hours of formal training; in addition, they rotate through all the possible jobs, from the parts storeroom, to diagnosis, to repair, to the packing and shipping of refurbished components. They are progressively introduced to every task required in the shop. Following this introduction, they are assigned a specific job in accordance with their interests and abilities, and all production jobs, except driving the delivery truck, are filled by trainees. During the last three weeks of their stay, they engage in a supervised job search, which is considered an integral part of the training process. At this stage they are not as intensively involved in production activities; in fact, they are permitted only a brief return to production – something perceived as a reward – in order to boost their morale when the job search proves difficult. After they complete the program, some informal follow-up takes place through social activities to which "alumni" are invited. Except for some basic short-term tracking of employment status, there is no systematic follow-up, although the director reports that many young people return to visit and share their news, both good and bad. More formalized follow-up might well prove beneficial, but it cannot be provided as the project's financial backers do not permit the readmission of a young person who has already benefited from the centre's services.

For the young trainees, their stay at the centre often provides them with their first experience of success, both personal and work-related. This success, the director believes, makes them realize that they are capable of completing a project and encourages them to try to repeat this positive experience (in some cases by resuming their studies).

At the end of the process, most centre "graduates" end up in a job unrelated to the computer field. Half end up working in warehouses, 30 percent in commerce and services (including some work in Internet Cafés), and 20 percent in computer-related jobs. Project personnel perceive this as an indication of the transferability of the acquired skills. Of the ten members of the cohort that entered in September 1999 and left in March 2000, five were already employed three months later, while the other five were actively job hunting. Paradoxically, the fact of undergoing training that is adapted to their needs has resulted in about one-quarter of the young people returning to school.

As emphasized by the director, the centre's mission is not merely to provide employers with better trained young workers but also to enable young people to obtain quality jobs that provide good pay and stability. To improve the quality of the jobs secured by its graduates, centre personnel work on developing networks of contacts among potential employers.

A Multidisciplinary Team

To effectively run its production and training activities, the centre has a number of employees with varied qualifications who perform different functions. The director and an administrative assistant carry out administrative duties. Responsibility for the project's business component lies with the production manager. Working on the training component is a job-entry program specialist who is, in fact, a psychosocial support worker; a technical trainer specializing in computers; and another trainer supervises the handling section. The handling specialist trains and supervises the participants during their work in the warehouse, teaching them how to use the lift truck and how to work in packing. These employees work most directly with the young people.

There are, in addition, three other technicians: one who has no supervisory duties and two who combine supervisory and production duties. There is also a truck driver, who delivers the merchandise and occasionally performs some coaching duties, and a sales representative, whose job is to sell the centre's production. All these workers are employed on one-year contracts and are not considered permanent employees. They are not unionized.

A Project Originating in the Community

December 1991, a time of economical restructuring and high unemployment across industrialized countries, saw the final closure, after repeated difficulties, of the Angus railway shops – a large industrial complex located in a working-class district of Montreal. The closure engendered a long process of mobilization as people strove to find solutions to the resulting crisis. In 1994 a citizens committee voted to purchase the Angus shops site, and thus it became community property managed by a non-profit development corporation established by the Corporation de développement économique (CDE) Rosemont-La Petite Patrie.

During discussions on how the site should be developed, a district workforce adjustment committee was created, the Comité d'adaptation de la main-d'oeuvre (CAMO)[6] Angus, which sat from September 1995 to September 1997. The committee, composed of about twenty partners, adopted a number of strategies and projects for dealing with the training and access to employment problems of the local workforce. As a result of these efforts, the CIFER Angus, a multi-level work-study project, was established on paper in 1997, although it became operational only in autumn 1998, with the centre's first employees beginning work in September. Given the challenge of organizing so ambitious a project from scratch, with no previous example to follow, the initiators decided to proceed in stages. Thus the work, or business, component of the project was established first, while the study, or school, component, which required a good deal more preparation and consultation with school and other authorities in order to obtain course content approval, was put on hold and ultimately dropped when the CIFER Angus officially became a job-entry firm and changed its name to Insertech Angus in April 2000.

The simplest approach was to set up a business and a job-entry program for poorly educated youth. With Emploi-Québec funding for the program and contributions from the Anti-Poverty Fund and other local funds, the project got off the ground.

Initially, the present director of the centre was the only employee. She focused her attention on seeking funding for the project in order to ensure its survival. As this activity took most of her time, she hired a temporary worker to set up the job-entry program. Once sufficient funding was obtained, additional staff was hired. The present team, including the director and the first temporary worker (who is now a regular employee) numbers about ten.

Partnership Links
The centre's original partners were representatives of the agencies comprising the district CAMO, the committee responsible for the industrial re-development of the Angus shops. These agencies included FEDEC, the Société de développement Angus, the Montreal French school board,[7] the CEGEP de Rosemont (college), financial groups such as the Fédération des travailleurs et travailleuses du Québec (FTQ) Solidarity Fund and the Caisses populaires credit unions, labour (Confédération des syndicats nationaux [CSN] and FTQ) and community representatives. These initial partners became members of the management board, to be joined later by other stakeholders.

The centre has a partnership link with the school board and with the CEGEP. Together, they have worked on a pilot project for developing bridges between the job-entry program and high school, searching for a way to achieve recognition (as a semi-skilled trade) for the learning acquired at the centre. This school component of the work-study project would enable the centre to achieve another part of its mission: to provide young people with qualifications. The centre director also believes that the presence of trainees from vocational schools or colleges would stimulate the participants of the job-entry program and make them see that they are capable of the same achievements as the students. Unfortunately, this part of the project is taking time to get off the ground, in part because of the time required for educational authorities to develop and recognize new types of training.

A Complex Financial Arrangement
Insertech Angus is a non-profit organization, existing largely thanks to start-up grants from Emploi-Québec and contributions from the Anti-Poverty Fund, which are used to pay the participants' wages.

The employees' wages, although all paid by the centre, are financed in different ways. Most of the wages are paid from the grants obtained for the job-entry program; thus, the wages of employees who work with the trainees come from the budget allocated for coaching. For employees who do not work with the young people, the wages are generated through self-financing.

The centre operates on a budget of approximately $1.3 million per year, split more or less equally between revenue from grants and revenue from sales ($700,000 in grants and $600,000 in sales). As the grants are diminishing, the centre is seeking to increase its sales. It is trying to diversify its markets as selling to educational institutions is not highly profitable.

A Fragile Success

Insertech Angus is primarily a business, but it aspires to increase its educational role, which already exists in an informal way. The establishment of bridges between high school or college and the centre, which was part of the initial project plan, is no longer such a priority as the job-entry program must first be assured of stable and recurrent funding. Under the present conditions, introduction of the school component would not only prove difficult because of the delays involved in working with educational authorities but it would also jeopardize the project's business component. The centre's current funding is based on a complex financial arrangement, which could be adversely affected by a change in its orientation.

Finances are one of the main sources of the centre's insecurity. There is a limit to its ability to generate economic activities that serve its mission of providing job-entry assistance while still permitting it to stay viable and even profitable. The centre is well aware that the search for profitability cannot be made at the expense of its educational mission. Thus, for example, computer recycling is a less profitable business than is the assembly of new computers, but working on recycling enables the young trainees to acquire a lot of transferable knowledge, which might not be the case if they assembled new computers. In addition, by working in recycling, the company avoids competing with the private sector, an essential requisite for its recognition as a socio-economic organization.

Other constraints are imposed by CIFER's sources of funding. Its training program is funded by Emploi-Québec, specifically through its Job Preparation[8] measure, which pays for coaching. The rest of the funding comes from the Anti-Poverty Fund, which restricts the selection of clients as the trainees must be eligible for the fund in order for their wages to be subsidized. The 1999 crisis at Emploi-Québec[9] showed the fragility of this type of funding, which is subject to the vagaries of politics and the management priorities of a ministry that is tending increasingly to reduce its allocations in favour of short-term training for individuals at the job access threshold.

The success that CIFER has experienced can be explained, in part, by its position within a particular niche of the social economy, which enables the business to be largely self-financed while remaining on the fringe of the market economy. An additional factor is the specific targeting of its clients, who are not burdened by excessive problems (they have knowledge of French and their own living arrangements) but who are nevertheless excluded from the labour market (young people who are too employable are not accepted). However, it must be said that a large part of the project's success rests on its highly media-friendly character, including its activity in two high-profile fields – computers and recycling – and its location in a well-known site in the heart of the city's historical working district. The project's media appeal has been fully exploited both by its management and by government members, who never miss a chance to cite it as a successful model and to associate themselves with it in the press; this, in turn, helps to ensure its funding. But this media-friendliness, while understandable in view of the initiative's real interest, is probably the Achilles heel of this model in terms of its wider application as a remedy for the social exclusion of youth with limited schooling. There is simply no place or any relevance in the eyes of politicians for hundreds of models of this same type. Moreover, to function effectively, this initiative requires significant investments and large amounts of working capital. These sums may appear prohibitive, although they probably represent the real price that must currently be paid to ensure to all citizens the place that is their due.

Notes

1 L. Moreau, "La pauvreté et le décrochage scolaire ou, La spirale de l'exclusion" [Literature review]: Direction de la recherche, de l'évaluation et de la statistique (Ministère de la Sécurité du revenu, Gouvernement du Québec, 1995).

2 R. Castel, *Métamorphose de la question sociale: Une chronique du salariat* (Paris: Fayard, 1995).

3 The English translation of Centre intégré de formation et de recyclage is Integrated Training and Retraining Centre.

4 This chapter is mostly based on data and observations made during the transition from CIFER Angus to Insertech Angus during the spring of 2000. Most of the time, this changing organization is referred to as the "centre," but observations apply to both entities since the evolution of the training model has been fluid.

5 B. Lahire, *Culture écrite et inégalités scolaires: sociologie de "l'échec scolaire" à l'école primaire* (Lyon: Presses universitaires de Lyon, 1993).

6 The English translation of Comité d'adaptation de la main-d'oeuvre is Workforce Adjustment Committee.

7 Commission scolaire de Montréal.

8 Préparation à l'emploi.

9 In the year following the transfer of funds and responsibility for training from Ottawa to Quebec, a series of problems resulted in an immense anticipated deficit for the training budget in mid-year, which led to a thorough reconsideration of the funding and drastic cuts to programs and allocations.

Bibliography

Books

Acker, J. *Doing Comparable Worth: Gender, Class and Pay Equity.* Philadelphia: Temple University Press. 1989.

Ainley, Patrick. *Learning Policy: Towards the Certified Society.* New York: St. Martin's Press. 1999.

Allard, M.A., R. Albelba, M.E. Colten, and C. Cosenza. *In Harm's Way? Domestic Violence, AFDC Receipt, and Welfare Reform in Massachusetts.* Boston: University of Massachusetts, McCormack Institute, Centre for Survey Research. 1997.

Allen, R. *The Economic Benefits of Post-Secondary Training and Education in B.C.: An Outcomes Assessment.* Vancouver: Department of Economics, University of British Columbia. 1996.

Anderson, Kim. *A Recognition of Being: Reconstructing Native Womanhood.* Toronto: Second Story Press. 2000.

Anisef, P., R. Sweet, G. Plickert, and D. Tom-Kun. *The Effects of Region and Gender on Educational Planning in Canadian Families.* Toronto: Laidlaw Foundation. 2001.

Anisef, P., P. Axelrod, E. Baichman-Anisef, C. James, and A. Turrittin. *Opportunity and Uncertainty: Life Course Experiences of the Class of '73.* Toronto: University of Toronto Press. 2001.

Armstrong, Pat, Hugh Armstrong, Ivy Bourgeault, Jacqueline Choiniere, Eric Mykhalovskiy, and Jerry P. White. *Heal Thyself: Managing Health Care Reform.* Aurora: Garamond. 2000.

Association of Service Providers for Employability and Career Training (ASPECT). *Analyzing the Impact and Challenging the Assumptions: A Report that Demonstrates the Impact of Government Policies on Unemployed Persons and on Community Service Deliverers.* Vancouver: ASPECT. 1999.

Bakker, Isabella. *Unpaid Work and Macroeconomics.* Ottawa: Status of Women Canada. 1998.

–, ed. "Introduction: The Gendered Foundations of Restructuring in Canada." *Rethinking Restructuring: Gender and Change in Canada.* Toronto: University of Toronto Press. 1996.

Barrett, Michele. *Women's Oppression Today: Problems in Marxist Feminist Analysis.* London: Verso. 1980.

Beck, U. *Risk Society: Towards a New Modernity.* London: Sage. 1992.

Betcherman, Gordon, Kathryn McMullen, Norm Leckie, and Christina Caron. *The Canadian Workplace in Transition.* Kingston: Industrial Relations Centre, Queen's University. 1994.

Betcherman, Gordon, Kathryn McMullen, and Katie Davidman. *Training for the New Economy.* Ottawa: Canadian Policy Research Networks. 1998.

Bird, Florence, chair. *Report of the Royal Commission on the Status of Women in Canada.* Ottawa: Information Canada. September 1970.

Bird, Pat, and Alice de Wolff. *Occupational Analysis: Clerical Occupations in Metropolitan Toronto.* Toronto: Clerical Workers Centre. December 1997.

Booth, Susan. *Bridges to Equity.* Toronto: City of Toronto. 1991.

Braid, Kate. "Invisible Women: Women in Non-Traditional Occupations in B.C." MA thesis, Simon Fraser University. 1979.

Braundy, Marcia, ed. *Surviving and Thriving: Women in Trades and Technology and Employment Equity.* Winlaw, BC: Kootenay Women in Trades and Technology (WITT). 1989.

Braverman, Harold. *Labour and Monopoly Capital: The Degradation of Work in the Twentieth Century.* London: Monthly Review Press. 1974.

Brouwer, Andrea. *Immigrants Need Not Apply.* Ottawa: The Caledon Institute. 1999.

Buchanan, R.M., and S. Koch-Schulte. *Gender on the Line: Technology Restructuring and the Reorganization of Work in the Call Centre Industry.* Ottawa: Status of Women. 2000.

Butterwick, Shauna. "The Politics of Needs Interpretation: A Study of Three CJS-Funded Job-Entry Programs for Women." PhD diss., University of British Columbia. 1993.

Callaghan, George S. *Flexibility, Mobility and the Labour Market.* Brookfield: Ashgate. 1997.

Canadian Congress for Learning Opportunities for Women. *CCLOW and the Social Security Reforms.* Toronto: CCLOW. 1994.

–, Canadian Research Institute for the Advancement of Women, National Organisation of Immigrant and Visible Minority Women, Canadian Farm Women's Education Council. *A Collaborative Response to the Green Paper on Social Security Reform from Four National Women's Groups.* Toronto: CCLOW/CRIAW/NOIVMW/CFWEC. 1994.

Canadian Labour Congress. "Statement by the CLC to the House of Commons Standing Committee on Human Resources on Bill C-2: An Act to Amend the Employment Insurance Act." Ottawa: Canadian Labour Congress. 1 March 2001.

Canadian Youth Foundation. *Youth Unemployment: Canada's Hidden Deficit.* Canadian Imperial Bank of Commerce Aid in Production. Ottawa: Canadian Youth Foundation. 1995.

–. *Youth Unemployment: Canada's Rite of Passage.* Ottawa: Canadian Youth Foundation. 1995.

Castel, R. *Métamorphose de la question sociale: Une chronique du salariat.* Paris: Fayard. 1995.

Centre for the Study of Living Standards. *Report on Creating a More Efficient Labour Market.* Ottawa: CSLS. 2001.

Chuchryk, Patricia, and Christine Miller, eds. *Women of the First Nations: Power, Wisdom, and Strength.* Winnipeg: University of Manitoba Press. 1996.

Cockburn, C. *Brothers: Male Dominance and Technological Change.* London: Pluto Press. 1983.

–. *In the Way of Women: Men's Resistance to Sex Equality in Organizations.* London: Macmillan. 1991.

Critoph, Ursule. *Background on the Training System in Canada.* Ottawa: Canadian Labour Congress. 1997.

–. *Training: Is There Still a Public Commitment?* Ottawa: National Union of Public and General Employees. 1996.

Crouch, Colin, David Finegold, and Mari Sako. *Are Skills the Answer? The Political Economy of Skills Creation in Advanced Industrial Countries.* New York: Oxford University Press. 1999.

Das Gupta, Tania. *Racism and Paid Work.* Toronto: Garamond. 1996.

Dunk, Thomas W., Stephen McBride, and Randle W. Nelsen, eds. *The Training Trap: Ideology, Training and the Labour Market.* Winnipeg/Halifax: Society for Socialist Studies/Fernwood. 1996.

Eisenberg, Susan. *We'll Call You If We Need You: Experiences of Women Working Construction.* Ithaca and London: ILR Press. 1998.

Ellul, Jacques. *The Technological Society.* Trans. John Wilkinson. New York: Knopf. 1964.

Epstein, D., J. Elwood, V. Hey, and J. Maw. *Failing Boys: Issues in Gender and Achievement.* Buckingham, UK: Open University Press. 1998.

Fay, Robert G. *Enhancing the Effectiveness of Active Labour Market Policies: Evidence From Program Evaluations in OECD Countries.* Labour Market and Social Policy Occasional Papers 18. Paris: OECD. 1996.

Fraser, Nancy. *Unruly Practice: Power Discourse and Gender in Contemporary Social Theory.* Minneapolis, MN: University of Minnesota Press. 1989.

Fudge, J., and P. McDermott, eds. *Just Wages: A Feminist Assessment of Pay Equity*. Toronto: University of Toronto Press. 1991.

Furlong, A., and F. Cartmel. *Young People and Social Change: Individualization and Risk in Late Modernity*. Buckingham, UK: Open University Press. 1997.

Gallagher, P. *Changing Course: An Agenda for Real Reform of Canadian Education*. Toronto: OISE Press. 1995.

Gaskell, J. *Gender Matters from School to Work*. Milton Keynes, UK/Philadelphia: Open University Press. 1992.

Goldberg, Sharon R. *Women in Construction: A Report on Access, Training and Retention in the Construction Trade*. Vancouver: Amalgamated Construction Association of BC. 1992.

Gregor, A., and G. Jasmin. *Higher Education in Canada*. Ottawa: Secretary of State. 1992.

Grubb, W. Norton. *Learning to Work: The Case for Reintegrating Job Training and Education*. New York: Russell Sage Foundation. 1996.

–. *Working in the Middle: Strengthening Education and Training for the Mid-Skilled Labor Force*. San Francisco: Jossey-Bass. 1996.

Grzetic, Brenda, Mark Shrimpton, and Sue Skipton. *Women, Employment Equity and the Hibernia Construction Project*. St. John's, NF: Women in Trades and Technology. June 1996.

Hayes, Kevin. *Left Out in the Cold: The End of UI for Canadian Workers*. Ottawa: Canadian Labour Congress. 1999.

Heinz, W. *Theoretical Advances in Life Course Research*. Weinheim: Deutscher Studien Verlag. 1991.

Horsman, Jenny. *Too Scared to Learn: Women, Violence, and Education*. Toronto: McGilligan Books. 1999.

Hughes, K. *Gender and Self-Employment in Canada: Assessing Trends and Policy Implications*. Ottawa: Canadian Policy Research Networks. 1999.

International Labour Office. *World Employment Report 1998-99: Employability in the Global Economy – How Training Matters*. Geneva: International Labour Organization. 1998.

Johnston, Catharine G., and Carolyn R. Fuqua. *Empowered People Satisfy Customers*. Ottawa: Conference Board of Canada. 1992.

Lahire, B. *Culture écrite et inégalités scolaires: sociologie de "l'échec scolaire" à l'école primaire*. Lyon: Presses universitaires de Lyon. 1993.

Lakoff, Robin. *Language and Women's Place*. New York: Harper Colophon. 1975.

Larson, Magali S. *The Rise of Professionalism: A Sociological Analysis*. Berkeley: University of California Press. 1977.

Lawrence, Bonita. "'Real' Indians and Others: Mixed-Race Urban Native People, the Indian Act, and the Rebuilding of Indigenous Nations." PhD diss., Ontario Institute for Studies in Education, April 1999.

Lazar, Harvey. *Shifting Roles: Active Labour Market Policy in Canada under the Labour Market Development Agreements*. Ottawa: Canadian Policy Research Networks. 2002.

Lee, David, Dennis Marsden, Penny Rickman, and Jean Duncombe. *Scheming for Youth: A Study of YTS in the Enterprise Culture*. Milton Keynes, UK/Philadelphia: Open University Press. 1990.

Lewis, J., M. Porter, and M. Shrimpton, eds. *Women, Work and Family in the British, Canadian and Norwegian Offshore Oilfields*. London: Macmillan. 1988.

Livingstone, David W. *The Educational Jobs Gap: Underemployment or Economic Democracy*. Toronto: Garamond. 1998.

Marquardt, Richard. *Enter at Your Own Risk: Canadian Youth and the Labour Market*. Toronto: Between the Lines. 1998.

Martin, John P. *What Works among Active Labour Market Policies: Evidence from OECD Countries' Experiences*. OECD Working Papers: Labour Market and Social Policy – Occasional Papers 6 (35). Paris: OECD. 1998.

McBride, Stephen. *Paradigm Shift: Globalization and the Canadian State*. Halifax: Fernwood. 2001.

–, and John Shields. *Dismantling a Nation: The Transition to Corporate Rule in Canada*. Halifax: Fernwood. 1997.

Messing, Karen. *One-Eyed Science: Occupational Health and Women Workers.* Philadelphia: Temple University Press. 1998.

Moser, Caroline. *Gender Planning and Development: Theory, Practice and Training.* London: Routledge. 1993.

Musisi, Nakanyike B., and Jane Turritin. *African Women and the Metropolitan Toronto Labour Market in the 1990s.* Toronto. June 1995.

Ng, Winnie. *Women's Work: A Report.* Ottawa: Canadian Labour Congress. March 1997.

Ontario Association of Interval and Transition Houses (OAITH). *Locked In, Left Out: Impacts of the Budget Cuts on Abused Women and Their Children.* Toronto: OAITH. 1996.

Ontario Network of Skills Training Projects. *A History of Community Based Training in Canada.* Toronto: ONESTEP. 1998.

Organisation for Economic Cooperation and Development. *Education and Policy Analysis.* Paris: OECD. 2001.

–. *Key Employment Policy Challenges Faced by OECD Countries.* OECD Working Papers. Labour Market and Social Policy Occasional Papers 6 (50). Paris: OECD. 1998.

Overend, Valerie. *Foundation for Success: The Story of the Women's Work Training Program in Saskatchewan.* Regina: Saskatchewan Women in Trades and Technology. 2000.

Parkin, Frank. *Marxism and Class Theory: A Bourgeois Critique.* New York: Columbia University Press. 1979.

Pendakur, Ravi. *Immigrants and the Labour Force.* Montreal and Kingston: McGill-Queen's University Press. 2000.

Raphael, Jodi, and Richard Tolman, eds. *Trapped by Poverty, Trapped by Abuse.* Michigan: Taylor Institute and the University of Michigan Research Development Center on Poverty Risk and Mental Health. 1997.

Razack, Sherene. *Looking White People in the Eye: Gender, Race and Culture in Courtrooms and Classrooms.* Toronto: University of Toronto Press. 1998.

Redclift, Michael, ed. *Life Chances and Livelihoods.* London: Routledge. 2000.

"Registered Apprenticeship and the National Skill Standards System." Washington, DC: American Federation of Labour/Congress of Industrial Organizations. 2000.

Rhode, D. *Justice and Gender: Sex Discrimination and the Law.* Cambridge: Harvard University Press. 1989.

Ryan, P. ed. *International Comparisons of Vocational Education and Training for Intermediate Skills.* New York: Falmer. 1991.

Scane, J., P. Staton, and M. Schneider, eds. *Strategies that Work: Women in Science, Trades, and Technology.* Toronto: Green Dragon Press. 1994.

Schetagne, S. *Building Bridges across Generations in the Workplace: A Response to Aging of the Workforce.* Ottawa: Canadian Council on Social Development. 2001.

Schuetze, H., and K. Rubenson. *Learning in the Classroom and at the Workplace: Elements of a Framework for the Analysis of Apprenticeship Training and Other Forms of "Alternation" Education and Training in Canada.* Vancouver: UBC Centre for Policy Studies in Education. 1996.

Schuetze, H., and R. Sweet, eds. *Integrating School and Workplace Learning in Canada: Principles and Practices of Alternation Education and Training.* Montreal: McGill-Queen's University Press. Forthcoming.

Sheets, Robert G., Stephen Nerd, and John J. Phelps. *The Impact of Service Industries on Unemployment in Metropolitan Economies.* Toronto: D.C. Heath and Company. 1987.

Simon, R., D. Dippo, and A. Schenke. *Learning Work: A Critical Pedagogy of Work Education.* Toronto: OISE Press. 1991.

Spender, Dale. *Man Made Language.* Boston: Routledge and Kegan Paul. 1980.

Tannen, Deborah. *You Just Don't Understand: Women and Men in Conversation.* New York: William Morrow and Company. 1990.

Teichler, U. *Thematic Debate: The Requirements of the World of Work.* Paper ED-98/CONF. 202/18. Geneva: International Labour Organization. 2000.

White, Julie. *Sisters and Solidarity: Women and Unions in Canada.* Toronto: Thompson Educational Publishing. 1993.

Williams, Raymond. *Keywords: A Vocabulary of Culture and Society.* New York: Oxford University Press. 1974.

Wismer, Susan. *Counting Ourselves In: Women's Contribution to the Canadian Economy*. Toronto: Canadian Women's Foundation. January 1997.

–. *Women's Education and Training: A Policy Analysis*. Toronto: Canadian Congress for Learning Opportunities for Women. 1988.

Wolfson, William. *The Second Century: Community-Based Training in Canada*. National Human Resources Study. Toronto: Canadian Coalition of Community-Based Training. 1997.

Wong, Linda. "The Foundations of British Columbia's Youth Employment Programs." MA thesis, Simon Fraser University. 2001.

Working Skills Centre. *Working Skills for Immigrant Women*. 2nd ed. Toronto: Working Skills Centre of Ontario. 1996.

Yalnizyan, Armine. *The Growing Gap: A Report on Growing Inequality between the Rich and the Poor in Canada*. Toronto: Centre for Social Justice. 1998.

Articles

Ainley, P., and J. Corbett. "From Vocationalism to Enterprise: Social and Life Skills Become Personable and Transferable." *British Journal of Sociology of Education* 15, 3 (1994): 365-74.

Albo, Greg. "'Competitive Austerity' and the Impasse of Capitalist Employment Policy." In *The Socialist Register 1994: Between Globalism and Nationalism*. Ed. Ralph Miliband and Leo Panitch, 144-70. London: Merlin Press. 1994.

–. "Cult of Training." In *Work and Idleness: The Political Economy of Full Employment*. Ed. J. Wheelock and J. Vail. Boston: Kluwer Academic Publishers. 1998.

Andres, L., P. Anisef, H. Krahn, D. Looker, and V. Thiessen. "The Persistence of Social Structure: Class and Gender Effects on the Occupational Aspirations of Canadian Youth." *Journal of Youth Studies* 2 (1999): 261-82.

Andres, L., and D. Looker. "Rurality and Capital: Educational Expectations and Attainments of Rural, Urban-Rural and Metropolitan Youth." *Canadian Journal of Higher Education*. Forthcoming.

Arat-Koc, Sedef. "Immigration Policies, Migrant Domestic Workers, and the Definition of Citizenship in Canada." In *Deconstructing a Nation: Immigration, Multiculturalism and Racism in '90s Canada*. Ed. Vic Satzewich, 229-42. Halifax: Fernwood. 1992.

Arriola, Elvira R. "'What's the Big Deal?' Women in the New York City Construction Industry and Sexual Harassment Law, 1970-1985." *Columbia Human Rights Law Review* 22, 1 (1990): 21-71.

Ash, Sylvia, Helen King, Dorothy Robbins, Gladys Watson, and WISE participants. "Women Interested in Successful Employment: Perspectives on a Bridging Program." *Women's Education des femmes* 7, 2 (1989): 30-34.

Ashton, D., M. Maguire, and J. Sung. "Institutional Structures and Provision of Intermediate Skills: Lessons from Canada and Hong Kong." *International Comparisons of Vocational Education and Training for Intermediate Skills*. Ed. P. Ryan. New York: Falmer. 1991.

Atkinson, John. "Manpower Strategies for Flexible Organisations." *Personnel Management* (August 1984): 28-31.

Bakan, Abigail B., and Daiva K. Stasiulis. "Foreign Domestic Worker Policy in Canada." *Science and Society* 58 (Spring 1994): 7-33.

Baptiste, Ian. "Educating Lone Wolves: Pedagogical Implications of Human Capital Theory." *Adult Education Quarterly* 51, 3 (2001): 184-201.

Bowers, Norman, Anne Sonnet, and Laura Bardone. "Background Report: Giving Young People a Good Start – The Experience of OECD Countries." *Preparing Youth for the 21st Century: The Transition from Education to the Labour Market – Proceedings of the Washington, D.C., Conference, 23-24 February 1999*. Paris: OECD. 1999.

Boyd, Monica. "Migration Policy, Female Dependency, and Family Membership: Canada and Germany." In *Women and the Canadian Welfare State*. Ed. Patricia M. Evans and Gerda R. Wekerle, 142-69. Toronto: University of Toronto Press. 1997.

Braid, Kate. "Neither Friendly nor Familiar: Language Styles, Stress and Macho." In *Surviving and Thriving: Women in Trades and Technology and Employment Equity – Proceedings of the Naramata Conference*. Winlaw, BC: Kootenay WITT, 61-68. 1988.

Byrd, Barbara. "Women in Carpentry Apprenticeship: A Case Study." *Labour Studies Journal* 24, 3 (1999): 3-22.

Charles, M., M. Buchmann, S. Halebsky, J. Powers, and M. Smith. "The Context of Women's Market Careers: A Cross-National Study." *Work and Occupations* 28 (2001): 371-96.

Cohen, Marjorie Griffin, and Kate Braid. "Training and Equity Initiatives on the British Columbia Vancouver Island Highway Project: A Model for Large-Scale Construction Projects." *Labor Studies Journal* 25, 3 (2000): 70-103.

Cohen, P. "Against the New Vocationalism." In *Schooling for the Dole: The New Vocationalism.* Ed. I. Bates, J. Clarke, P. Cohen, D. Finn, R. Moore, and P. Willis, 104-69. Basingstoke, UK: Macmillan. 1984.

Collinson, D.L. "Shift-ing Lives: Work-Home Pressures in the North Sea Oil Industry." *Canadian Review of Sociology and Anthropology* 35, 3 (1998): 301-24.

Conger, Stuart, and D. Mullen, "Life skills." *International Journal of Advising Counseling* 4 (1981): 305-19.

Finnie, R. "Holding Their Own: Employment and Earnings of Post-Secondary Graduates." *Education Quarterly Review* 7 (2001): 21-37.

Fraser, Nancy, and Linda Gordon. "A Genealogy of 'Dependency': Tracing a Keyword of the U.S. Welfare State." In *Justice Interruptus: Critical Reflections on the "Postsocialist Condition."* Ed. Nancy Fraser, 309-36. New York: Routledge. 1997.

Freeman, Richard B. "The Youth Job Market Problem at Y2K." *Preparing Youth for the 21st Century: The Transition from Education to the Labour Market – Proceedings of the Washington, D.C., Conference, 23-24 February 1999.* Paris: OECD. 1999.

Gale, Andrea W. "Women in Non-Traditional Occupations: The Construction Industry." *Women in Management Review* 9, 2 (1994): 3-14.

Gallagher, P., and R. Sweet. "Intermediate Skill Development in British Columbia: Policy Options for a Post-Industrial Era." *Canadian Journal of Higher Education* 27 (1997): 181-212.

Gaskell, J. "Conceptions of Skill and the Work of Women: Some Historical and Political Issues." In *Politics of Diversity.* Ed. M. Barrett and R. Hamilton, 361-80. London: Verso Editions. 1986.

Giddens, A. "Living in a Post-Traditional Society." In *Reflexive Modernization: Politics, Tradition and Aesthetics in the Modern Social Order.* Ed. U. Beck, A. Giddens, and S. Lash, 56-109. Stanford: Stanford University Press. 1994.

Griffith, Allison. "Skilling for Life/Living for Skill: The Social Construction of Life Skills in Ontario Schools." *Journal of Educational Thought* 22, 2A (1988): 198-208.

Grinspun, Ricardo, and Robert Kreklewich. "Consolidating Neoliberal Reforms: 'Free Trade' as a Conditioning Framework." *Studies in Political Economy* 43 (1994): 33-61.

Grubb, W. Norton. "Lessons from Education and Training for Youth: Five Precepts." *Preparing Youth for the 21st Century: The Transition from Education to the Labour Market – Proceedings of the Washington, D.C., Conference, 23-24 February 1999.* Paris: OECD. 1999.

Haddow, Rodney S. "How Malleable Are Political-Economic Institutions? The Case of Labour Market Decision-Making in BC." *Canadian Public Administration* 43, 4 (2000): 387-411.

–. "Regional Development Policy: A Nexus of Policy and Politics." In *How Ottawa Spends 2001-2002: Power in Transition.* Ed. Leslie A. Pal, 247-75. Don Mills: Oxford University Press. 2001.

Hadley, Karen. *"And We Still Ain't Satisfied": Gender Inequality in Canada – A Status Report for 2001.* Toronto: National Action Committee on the Status of Women and the CSJ Foundation for Research and Education. June 2001.

Heinz, W. "Job-Entry Patterns in a Life Course Perspective." In *From Education to Work: Cross-National Perspectives.* Ed. W. Heinz, 214-31. Cambridge: Cambridge University Press. 1999.

Hollands, Robert. "Crap Jobs, 'Govy Schemes' and 'Trainspotting': Reassessing Youth, Employment and Idleness Debate." In *Work and Idleness: The Political Economy of Full Employment.* Ed. J. Wheelock and J. Vail, 99-117. Boston: Kluwer Academic Publishers. 1988.

"I'm a Lumberjack and I'm Okay." *Globe and Mail,* 17 November 1999, B3.

Jackson, N. "Skill Training in Transition: Implications for Women." *Women and Education.* 2nd ed. Ed. J. Gaskell and A. McLaren, 351-70. Calgary: Detselig. 1991.

James, N. "Emotional Labour: Skill and Work in the Social Regulation of Feelings." *Sociological Review* 37, 1 (1989): 15-32.

Jansen, Theo, and Danny Wildemeersch. "Beyond the Myth of Self-Actualization: Reinventing the Community Perspective of Adult Education." *Adult Education Quarterly* 48, 4 (1998): 216-26.

Jenson, J. "Shifting the Paradigm: Knowledge and Learning for Canada's Future." *CPRN Discussion Paper No. F18.* Ottawa: Canadian Policy Research Networks. 2001.

Johnson, Wendy. "Model Programs Prepare Women for the Skilled Trades." In *Women, Work and School: Occupational Segregation and the Role of Education.* Ed. Leslie R. Wolfe, 140-52. Boulder: Westview Press. 1991.

Johnston, Betty. "Women in Charge on Mt. Lemmon Highway Job." *Rocky Mountain Construction,* 30 September 1997, 20-23.

Klassen, Thomas. "The Federal-Provincial Labour Market Development Agreements: Brave New Model of Cooperation." In *Federalism, Democracy and Labour Market Policy in Canada.* Ed. Tom McIntosh, 159-203. Kingston: McGill-Queen's University Press. 2001.

Lawrence, Bonita. "Mixed-Race Urban Native Identity: Surviving a Legacy of Genocide." *Kinesis,* Native Women's Issue, December 1999/January 2000: 15, 18.

Lee, David. "Poor Work and Poor Institutions: Training and the Youth Labour Market." In *Poor Work: Disadvantage and the Division of Labour.* Ed. Phillip Brown and Richard Scase, 88-102. Philadelphia: Open University Press. 1991.

Lenhardt, G. "School and Wage Labour." *Economics and Industrial Democracy* 2 (1981): 191-222.

Little, Margaret. "A Litmus Test for Democracy: The Impact of Ontario Welfare Changes on Single Mothers." *Studies in Political Economy,* forthcoming.

Livingstone, David W. "Wasted Education and Withered Work: Reversing the 'Postindustrial' Education-Jobs Optic." In *The Training Trap: Ideology, Training and the Labour Market.* Ed. Thomas W. Dunk, Stephen McBride, and Randle W. Nelsen, 73-99. Winnipeg/Halifax: Society for Socialist Studies/Fernwood. 1996.

Looker, D. "In Search of Credentials: Factors Affecting Young Adults' Participation in Postsecondary Education." *Canadian Journal of Education* 27 (1997): 1-36.

–, and V. Thiessen. "Images of Work: Women's Work, Men's Work, Household Work." *Canadian Journal of Sociology* 24, 2 (1999): 225-54.

Lowe, Graham S. "The Future of Work: Implications for Unions." *Industrial Relations* 53 (1998): 235-57.

–, and H. Krahn. "Work Aspirations and Attitudes in an Era of Labour Market Restructuring: A Comparison of Two Canadian Cohorts." *Work, Employment and Society* 14 (2000): 1-22.

McBride, Stephen. "Policy from What?" In *Critical Perspectives on Canadian Public Policy: Restructuring and Resistance.* Ed. Mike Burke, Colin Mooers, and John Shields, 159-77. Halifax: Fernwood. 2000.

–, and Russell A. Williams. "Globalization, the Restructuring of Labour Markets and Policy Convergence: The OECD 'Jobs Strategy'." *Global Social Policy* 1 (2000): 283-311.

McFarland, Joan. "Combining Economic and Social Policy through Work and Welfare: The Impact on Women." In *Papers on Economic Equality.* 147-64. Ottawa: Status of Women Canada. 1994.

–, and Bob Mullaly. "NB Works: Image vs. Reality." *Remaking Social Policy: Social Security in the Late 1990s.* Ed. Jane Pulkingham and Gordon Ternowetsky, 202-19. Halifax: Fernwood. 1996.

MacKeracher, Dorothy. "CASP! Do You Really Want One in Your Neighbourhood?" *Women's Education des femmes* 11, 1 (1994): 47-52.

Mason, G. "The Mix of Graduate and Intermediate-Level Skills in Britain: What Should the Balance Be?" *Journal of Education and Work* 14 (2001): 5-27.

–, and D. Finegold. "Productivity, Machinery and Skills in the United States and Western Europe." *National Institute Economic Review* 162 (1997): 85-98.

Mhatre, S.L., and R.B. Deber. "From Equal Access to Health Care to Equitable Access to Health: A Review of Canadian Provincial Health Commissions and Reports." *International Journal of Health Services* 22, 4 (1992): 645-68.

"Minister Announces KPI Launch," *kpi express,* 1, 1 (1998): 1. Ontario Ministry of Education and Training/Association of Colleges of Applied Arts and Technology of Ontario.

Moore Milroy, Beth, and Susan Wismer. "Communities, Work and Public/Private Sphere Models." *Gender, Place and Culture* 1, 1 (January 1994): 71-90.

Mosher, Janet. "Managing the Disentitlement of Women: Glorified Markets, the Idealized Family and the Undeserving Other." In *Restructuring Caring Labour: Discourse, State Practice, and Everyday Life.* Ed. Sheila M. Neysmith. Toronto: Oxford University Press. 2000.

Nelson, Sharon. "Women in Business." *Nation's Business,* October 1991, 41-44.

Ng, Roxana. "Racism, Sexism and Immigrant Women." In *Changing Patterns: Women in Canada.* 2nd ed. Ed. Sandra Burt, Lorraine Code, and Lindsay Dorney, 279-301. Toronto: McClelland and Stewart. 1993,

Noble, David. "Let Them Eat Skills." In *Education and Cultural Studies: Toward a Performative Practice.* Ed. Henry Giroux, 198-212. New York: Routledge. 1997.

Phillips, A., and B. Taylor. "Sex and Skill: Notes Towards a Feminist Economics." *Feminist Review* 6 (1980): 79-88.

Picot, G., A. Heisz, and A. Nakamura. "Were 1990s Labour Markets Really Different?" *Policy Options* July/August (2000): 15-26.

Raudenbush, S., and R. Kasim. "Cognitive Skill and Economic Inequality: Findings from the National Adult Literacy Survey." *Harvard Education Review* 68 (1998): 33-79.

Rockhill, Kathleen. "Literacy as Threat/Desire." *Women's Education des femmes* 5, 3 (1987): 9-12.

Rudd, P. "From Socialization to Post-Modernity: A Review of Theoretical Perspectives on the School-to-Work Transition." *Journal of Education and Work* 10 (1997): 257-78.

Scheurich, James Joseph. "Policy Archeology: A New Policy Studies Methodology." *Journal of Education Policy* 9, 4 (1994): 297-316.

Schneider, M. "Women in Non-Traditional Occupations: Educational Strategies that Work." *Education and Work.* Vol 2: *Proceedings of the International Conference Linking Research and Practice.* Ed. D. Corson and S. Lawton, 40-48. Toronto: OISE. 1990.

Schuetze, H. "Alternation Education and Training in Canada." In *Preparing for Work in the New Economy: Alternation Education and Training in Canada.* Montreal: McGill-Queen's University Press. Forthcoming.

Shields, John. "Flexible Work, Labour Market Polarization, and the Politics of Skills, Training and Enhancement." In *The Training Trap: Ideology, Training and the Labour Market.* Ed. Thomas W. Dunk, Stephen McBride, and Randle W. Nelsen, 53-72. Winnipeg/Halifax: Society for Socialist Studies/Fernwood. 1996.

Skof, K. "Women in Registered Apprenticeship Training Programs." *Education Quarterly Review* 1 (1994): 26-35.

Smith, M. "Technological Change, the Demand for Skills, and the Adequacy of Their Supply." *Canadian Public Policy* 27 (2001): 1-22.

Sussman, Deborah. "Barriers to Job-related Training." *Perspectives on Labour and Income* 14, 2 (2002): 25-32.

Swift, James, and David Peerla. "Attitude Adjustment: The Brave New World of Work and the Revolution of Falling Expectations." In *The Training Trap: Ideology, Training and the Labour Market.* Ed. Thomas W. Dunk, Stephen McBride, and Randle W. Nelsen, 29-51. Winnipeg/Halifax: Society for Socialist Studies/Fernwood. 1996.

Taylor, Allison. "Employability Skills: From Corporate 'Wish List' to Government Policy." *Journal of Curriculum Studies* 30, 2 (1998): 143-64.

Thomson, Aisla. "Editorial: Training for Whom?" *Women's Education des femmes.* Special Issue: *What's Happening with Women's Training in Canada?* 10, 3/4 (1993).

Tulloch, Elspeth. "Where Are the Women? Federal Training Policy and the Gender Factor." *Women's Education des femmes.* Special Issue: *What's Happening to Women's Training in Canada?* 10, 3/4 (1993): 4-7.

Warburton, William P., and Rebecca N. Warburton, "Measuring the Performance of Government Training Programs." *C.D. Howe Institute Commentary* 165 (June 2002).

Wellmeier, Ingrid. "Transitions Research by the Women's Reference Group." *Women's Education des femmes* 10, 3/4 (1993): 36-39.

Wells, David. "Speak Softly and Carry a Big Carrot: Why the High Road to Competitiveness is the Wrong Road." *Canadian Dimension* 31 (1997): 23-25.

Wilensky, Harold. "The Professionalisation of Everyone." *American Journal of Sociology* 70, 2 (1964): 137-58.

Wismer, Susan, and Karen Lior, "Shopping for Training." *Canadian Women's Studies* 17, 4 (1998): 122-26.

Zeytinoglu, Isik U., and Jacinta K. Muteshi. "Gender, Race and Class Dimensions of Non-standard Work." *Industrial Relations* 55 (2000): 133-67.

Government Documents

"A Growing Gap: Why Are Lone Mothers with Young Children Falling Behind in the Labour Market?" *Bulletin* 1, 2. Applied Research Branch, Strategic Policy, Human Resources Development Canada. 1995.

Adult Education and Training in Canada: Report of the 1994 Adult Education and Training Survey. Ottawa: Human Resources Development Canada and Statistics Canada. February 1997.

Amalgamated Construction Association of BC and Employment and Immigration Canada. *Women, Native Indians, Visible Minorities, and People with Disabilities Working for Employers*. Vancouver: Employment and Immigration Canada. 1990.

Arnopoulos, Sheila McLeon. *Problems of Immigrant Women in the Canadian Labour Force*. Ottawa: Advisory Council on the Status of Women. January 1979.

Boothby, D. *The Trade-Vocational Educational Pathway in Canada: 190 Trade-Vocational Graduates in the 1992 National Graduates and 1995 Follow-Up Surveys*. Ottawa: Centre for Educational Statistics, Statistics Canada. 2000.

BC Council of Human Rights. Decision on *Karen Burton* vs. *Chalifour Bros. Construction Ltd., Thomas Chailfour and Edward Tai*. Vancouver, 9 March 1994.

British Columbia. *A British Columbia Skills Development Strategy*. Report of the Skills Development Advisory Committee. Victoria: Queen's Printer. 1989.

–. Industry Training and Apprenticeship Commission. *Ensuring a Skilled Workforce for British Columbia*. Victoria: Industry Training and Apprenticeship Commission. 2001.

–. Labour Force Development Board. *Training for What?* Victoria: Queen's Printer. 1995.

–. Premier's Business Advisory Committee on Youth Employment. *Working Together, Working Now: Combating Youth Unemployment*. Victoria: Premier's Business Advisory Committee on Youth Employment. 1998.

Butterwick, Shauna, with Mutindi Ndunda. *What Works and What Doesn't Work in Training: Lessons Learned from a Review of Selected Studies of Labour Market Training Programs*. Vancouver: British Columbia Labour Force Development Board. December 1996.

Canada. *Knowledge Matters: Skills and Learning for Canadians*. Ottawa: Supply and Services. 2002.

–. *Report of the Royal Commission on Equality in Employment*. Ottawa: Supply and Services. 1984.

Canadian Employment Insurance Commission (CEIC). *1998 Employment Insurance Monitoring and Assessment Report*. Ottawa: Queen's Printer. 1998.

–. *Program Evaluation Report: Evaluation of Job Entry Program. Final Report*. July 1989. Ottawa: CEIC. July 1989.

Canadian Labour Force Development Board. *Inventory of Programs and Services, 1995/96*. Ottawa: Canadian Labour Force Development Board. 1997.

Carroll, B., and F. Cherry. *Some Advice for Overcoming Barriers to Women's Achievement in Non-Traditional Occupations*. Ottawa: Women's Employment Directorate, EIC. 1985.

Conger, Stuart. "Life Skills Training: A Social Invention." In *Readings in Life Skills*, 1-5. Training Research and Development Station. Prince Albert, SK: Saskatchewan NewStart Incorporated, Training Research and Development Station, Department of Manpower and Immigration. 1973.

Council of Ministers of Education Canada. *The Transition from Initial Education to Working*

Life: A Canadian Report for an OECD Thematic Review. Toronto: Council of Ministers of Education Canada. 1998.

Critoph, Ursule. *Background on Training.* Ottawa: Canadian Labour Force Development Board. 1997.

–. "Recent Labour Market Policy and Program Changes: A Synthesis of the Impacts and Implications for Women," Unpublished. Ottawa: Prepared for the Status of Women Canada. October 1999.

–. *Resource Package on Changes in Labour Market Programming, including Bill C-12, Federal Withdrawal from Training and Offer to the Provinces/Territories.* Ottawa: Canadian Labour Force Development Board. 1996.

Economic Council of Canada. *A Lot to Learn.* Ottawa: Economic Council of Canada. 1992.

Federal/Provincial/Territorial Ministers Responsible for the Status of Women. *Economic Gender Equality Indicators.* Ottawa: Status of Women Canada. Cat. no. SW21-17/1997E. 1997.

Government of Newfoundland and Labrador. *Investigative Summary: Complaints Received Regarding Hibernia Referral and Hiring Procedures Related to Women.* Unpublished. St. John's. 1994.

Gunderson, Morley. *Women and the Canadian Labour Market.* Ottawa: Statistics Canada. 1998.

Guppy, N., and S. Davies. *Education in Canada: Recent Trends and Future Challenges.* Ottawa: Statistics Canada. 1998.

Hibernia Construction Sites Environmental Management Committee. *Socio-Economic Review Hibernia Development Project.* St. John's: Government of Newfoundland and Labrador. 1995.

Hughes, K. "Women in Non-Traditional Occupations." *Perspectives on Labour and Income* 7 (1995): 14-19.

Human Resources Development Canada (HRDC). *1998 Employment Insurance Monitoring and Assessment Report.* Ottawa: Human Resources Development Canada. February 1999.

–. "Behind in the Labour Market?" *Bulletin* 1, 2. Ottawa: Applied Research Branch, Strategic Policy, Human Resources Development Canada. Summer 1995.

–. *Closing the Skills Gap: Developing Career Awareness in Our Schools.* Ottawa: Minister of Public Works and Government Services Canada. 1997.

–. "Earnings, Education and ... The Low End Goes Lower." *Bulletin* 1, 2. Ottawa: Applied Research Branch, Strategic Policy, Human Resources Development Canada. Summer 1995.

–. *Employment Insurance: 2001 Monitoring and Assessment Report.* Annex 1. Ottawa: HRDC. 2002.

–. "The Future of Work: Trends in the Changing Nature of Employment." *Bulletin* 1, 2. Ottawa: Applied Research Branch, Strategic Policy, Human Resources Development Canada. Summer 1995.

–. *High School May Not Be Enough: An Analysis of Results from the School Leavers Follow-Up Survey, 1995.* Ottawa: Minister of Public Works and Government Services Canada. 1998.

–. *National Apprenticed Trades Survey.* Ottawa: Standards, Planning and Analysis Division, Human Resources Development Canada. 1994.

–. Applied Research Branch, Strategic Policy. *An Analysis of Employment Insurance Benefit Coverage,* Working Papers. Ottawa: Human Resources Development Canada. October 1998.

–, and Statistics Canada. *Adult Education and Training in Canada: Report of the 1994 Adult Education and Training Survey.* Ottawa: Human Resources Development Canada and Statistics Canada. February 1997.

Joint Federal/Provincial/Territorial Working Group. *Rethinking Training.* Ottawa: FTP Working Group/Status of Women Canada. 1994.

Kapsalis, Constantine. *Employee Training: An International Perspective.* Ottawa: Statistics Canada. 1997.

Krahn, H. *School-Work Transitions: Changing Patterns and Research Needs.* Ottawa: Applied Research Branch, Human Resources Development Canada. 1996.

Léonard, André. *Why Did the Participation Rate in Job-Related Training Decline during the 1990s in Canada?* Ottawa: Human Resources Development Canada. October 2001.

Lin, Z., R. Sweet, P. Anisef, and H. Schuetze. "Consequences and Policy Implications for University Students Who Have Chosen Liberal or Vocational Education: Labour Market Outcomes and Employability Skills." *Applied Research Branch – Research Paper R-00-2-3E.* Ottawa: Human Resources Development Canada. 2000.

Lochhead, Clarence, and Katherine Scott. *The Dynamics of Women's Poverty in Canada.* Ottawa: Status of Women Canada. 2000.

Manitoba. *Inventory of Canada's Youth Employment Programs and Services.* Youth Programs Branch. Training and Continuing Education Divisions of Manitoba Education and Training. 1999.

Menozzi, Annamarie, and Associates, and Quail Community Consulting Ltd. *Metro Toronto Immigrant Employment Services Review.* Ottawa: HRDC. January 1997.

Moreau, L. *La pauvreté et le décrochage scolaire ou La spirale de l'exclusion* [literature review]: *Direction de la recherche, de l'évaluation et de la statistique.* Québec: Ministère de la Sécurité du revenu, Gouvernement du Québec. 1995.

National Women's Reference Group on Labour Market Issues. "Canada Given a Failing Grade by UN Committee." In *Over the Fence,* 11-14. Toronto: Winter 1999.

–. *Voices from the Field: Impacts of the Changing Federal Funding Context on Women's Access to Training.* Ottawa: Canadian Labour Force Development Board. 1998.

New Brunswick. Literacy NB. *Final Report. CASP! Evaluation Program.* Fredericton: Baseline Market Research for Literacy NB. December 1997.

–. Department of Education (various years). *New Brunswick Student Aid: Statistical Profile.* (Title later changed to *New Brunswick Student Financial Assistance Program: Overview.*)

O'Hara, S., and F. Evers. *Opportunity in Apprenticeship: An Analysis of the 1994/95 National Apprenticed Trades Survey.* Ottawa: Standards, Planning and Analysis Division, Human Resources Development Canada. 1996.

Ontario Premier's Council. *People and Skills in the New Global Economy.* Toronto: Queen's Printer. 1990.

Riddle, D. *Assessment of HRDC's Designated Group Policy.* Ottawa: Government of Canada. 1995.

Saskatchewan Health Employer Survey Summary Report. *Saskatchewan Health.* Regina: Policy and Planning Branch. 1997.

–. *Saskatchewan Health.* Regina: Policy and Planning Branch. 1994-99.

Sharpe, A. *Apprenticeship in Canada: A Training System under Siege?* Ottawa: National Apprenticeship Committee, Canadian Labour Force Development Board. 1999.

Social Research and Demonstration Corporation. *When Financial Incentives Encourage Work: Complete 18 Month Findings from the Self-Sufficiency Project.* Vancouver: Social Research and Demonstration Corporation for HRDC. 1998.

Statistics Canada. *1996 Census: Labour Force Activity, Occupation and Industry, Place of Work, Mode of Transportation to Work, Unpaid Work.* Ottawa: Statistics Canada. 1996.

–. *Education in Canada.* Ottawa: Statistics Canada. 1996.

–. Labour Force Historical Review. *Table 1: Labour Force Estimates by Detailed Age, Sex, Canada/Provinces, Annual Averages.* Ottawa: Statistics Canada. 1999.

–. *Labour Force Survey.* Ottawa: Statistics Canada. 1999.

–. *Labour Force Update.* Ottawa: Statistics Canada. Summer 1998. Cat 71-005-XPB.

–. *Labour Force Update: An Overview of Average Wages and Wage Distribution in the Late 1990s.* Vol. 4, no. 2, 2000. Cat 71-005-XPB.

–. *Labour Force Update: Youth and the Labour Market, 1998-1999.* Autumn 1999. Cat No. 71-005-XPB.

–. "Key Labour and Income Facts." *Perspectives on Labour and Income* 10, 2 (1998): 53-65.

–. *The Nation Series 1996.* Ottawa: Government of Canada. 1998.

–. "Registered Apprenticeship Training Survey." *The Daily.* 4 August 1999. 10-11.

–, and the Council of Ministers of Education, Canada (CMEC). *Education Indicators in Canada: Report of the Pan-Canadian Education Indicators Program, 1999,* Cat. No. 81-582. Toronto: Statistics Canada, Council of Ministers of Education, Canada. 2001.

Status of Women Canada. *Women's Economic Independence and Security: A Federal/Provincial/Territorial Strategic Framework.* Ottawa: Status of Women Canada. 2001.

Sweet, R., P. Anisef, and Z. Lin. *Exploring Family Antecedents of Participation in Post-Secondary Education.* Ottawa: Learning and Literacy Directorate, Human Resources Development Canada. 2000.

Sweet, R., and P. Gallagher. *Women and Apprenticeships: An Analysis of the 1994 National Apprenticed Trades Survey.* Ottawa: Standards, Planning and Analysis Division, Human Resources Development Canada. 1997.

Thiessen, V., and C. Nickerson. *Canadian Gender Trends in Education and Work.* Ottawa: Applied Research Branch, Human Resources Development Canada. 1999.

Toupin, Louise. *Social and Community Indicators for Evaluating Women's Work in Communities.* Ottawa: Status of Women Canada. 2001.

Tulloch, Elspeth, for the New Brunswick Advisory Council on the Status of Women. *Background Paper: Women's Training Needs in New Brunswick.* Document 2. Moncton: New Brunswick Advisory Council on the Status of Women. 1993.

Wills, J. *Standards: Making Them Useful and Workable for the Education Enterprise.* Washington, DC: Office of Vocational and Adult Education, US Department of Education. 1997.

Windsor Women's Incentive Centre (WIC). *Submission to the Parliamentary Standing Committee on Human Resources Development.* Windsor: WIC. 1994.

Wismer, Susan, and Karen Lior. *Meeting Women's Training Needs: Case Studies in Women's Training, Phase 2 Report.* Ottawa: FTP Working Group/Status of Women Canada. 1994.

Wismer, Susan, and Linda Szeto. *Towards a Women's Agenda on Training.* Toronto: National Women's Reference Group on Labour Market Issues/Canadian Congress for Learning Opportunities for Women. 1991.

Women's Economic Independence and Security. *A Federal Provincial/Territorial Strategic Framework.* Ottawa: Status of Women Canada. 2001.

Conference Papers, Pamphlets, and Reports

Act Inc. *Work Keys Technical Handbook.* Iowa City: ACT Publications. 1997.

Advocates for Community-Based Training and Education for Women (ACTEW). *Building the Capacity of the Women's Training and Education Community: A Plan for Sustainable Action.* Toronto: ACTEW. 2001.

–. *Employers' Guide to Community-Based Training.* Toronto: ACTEW. 1991.

–. "Think Tank Highlights." Unpublished discussion paper. Toronto: ACTEW. June 2001.

The Association of Service Providers for Employability and Career Training (ASPECT). *Analysing the Impact and Challenging the Assumptions: A Report that Demonstrates the Impact of Government Policies on Unemployed Persons and on Community Service Deliverers.* Vancouver: ASPECT. 1999.

Business and Administrative Services. *Recommendations to the National Skill Standard Board.* Washington, DC: National Alliance of Business. 1998.

Business Council of British Columbia. *The Third Option: Rewarding Careers Via Non-University Pathways.* Vancouver: Business Council of British Columbia. 2001.

Calvert, John. "Maximizing Social, Training and Economic Development Spin-Offs from Public Capital Spending: The Experience of the Vancouver Island Highway Project," Unpublished paper. 1997.

Canadian Association for Prior Learning Assessment. *A Slice of the Iceberg: Cross-Canada Study on Prior Learning Assessment and Recognition.* Tyendinaga Mohawk Territory, ON: CAPLA. 1999.

Canadian Coalition of Community-Based Training. *A Study to Investigate, Analyse and Organise Community-Based Training Roles in Canada.* Ottawa: CCCBT/HRDC. 2000.

Carney, Diana. *Livelihoods Approaches Compared.* Rev. Report prepared for the United Nations Development Program. February 2000.

Cohen, Marcy. *Report to the Second Annual Consultation of the Women's Reference Group on Labour Market Issues.* Ottawa: National Women's Reference Group J. 1993.

Cohen, Marjorie. *Evaluation of the Working Skills Centre.* Toronto: Working Skills Centre. 1979.

Committee for Alternative Training and Education for Women (ACTEW [formerly known as CATEW]). "Proposal to Secretary of State." Toronto: CATEW. 1985.

Critoph, Ursule. "Recent Labour Market Policy and Program Changes: A Synthesis of the Impacts and Implications for Women." Unpublished paper prepared for the Status of Women Canada. October 1999.

–. *Training: Is There Still a Public Commitment?* Ottawa: National Union of Public and General Employees. 1996.

de Wolff, Alice. *Breaking the Myth of Flexible Work: Contingent Work in Toronto.* Toronto: Contingent Workers Project. 2000.

–. *The Impact of E-Business on Office Work.* Toronto: Office Workers Career Centre. 2000.

–. *Job Loss and Entry-Level Information Workers: Training and Adjustment Strategies for Clerical Workers in Metropolitan Toronto.* Toronto: Metro Toronto Clerical Workers Labour Adjustment Committee. 1995.

Frangos, P., S. Gardias, and C. Hookey. "Response to the Findings of the Investigation into Women's Concerns about Hiring Practices on the Hibernia Construction Project," Unpublished paper. St. John's, NF. 1994.

Glenday, Daniel, Ann Duffy, and Norene Pupo. "Do Unions Make a Difference? Unions and the Introduction of Information Technology into Clerical Occupations." Presented to the Advanced Research Seminar, Women and Unions: Industrial Relations Collective Bargaining and Union Militancy, York University, 24 January 1992.

Haiven, Larry. "Professionalization and Unionization among Paramedical Occupations: National Regulation and the Challenge of Globalization." Paper delivered at Canadian Industrial Relations Association Conference, June 1998.

Hewitt-Ferris and Associates. "A Review of the Equity Component of the Vancouver Island Highway Project." Unpublished paper, Highway Constructors Ltd. May 1997.

Highway Constructors Ltd. *Vancouver Island Collective Agreement between Highway Constructors Ltd. and British Columbia Highway and Related Construction Council.* April 1997.

Husky Oil. *White Rose Oilfield Development Application.* Vol. 1: *Canada-Newfoundland Benefits Plan.* St. John's, NF: Husky Oil Operations Ltd. 2001.

–. *White Rose Oilfield Development Application: Response to Additional Requests from the White Rose Public Review Commission.* St. John's, NF: Husky Oil Operations Ltd. 2001.

International Labour Organization (ILO). *Learning and Training for Work in the Knowledge Society.* Report 4, 1. Geneva: International Labour Office. 2002.

Jackson, Nancy, and Steven Jordan. *Skills Training: Who Benefits?* Toronto: Labour Education and Training Research Network, Centre for Research on Work and Society, York University. 2000.

Labour Education and Training Research Network. "The Provision of Training in Canada: Regional Comparisons, National Perspectives – Conference 2000 Report." *Newsletter of the Labour Education and Training Research Network no. 5. Training Matters/Recherche en Formation.* Toronto: York University, Labour Education and Training Research Network. Spring 2001.

Lackey, Laura. "We've Got to Have Skills: Exploring Meanings, Contradictions and Implications of British Columbia's Skills Now Policy." *The Western Research Network on Education and Training Home Page.* April 2000.

Legault, Marie-Josée. "Workers' Resistance to Women in Non-Traditional Sectors of Employment and the Role of Unions." Unpublished paper. Montreal: Université du Québec à Montréal. 2001.

Livingstone, David. "Wasted Education and Withered Work: Reversing the 'Post-Industrial' Education – Jobs Optic." Paper prepared for the International Workshop Conference, Human Resources Development in a Changing Economy, University of British Columbia, 19-21 August 1996.

Lyon, Eleanor. "Poverty, Welfare and Battered Women: What Does the Research Tell Us?" Welfare and Domestic Violence Technical Assistance Initiative. National Resource Centre on Domestic Violence. <www.vaw.umn.edu/vawnet/welfare.htm> (December 2002).

McBride, Stephen. "The Political Economy of Training in Canada." Training Matters: Working Paper Series 98-07, Labour Education and Training Research Network. Working

Paper Series 98-07, Labour Education and Training Research Network, Centre for Research on Work and Society, York University. 1998.

McFarland, Joan. "Recent Changes in Training Policy and Structure in New Brunswick." Training Matters: Newsletter of the Labour Education and Training Research Network, No. 2., Centre for Research on Work and Society, York University. Winter 1998/99.

–. "Women's Access to Training in New Brunswick." Training Matters: Working Paper Series, Labour Education and Training Research Network, Centre for Research on Work and Society, York University. May 1999.

–, and Abdella Abdou. "What's Happening with Training in New Brunswick?" Training Matters: Working Paper Series, Labour Education and Training Research Network, Centre for Research on Work and Society, York University. May 1998.

Moore, Diane. "Office Professionals in Transition. Preparing for the Millennium." Presented to the 1999 American Society for Training and Development International Conference, Atlanta, Georgia.

Murphy, P. Submission to the White Rose Public Review Commission, Submission MR-087. St. John's, 2001.

National Action Committee on the Status of Women. *Training and the Social Security Review*. Fact Sheet 2. Toronto: NAC. 1994.

Ontario Association of Interval and Transition Houses (OAITH). *Some Impacts of the Ontario Works Act on Survivors of Violence against Women*. Toronto: OAITH, Standing Committee on Social Development. 1997.

Peluso, Maria. "Labour Market Issues for Women in Quebec." Presentation to the NWRG, Montreal, Quebec, October 1998.

Stephen, Jennifer. *Access Diminished: A Report on Women's Training and Employment Services in Ontario*. Toronto: ACTEW. 2000.

Sweet, R. "Women and Apprenticeships: The Role of Personal Agency in Transition Success." Training Matters: Working Paper Series, Labour Education and Training Research Network, Centre for Research on Work and Society, York University. 2000.

–, and Z. Lin. "Union Membership and Apprenticeship Completion." Working Paper. Training Matters: Working Paper Series, Labour Education and Training Research Network, Centre for Research on Work and Society, York University. 1999.

Viswanathan, Leela. *Toronto Training Board 2000-2001 Environmental Scan: Training for Toronto's New Economy*. Toronto: Toronto Training Board. 2000.

Women in Resource Development Committee. *Where Are the Women?* St. John's, NF: Women in Resource Development Committee. 2001.

Workfare Watch. *Broken Promises: Welfare Reform in Ontario*. Toronto: Welfare Watch. 1999.

Zelechow, Ann, and Anne Morais. *ACTEW Survey of Training and Employment Programs for Women in Metro Toronto*. Toronto: ACTEW. 1997.

Contributors

Sylvain Bourdon is a professor of sociology and research methodology in the Faculty of Education of Sherbrooke University. His research focuses on the social aspects of the school-work relationship, particularly on youth's transition from school to work. His current work tackles such aspects of this field as youth's work in community organizations, marginalized youth and the written text, and the evolution of training practices in organizations aimed at helping youth employment.

Kate Braid is a journey carpenter, teacher, and writer who has worked as a union carpenter building bridges, commercial, and industrial buildings. She also ran her own company, Sisters Construction, doing renovations and residential housing. She is a founder of Vancouver Women in Trades and of the Women in Trades and Technologies National Network. She was the first woman elected to the executive of the Vancouver local of the International Brotherhood of Carpenters and Joiners of America, and the first woman to teach trades full-time at the British Columbia Institute of Technology. She has written two biographies and three award-winning books of poetry and currently teaches creative writing at Malaspina University-College in Nanaimo, British Columbia.

Shauna Butterwick is an assistant professor in the Adult Education Program, Department of Educational Studies, University of British Columbia. Her research interests include feminist analysis of employment-related policies and programs for women, community-based and action-oriented research, learning in social movements (particularly the role of popular theatre/education), coalition building, and life skills training. She teaches within and across several departmental program areas, including adult education, feminist theory, and leadership and policy.

Marjorie Griffin Cohen is an economist and professor of political science and women's studies at Simon Fraser University. She is a research associate with the Canadian Centre for Policy Alternatives and writes on various issues dealing with labour, the Canadian economy, women and public policy, and international trade agreements.

Ursule Critoph, an economist by training, is an independent consultant, researcher, and activist with a special focus on training and labour market issues. She is the author of a course on the training system in Canada, which is taught at Athabasca University. As a senior associate at the now defunct Canadian Labour Force Development Board, she undertook an extensive review of how federal funding cuts and the transfer of responsibility to the provinces has affected training. Over the years she has worked with a number of Aboriginal and women's groups in the communities in which she has lived.

Frédéric Deschenaux is a doctoral student in education sociology at Sherbrooke University. His dissertation focuses on college and university graduates moving from school to work in community organizations.

Alice de Wolff is community co-director for the Alliance on Contingent Employment at York University. Alice is a researcher and policy analyst who has worked with community, labour, and women's organizations for many years. She has conducted research on office work in Toronto since the mid-1990s and is currently a board member of the Office Workers Career Centre.

Larry Haiven is an associate professor in the Department of Management, Faculty of Commerce, St. Mary's University, Halifax, Nova Scotia. He specializes in the field of health care, including industrial relations, interprofessional relations, and training.

Susan Hart is an associate professor in industrial relations, Faculty of Business Administration, Memorial University, St. John's, Newfoundland. Her research interests include equality bargaining and worker involvement in health and safety in the offshore oil and gas industry.

Maureen Hynes is coordinator of the School of Labour at George Brown College in Toronto. Since 1992 she has coordinated this partnership with the Toronto and York Region Labour Council and has implemented many curriculum, PLAR, and labour adjustment projects, including the Office Workers' Career Centre. With her colleagues, she is now in the process of developing a labour studies diploma program.

Karen Charnow Lior is the national representative of training for the Canadian Labour Congress. With Susan Wismer, she is the co-author of "Meeting Women's Training Needs: Case Studies in Women's Training" and "Shopping for Training." She has also written other articles on women's training issues. She has a master's degree from York University and is an adult educator and community activist.

Margaret Hillyard Little is an anti-poverty activist and academic who works in the area of single mothers on welfare, welfare and workfare reform, and retraining for women on welfare. She is jointly appointed to women's studies and political studies at Queen's University.

Stephen McBride is a professor of political science at Simon Fraser University. He has published widely on political economy and public policy. His most recent book is *Paradigm Shift: Globalization and the Canadian State* (Fernwood Books, 2001).

Joan McFarland is a professor of economics and gender studies at St. Thomas University in Fredericton, New Brunswick Her research interests include the political economy of women and social policy. She is a member of the Labour Education and Training Research Network.

Margaret Menton Manery, who has a master's degree in political science from Simon Fraser University, is an independent researcher. She has conducted postgraduate research for the BC Human Rights Commission publication, *Factors Affecting the Economic Status of Older Women in Canada: Implications for Mandatory Retirement,* as well as for the Hospital Employees' Union publication, *Do Comparisons between Hospital Support Workers and Hospitality Workers Make Sense?*

Elizabeth Quinlan is a doctoral candidate in interdisciplinary studies at the University of Saskatchewan and a member of the Women's Reference Group to the Saskatchewan Labour Force Development Board. She has taught mathematics, communications, and computer literacy in a variety of adult training, pre-employment, and upgrading courses.

Mark Shrimpton is principal of Community Resource Services Ltd., a Newfoundland-based socio-economic consulting company, and an adjunct professor of geography at Memorial University. He is also the author of numerous reports and papers on the social and economic effects and management of the oil industry and resource development projects. With Jane Lewis and Marilyn Porter he co-edited *Women, Work and Family in the British, Canadian and Norwegian Offshore Oilfields* (Macmillan, 1988).

Robert Sweet teaches educational psychology at Lakehead University. His research interests include youth transitions, postsecondary access, and equity issues. Currently he is involved in a national study of the role of families in supporting their children's postsecondary education.

Susan Wismer is an associate professor in the Department of Environment and Resource Studies at the University of Waterloo. She has over twenty years' experience in the field of women's education and training as a practitioner, researcher, and policy analyst. She has a particular interest in community-based training.

Linda Wong is a policy/research fellow at the University of British Columbia.

Index